Learning
MATLAB 6.5

MATLAB®
STUDENT VERSION
with SIMULINK®

The MathWorks

How to Contact The MathWorks:

www.mathworks.com	Web
comp.soft-sys.matlab	Newsgroup

suggest@mathworks.com	Product enhancement suggestions
bugs@mathworks.com	Bug reports
doc@mathworks.com	Documentation error reports

ISBN 0-9672195-7-4

Printing History:	August 1999	First printing	New manual
	January 2001	Second printing	Revised for MATLAB 6.0 (Release 12)
	November 2002	Third printing	Revised for MATLAB 6.5 (Release 13)

Contents

Introduction

1

i

Installation

2

Development Environment

3

Getting Started

4

Graphics

5

Programming with MATLAB

6

MATLAB Programming Tips

7

Introducing the Symbolic Math Toolbox

8

Using the Symbolic Math Toolbox

9

MATLAB Quick Reference

A

Symbolic Math Toolbox Quick Reference

B

1

Introduction

This chapter introduces the MATLAB Student Version and provides resources for using it.

Quick Start

Install MATLAB. If you need help with the installation, see Chapter 2, "Installation."

If you are new to MATLAB, you should start by reading Chapter 4, "Getting Started." The most important things to learn are how to enter matrices, how to use the : (colon) operator, and how to invoke functions. After you master the basics, you should read the rest of the sections below and run the demos.

At the heart of MATLAB is a new language you must learn before you can fully exploit its power. You can learn the basics of MATLAB quickly, and mastery comes shortly after. You will be rewarded with high-productivity, high-creativity computing power that will change the way you work.

- "Introduction" — Describes the Student Version and the components of the MATLAB system.
- "Installation" — Covers installing the Student Version on Microsoft Windows, Macintosh OS X, and Linux platforms.
- "Development Environment" — Introduces the MATLAB development environment, including information about tools and the MATLAB desktop.
- "Getting Started" — Introduces how to use MATLAB to generate matrices and perform mathematical operations on matrices.
- "Graphics" — Introduces MATLAB graphic capabilities, including information about plotting data, annotating graphs, and working with images.
- "Programming with MATLAB" — Describes how to use the MATLAB language to create scripts and functions, and manipulate data structures, such as cell arrays and multidimensional arrays.
- "MATLAB Programming Tips" — Provides a compilation of tips for the MATLAB programmer.

About the Student Version

MATLAB® and Simulink® are premier software packages for technical computation in education and industry. The MATLAB Student Version provides all of the features of professional MATLAB, with no limitations, and the full functionality of professional Simulink, with model sizes up to 300 blocks. The Student Version gives you immediate access to the high-performance numeric computing, modeling, and simulation power you need.

MATLAB allows you to focus on your course work and applications rather than on programming details. It enables you to solve many numerical problems in a fraction of the time it would take you to write a program in a lower level language. MATLAB helps you better understand and apply concepts in applications ranging from engineering and mathematics to chemistry, biology, and economics.

Simulink, included with the Student Version, is a block diagram tool for modeling and simulating dynamic systems, including controls, signal processing, communications, and other complex systems.

The Symbolic Math Toolbox, also included with the Student Version, is based on the Maple® 8 symbolic kernel and lets you perform symbolic computations and variable-precision arithmetic.

MATLAB products are used in a broad range of industries, including automotive, aerospace, electronics, environmental, telecommunications, computer peripherals, finance, and medical. More than 500,000 technical professionals at the world's most innovative technology companies, government research labs, financial institutions, and at more than 2,000 universities, rely on MATLAB and Simulink as the fundamental tools for their engineering and scientific work.

Student Use Policy

This Student License is for use in conjunction with courses offered at a degree-granting institution. The MathWorks offers this license as a special service to the student community and asks your help in seeing that its terms are not abused.

To use this Student License, you must be a student using the software in conjunction with courses offered at degree-granting institutions.

You may not use this Student License at a company or government lab. Also, you may not use it for research or for commercial or industrial purposes. In these cases, you can acquire the appropriate professional or academic version of the software by contacting The MathWorks.

Differences Between the Student Version and the Professional Version

MATLAB

The MATLAB Student Version provides full support for all language features as well as graphics, external interface and Application Program Interface (API) support, and access to every other feature of the professional version of MATLAB.

MATLAB Differences. There are a few small differences between the Student Version and the professional version of MATLAB:

- The MATLAB prompt in the Student Version is

  `EDU>>`

- The window title bars include the words

  `<Student Version>`

- All printouts contain the footer

  `Student Version of MATLAB`

  This footer is not an option that can be turned off; it will always appear in your printouts.

- The Documentation CD must be in your CD-ROM drive to start MATLAB. Once MATLAB starts, you can remove the CD. However, to access the online documentation, the CD must be in the CD-ROM drive.

Simulink

This Student Version contains the complete Simulink product, which is used with MATLAB to model, simulate, and analyze dynamic systems.

Simulink Differences.

- Models are limited to 300 blocks.

Note You may encounter some demos that use more than 300 blocks. In these cases, a dialog will display stating that the block limit has been exceeded and the demo will not run.

- The window title bars include the words

  \<Student Version>

- All printouts contain the footer

  Student Version of MATLAB

  This footer is not an option that can be turned off; it will always appear in your printouts.

Note The Using Simulink documentation, which is accessible from the Help browser, contains all of the relevant information in the Learning Simulink book plus additional advanced information.

Symbolic Math Toolbox

The Symbolic Math Toolbox included with this Student Version lets you access all of the functions in the professional version of the Symbolic Math Toolbox except maple, mapleinit, mfun, mfunlist, and mhelp. For a complete list of all the available functions, see Appendix B, "Symbolic Math Toolbox Quick Reference."

Other Products

SimMechanics. With this product, you can build models with up to 20 mechanical bodies. This limit will accommodate models with as many as 120 degrees of freedom (a computationally intense simulation).

Obtaining Additional MathWorks Products

Many college courses recommend MATLAB as their standard instructional software. In some cases, the courses may require particular toolboxes, blocksets, or other products. Many of these products are available for student use. You may purchase and download these additional products at special student prices from the MathWorks Store at www.mathworks.com/store.

Some of the products you can purchase include

- Communications Blockset
- Control System Toolbox
- Fuzzy Logic Toolbox
- Image Processing Toolbox
- Neural Network Toolbox
- Optimization Toolbox
- Signal Processing Toolbox
- Statistics Toolbox
- Fixed-Point Blockset
- Stateflow® (A demo version of Stateflow is included with your Student Version.)

For an up-to-date list of available toolboxes and blocksets, visit the MathWorks Store.

Note The toolboxes and blocksets that are available for the MATLAB Student Version have the same functionality as the full, professional versions. The only restrictions are those described in "Differences Between the Student Version and the Professional Version" on page 1-4. Also, the student versions of the toolboxes and blocksets will only work with the Student Version. Likewise, the professional versions of the toolboxes and blocksets will not work with the Student Version.

Getting Started with MATLAB

What I Want	What I Should Do
I need to install MATLAB.	See Chapter 2, "Installation" in this book.
I want to start MATLAB.	On all operating systems, your MathWorks Documentation CD must be in your CD-ROM drive to start MATLAB.
	(Microsoft Windows) Double-click the MATLAB icon on your desktop.
	(Macintosh OS X) Double-click the LaunchMATLAB icon on your desktop.
	(Linux) Enter the matlab command at the command prompt.
I'm new to MATLAB and want to learn it quickly.	Start by reading Chapter 3, "Development Environment" through Chapter 6, "Programming with MATLAB" of Learning MATLAB. The most important things to learn are how to enter matrices, how to use the : (colon) operator, and how to invoke functions. You will also get a brief overview of graphics and programming in MATLAB. After you master the basics, you can access the rest of the documentation through the online help facility (Help).
I want to look at some samples of what you can do with MATLAB.	There are numerous demonstrations included with MATLAB. You can see the demos by clicking **Demos** in the Help Navigator or selecting **Demos** from the **Help** menu. There are demos in mathematics, graphics, visualization, and much more. You also will find a large selection of demos at www.mathworks.com/demos.

Finding Reference Information

What I Want	What I Should Do
I want to know how to use a specific function.	Use the online help facility (Help). To access Help, use the command helpbrowser or use the **Help** menu. "MATLAB Functions: Volume 1 (A-E), Volume 2 (F-O), and Volume 3 (P-Z)" is also available from Help in PDF format (**MATLAB -> Printable Documentation (pdf)**) if you want to print any of the function descriptions in high-quality form. **Note:** Your MathWorks Documentation CD must be in your CD-ROM drive to access Help.
I want to find a function for a specific purpose but I don't know its name.	There are several choices: • See Appendix A, "MATLAB Quick Reference," in this book for a list of MATLAB functions. • From Help, peruse the MATLAB functions using the **Category** or **Alphabetical** option. • Use lookfor (e.g., lookfor inverse) from the command line. • Use **Index** or **Search** from Help.
I want to learn about a specific topic like sparse matrices, ordinary differential equations, or cell arrays.	Use Help to locate the appropriate sections in the MATLAB documentation, for example, **MATLAB -> Mathematics -> Sparse Matrices**.

What I Want	What I Should Do
I want to know what functions are available in a general area.	Use Help to see "Functions - By Category" under MATLAB or see Appendix A, "MATLAB Quick Reference," in this book for a list of MATLAB functions. Help provides access to the reference pages for the hundreds of functions included with MATLAB.
I want to learn about the Symbolic Math Toolbox.	See Chapter 8, "Introducing the Symbolic Math Toolbox," Chapter 9, "Using the Symbolic Math Toolbox," and Appendix B, "Symbolic Math Toolbox Quick Reference," in this book. For complete descriptions of the Symbolic Math Toolbox functions, use Help and select **Function Reference** from **Symbolic Math Toolbox**.

Troubleshooting and Other Resources

What I Want	What I Should Do
I have a MATLAB specific problem I want help with.	Visit the Technical Support section (www.mathworks.com/support) of the MathWorks Web site.
I want to report a bug or make a suggestion.	Use Help or send e-mail to bugs@mathworks.com or suggest@mathworks.com.

Documentation Library

Your MATLAB Student Version contains much more documentation than the two printed books, Learning MATLAB and Learning Simulink. On your Documentation CD is a personal reference library of every book and reference page that is available for the Student Version. Access this documentation library from Help.

Note For an up-to-date list of products that are available for the Student Version, visit the MathWorks Store (www.mathworks.com/store). At the store you can also purchase printed manuals for the MATLAB family of products.

Accessing the Online Documentation

Access the online documentation directly from your Documentation CD. (Refer to Chapter 2, "Installation" for specific information on configuring and accessing the online Help from the CD.)

1 Place the CD in your CD-ROM drive.

2 Select **Full Product Family Help** from the **Help** menu.

Help appears in a separate window.

Tutorials and reference for MATLAB

Tutorials and reference for Symbolic Math Toolbox

Tutorials and reference for Simulink

Tutorials and reference for Stateflow

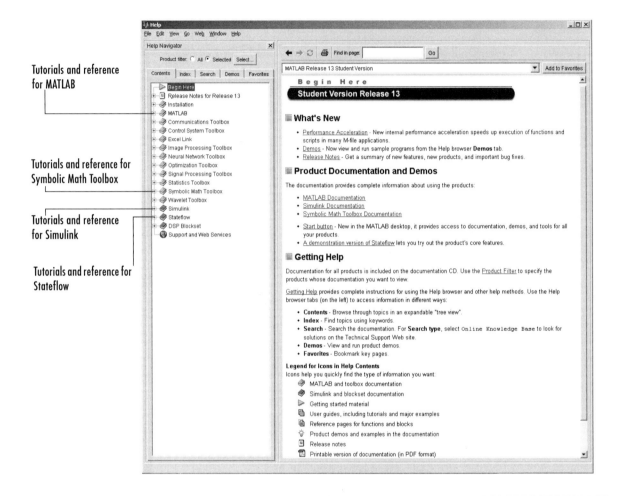

Note When you start MATLAB for the first time, the Help Navigator displays entries for additional products. To learn how to change the displayed product list, see the "Product Filter" on page 3-9.

MathWorks Web Site

Use your browser to visit the MathWorks Web site, www.mathworks.com. You'll find lots of information about MathWorks products and how they are used in education and industry, product demos, and MATLAB based books. From the Web site you will also be able to access our technical support resources, view a library of user and MathWorks supplied M-files, and get information about products and upcoming events.

MathWorks Education Web Site

This education-specific Web site, www.mathworks.com/education, contains many resources for various branches of engineering, mathematics, and science. Many of these include teaching examples, books, and other related products. You will also find a comprehensive list of links to Web sites where MATLAB is used for teaching and research at universities.

MATLAB Related Books

Hundreds of MATLAB related books are available from many different publishers. An up-to-date list is available at www.mathworks.com/support/books.

MathWorks Store

The MathWorks Store (www.mathworks.com/store) gives you an easy way to purchase add-on products and documentation.

MATLAB Central — File Exchange/Newsgroup Access

MATLAB Central (www.mathworks.com/matlabcentral) provides Web-based access to the MATLAB specific Usenet newsgroup (comp.soft-sys.matlab) as well as an extensive library of user-contributed files called the MATLAB File Exchange.

The newsgroup, comp.soft-sys.matlab, is a gathering of professionals and students who use MATLAB and have questions or comments about it and its associated products. This is a great resource for posing questions and answering those of others. MathWorks staff also participates actively in this newsgroup.

MathWorks Web-Based Technical Support

You can access MathWorks technical support from the Support link on our Web site. You can peruse information by product or search for particular information in Technical Notes, Solutions, documentation, and more. You will find numerous examples of graphics, mathematics, API, Simulink models, and other topics. You can answer many of your questions by spending a few minutes with this around-the-clock resource.

Technical Support

Telephone and e-mail access to our technical support staff is not available for students running the Student Version of MATLAB unless you are experiencing difficulty installing or downloading MATLAB or related products. There are numerous other vehicles of technical support that you can use. The "Additional Sources of Information" section in the CD holder identifies the ways to obtain support.

After checking the available MathWorks sources for help, if you still cannot resolve your problem, you should contact your instructor. Your instructor should be able to help you, but if not, there is telephone and e-mail technical support for registered instructors who have adopted the MATLAB Student Version in their courses.

Product Registration

Visit the MathWorks Web site (www.mathworks.com/student) and register your Student Version.

Registered users of the MATLAB Student Version can search our Solutions Database, get answers to Hot Topics, or use the Index of Examples located on the Technical Support Web site at www.mathworks.com/support to answer product questions.

About MATLAB and Simulink

What Is MATLAB?

MATLAB is a high-performance language for technical computing. It integrates computation, visualization, and programming in an easy-to-use environment where problems and solutions are expressed in familiar mathematical notation. Typical uses include

- Math and computation
- Algorithm development
- Modeling, simulation, and prototyping
- Data analysis, exploration, and visualization
- Scientific and engineering graphics
- Application development, including graphical user interface building

MATLAB is an interactive system whose basic data element is an array that does not require dimensioning. This allows you to solve many technical computing problems, especially those with matrix and vector formulations, in a fraction of the time it would take to write a program in a scalar noninteractive language such as C or Fortran.

The name MATLAB stands for *matrix laboratory*. MATLAB was originally written to provide easy access to matrix software developed by the LINPACK and EISPACK projects. Today, MATLAB uses software developed by the LAPACK and ARPACK projects, which together represent the state-of-the-art in software for matrix computation.

MATLAB has evolved over a period of years with input from many users. In university environments, it is the standard instructional tool for introductory and advanced courses in mathematics, engineering, and science. In industry, MATLAB is the tool of choice for high-productivity research, development, and analysis.

Toolboxes

MATLAB features a family of application-specific solutions called *toolboxes*. Very important to most users of MATLAB, toolboxes allow you to *learn* and *apply* specialized technology. Toolboxes are comprehensive collections of MATLAB functions (M-files) that extend the MATLAB environment to solve particular classes of problems. Areas in which toolboxes are available include signal processing, control systems, neural networks, fuzzy logic, wavelets, simulation, and many others.

The MATLAB System

The MATLAB system consists of five main parts:

Development Environment. This is the set of desktop tools and facilities that help you use MATLAB functions and files. Many of these tools are graphical user interfaces, including the Command Window, Command History, **Start** button, Editor/Debugger, Profiler for improving performance, and browsers for viewing help, the current directory, files, the workspace, arrays, and the search path.

The MATLAB Mathematical Function Library. This is a vast collection of computational algorithms ranging from elementary functions like sum, sine, cosine, and complex arithmetic, to more sophisticated functions like matrix inverse, matrix eigenvalues, Bessel functions, and fast Fourier transforms.

The MATLAB Language. This is a high-level matrix/array language with control flow statements, functions, data structures, input/output, and object-oriented programming features. It allows both "programming in the small" to rapidly create quick and dirty throw-away programs, and "programming in the large" to create complete large and complex application programs.

Handle Graphics®. This is the MATLAB graphics system. It includes high-level commands for two-dimensional and three-dimensional data visualization, image processing, animation, and presentation graphics. It also includes low-level commands that allow you to fully customize the appearance of graphics and to build complete graphical user interfaces on your MATLAB applications.

The MATLAB Application Program Interface (API). This is a library that allows you to write C and Fortran programs that interact with MATLAB. It include facilities for calling routines from MATLAB (dynamic linking), calling MATLAB as a computational engine, and reading and writing MAT-files.

What Is Simulink?

Simulink is an interactive tool for modeling, simulating, and analyzing dynamic, multidomain systems. It lets you build a block diagram, simulate the system's behavior, evaluate its performance, and refine the design. Simulink integrates seamlessly with MATLAB, providing you with immediate access to an extensive range of analysis and design tools. These benefits make Simulink the tool of choice for control system design, DSP design, communications system design, and other simulation applications.

Blocksets are collections of application-specific blocks that support multiple design areas, including electrical power-system modeling, digital signal processing, fixed-point algorithm development, and more. These blocks can be incorporated directly into your Simulink models.

Real-Time Workshop® is a program that generates optimized, portable, and customizable ANSI C code from Simulink models. Generated code can run on PC hardware, DSPs, microcontrollers on bare-board environments, and with commercial or proprietary real-time operating systems.

What Is Stateflow?

Stateflow is an interactive design tool for modeling and simulating complex reactive systems. Tightly integrated with Simulink and MATLAB, Stateflow provides Simulink users with an elegant solution for designing embedded systems by giving them an efficient way to incorporate complex control and supervisory logic within their Simulink models.

With Stateflow, you can quickly develop graphical models of event-driven systems using finite state machine theory, statechart formalisms, and flow diagram notation. Together, Stateflow and Simulink serve as an executable specification and virtual prototype of your system design.

Note Your MATLAB Student Version includes a demo version of Stateflow.

Installation

This chapter describes how to install the MATLAB Student Version.

Installing on Windows

System Requirements

Note For the most up-to-date information about system requirements, see the system requirements page, available in the Support area at the MathWorks Web site (www.mathworks.com).

MATLAB and Simulink

- Intel-based Pentium, Pentium Pro, Pentium II, Pentium III, Pentium IV, Xeon PIII or AMD Athlon, Athlon XP-based personal computer

- Microsoft Windows 98, Windows Millennium Edition, Windows NT 4.0 (with Service Pack 5, 6a), Windows 2000 (with Service Pack 1, 2, or 3), or Windows XP

- CD-ROM drive for installation, program startup, and online documentation

- Disk space varies depending on size of partition. The MathWorks Installer will inform you of the disk space requirement for your particular partition, for example, a partition with a 4K byte cluster size requires 120 MB for MATLAB only.

- 128 MB RAM minimum, 256 MB RAM recommended

- Netscape Navigator 4.0 or higher, or Microsoft Internet Explorer 4.0 or higher is required.

- Adobe Acrobat Reader 3.0 or higher is required to view and print the MATLAB online documentation that is in PDF format.

- Microsoft Word 8.0 (Office 97), Office 2000, or Office XP is required to run MATLAB Notebook, Excel Link, and Database Toolbox.

MEX-Files

MEX-files are dynamically linked subroutines that MATLAB can automatically load and execute. They provide a mechanism by which you can call your own C and Fortran subroutines from MATLAB as if they were built-in functions.

For More Information "External Interfaces/API" in the MATLAB documentation provides information on how to write MEX-files. "External Interfaces/API Reference" in the MATLAB documentation describes the collection of API functions. Both of these are available from Help.

If you plan to build your own MEX-files, one of the following is required:

- Borland C/C++ Version 5.0 or 5.02
- Borland C++Builder Version 3.0, 4.0, 5.0, or 6.0
- Compaq Visual Fortran Version 6.1 or 6.6
- Digital Visual Fortran Version 5.0 or 6.0
- Lcc C Version 2.4 (included with MATLAB)
- Microsoft Visual C/C++ Version 5.0, 6.0, or 7.0
- Watcom C/C++ Version 10.6 or 11

Note For an up-to-date list of all the compilers supported by MATLAB, see the MathWorks Technical Support Department's Technical Notes at

http://www.mathworks.com/support/tech-notes/v5/1600/1601.shtml

Installing MATLAB

This list summarizes the steps in the standard installation procedure. You can perform the installation by simply following the instructions in the dialog boxes presented by the installation program; it walks you through this process:

1 Exit any existing copies of MATLAB you have running.

2 Insert the MathWorks Product CD in your CD-ROM drive. The installation program starts automatically when the CD-ROM drive is ready. You can also run `setup.exe` from the product CD.

3 Install the Microsoft Java Virtual Machine (JVM), if prompted. The MathWorks Installer requires the Microsoft JVM.

Note: The Java installation requires a system reboot.

4 View the **Welcome** screen and review the Software License Agreement.

5 Review the Student Use Policy.

6 Enter your name and school name.

7 On the **Product List** screen, specify the destination directory, that is, the directory where you want to save the files on your hard drive. To change directories, use the **Browse** button. To install the complete set of software (MATLAB, Simulink, and the Symbolic Math Toolbox), make sure all of the products are selected.

8 When the installation is complete, verify the installation by starting MATLAB and running one of the demo programs. To start MATLAB, double-click on the MATLAB icon that the installer creates on your desktop. To run the demo programs, select **Demos** from **Help**.

Note The MathWorks Documentation CD must be in your CD-ROM drive to start MATLAB.

---

9 Customize any MATLAB environment options, if desired. For example, to include default definitions or any MATLAB expressions that you want executed every time MATLAB is invoked, create a file named `startup.m` in the $MATLAB\toolbox\local directory, where $MATLAB is the name of your MATLAB installation directory. MATLAB executes this file each time MATLAB is invoked.

10 Perform any additional configuration by typing the appropriate command at the MATLAB command prompt. For example, to configure the MATLAB Notebook, type notebook -setup. To configure a compiler to work with the MATLAB Application Program Interface, type mex -setup.

For More Information The MATLAB Installation Guide for Windows documentation provides additional installation information. This manual is available from Help.

Installing Additional Toolboxes

To purchase additional toolboxes, visit the MathWorks Store at (www.mathworks.com/store). Once you purchase a toolbox, it is downloaded to your computer.

When you download a toolbox, you receive an installation program for the toolbox. To install the toolbox, run the installation program by double-clicking on its icon. After you successfully install the toolbox, all of its functionality will be available to you when you start MATLAB.

Note Some toolboxes have ReadMe files associated with them. When you download the toolbox, check to see if there is a ReadMe file. These files contain important information about the toolbox and possibly installation and configuration notes. To view the ReadMe file for a toolbox, use the whatsnew command.

Accessing the Online Documentation (Help)

Access the online documentation (Help) directly from your Documentation CD:

1 Place the Documentation CD in your CD-ROM drive.

2 Select **Full Product Family Help** from the **Help** menu in the MATLAB Command Window. You can also type helpbrowser at the MATLAB prompt.

The Help browser appears.

Installing on Mac OS X

For More Information The Installing and Using MATLAB on Mac OS X documentation provides Macintosh-specific information for this release of MATLAB and its related products. This manual is available from Help.

System Requirements

Note For the most up-to-date information about system requirements, see the system requirements page, available in the Support area at the MathWorks Web site (www.mathworks.com).

MATLAB and Simulink

- Power Macintosh with G3 or G4 processor (G4 recommended)
- Mac OS X version 10.1.4 or higher
- 128 MB RAM minimum, 256 MB RAM recommended
- 90 MB free disk space for MATLAB only
- X Windows. The only supported version is the XFree86 4.2 X server (XDarwin) with the OroborOSX (Version 0.8 preview 3) window manager; both are included with MATLAB. (Note: XFree86 requires approximately 100 MB after it is uncompressed and installed onto your disk. To uncompress and install it onto your disk, you need an additional 40 MB for the uncompressed file and 40 MB for the actual installer. This space (80 MB) is not needed after XFree86 is installed.)
- CD-ROM drive for installation, program startup, and online documentation
- Netscape Navigator 4.7 or higher, or Microsoft Internet Explorer 5.1 or higher, is required.

MEX-Files

MEX-files are dynamically linked subroutines that MATLAB can automatically load and execute. They provide a mechanism by which you can call your own C and Fortran subroutines from MATLAB as if they were built-in functions.

For More Information "External Interfaces/API" in the MATLAB documentation provides information on how to write MEX-files. "External Interfaces/API Reference" in the MATLAB documentation describes the collection of API functions. Both of these are available from Help.

If you plan to build your own MEX-files, one of the following is required:

- gcc compiler as provided on Apple's Development Tools CD to build C MEX-files
- Absoft Pro Fortran v7.0 for OS X to build Fortran MEX-files

---

Note For an up-to-date list of all the compilers supported by MATLAB, see the MathWorks Technical Support Department's Technical Notes at

http://www.mathworks.com/support/tech-notes/v5/1600/1601.shtml

---

Installing MATLAB

The Student Version of MATLAB installs

- X Windows (XFree86/XDarwin)
- X Window Manager (OroborOSX)
- MATLAB, Simulink, and Symbolic Math Toolbox

The installation utility installs all the components necessary for a complete installation. The following sections fully describe the steps you must follow to install the products.

Note If you want to install MATLAB in a particular directory, you must have the appropriate permissions. For example, to install MATLAB in the Applications directory, you must have Administrator status. To create symbolic links in a particular directory, you must have the appropriate permissions. For information on setting permissions (privileges), see Macintosh Help (**Command+?** from the desktop).

1 Place the MathWorks Product CD in the CD-ROM drive. When the MATLAB_SV13 icon appears on the desktop, open it by double-clicking.

2 Double-click Install_for_Mac_OS_X.dmg to prepare for installation. A window opens containing the Install for Mac OS X installation utility and an Install for Mac OS X icon appears on the desktop.

3 Double-click the Install for Mac OS X icon in the window to begin the installation.

Note Use the Install for Mac OS X icon in the window, not on the desktop.

4 A welcome message appears. Click **Begin Installing** to begin the installation.

5 If you are not an Administrator, you will see this dialog.

You have two choices.

- If you continue the installation process as a non-Administrator, you will not be able to install MATLAB in the Applications directory. You will be able to install MATLAB in your Home directory.
- You can stop the installation, log out, and log in as an Administrator and then restart the installation.

6 If you are an Administrator, you will see this dialog.

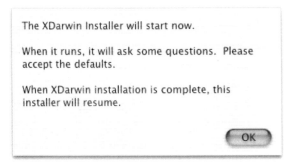

> MATLAB requires the X Server application XDarwin to run successfully.
>
> If you have a different X Server installed, you should remove that from the system before installing.
>
> Do you want to install XDarwin?
>
> (Skip XDarwin Installation)   (Install XDarwin)

Select **Install XDarwin**.

7 To start the XDarwin installation, click **OK** in this dialog.

> The XDarwin Installer will start now.
>
> When it runs, it will ask some questions. Please accept the defaults.
>
> When XDarwin installation is complete, this installer will resume.
>
> (OK)

Note The XDarwin installation can take several minutes.

As the XDarwin Installer runs, you will be asked for some information. The requested information includes these choices:

- Enter an Administrator password to authenticate.
- Select **English** as the language.
- Select **Full Install**.
- Do not create aliases.

At the conclusion of the XDarwin installation, this Install for Mac OS X utility will continue.

8 The next dialog lets you select where you want to install your MathWorks products and X Windows software.

> Now, you must choose where you want to install the MathWorks products and a new window manager for X Windows.
>
> We recommend that you create a new folder called MATLAB_SV13 in the Applications folder.
>
> (Cancel)   (Let me choose)   (**Do it for me**)

- If you are an Administrator, the Installer suggests you install the products in the Applications directory.
- If you are not an Administrator, the Installer suggests you install the products in your Home directory.

In either case, clicking **Do it for me** creates the new directory. You also have the option of choosing your own directory.

Note Your installation directory name cannot contain spaces, the @ character, or the $ character. Also, you cannot have a directory named private as part of the installation path. To create this directory in this location on your system, you must have administrative privileges. For information on setting privileges, see Macintosh Help (**Command+?** from the desktop).

---

9 This dialog lets you install and start the X Window Manager, called OroborOSX.

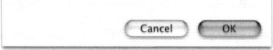

Click **OK** to start the X Window Manager OroborOSX. This window manager is required for the installation to proceed.

Installing and running OroborOSX may take a minute. After it is started, the installation of your MathWorks products will continue.

Cancel   OK

Click **OK**. This will install OroborOSX on your system and then start it.

10 When the OroborOSX installation is complete, OroborOSX starts and opens a window. When this dialog displays, click **OK** to start the MATLAB installation.

Click OK to run the MATLAB Installer.

Cancel   OK

11 When the installation script displays a welcome screen similar to this, click **OK**.

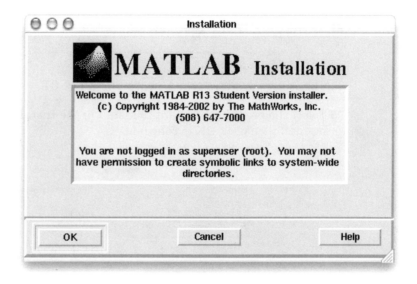

12 Accept or reject the software licensing agreement displayed. If you accept the terms of the agreement, you may proceed with the installation.

13 Verify the name of the installation directory in the **MATLAB Root Directory** dialog box and then click **OK** to continue. If you specify a directory that does not exist, the installer creates it. This book refers to this MATLAB installation directory as $MATLAB.

Note Do not install MATLAB 6.5 over any previous version of MATLAB.

---

14 The system displays your License File. Click **OK**.

15 Select the products you want to install in the **Installation Options** dialog box and then click **OK** to continue.

This dialog box lists all the products you are licensed to install in the **Items to Install** box. To remove an item from the **Items to install** list, select it and click the **Remove** button. (A MATLAB installation includes MATLAB, the MATLAB Toolbox, and the MATLAB Kernel.)

16 The **Installation Data** dialog box lets you specify where you want to put symbolic links to matlab and mex scripts. Leave the checkbox unselected and click **OK** to continue. The preferred method for starting MATLAB is to use the LaunchMATLAB application, which is described at the end of this installation process on page 2-16.

17 Click **OK** to begin the MATLAB installation.

18 After the installation is complete, the installer displays the **Installation Complete** dialog box, assuming your installation is successful. This dialog box informs you of some optional post-installation setup and configuration steps you may want to perform. See "After You Install" in the Installing and Using MATLAB on Mac OS X documentation for more information. Click **Exit** to dismiss the installer.

19 When the installation is complete, you can remove the CD. To do so:

- Drag the Install for Mac OS X icon from the desktop to the Trash.
- Then, drag the CD's icon to the Trash.

20 To start MATLAB, you can use the LaunchMATLAB application. The installation process puts the LaunchMATLAB application in the $MATLAB/bin directory. You can drag the icon to your dock or make an alias to it on your desktop for easy access.

Note Do not drag the LaunchMATLAB application to your desktop. The application must remain in the $MATLAB/bin directory.

Note The MathWorks Documentation CD must be in your CD-ROM drive to start MATLAB.

Double-click LaunchMATLAB to start MATLAB. The LaunchMATLAB application starts X Windows and then runs MATLAB.

21 To specify the path to the online documentation (Help), select **Preferences** from the **File** menu and then select **Help**. Change the **Documentation location** to /Volumes/MATLAB_SV13_DOC/help. Click **OK** to complete the process.

For More Information The Installing and Using MATLAB on Mac OS X documentation provides additional installation information. This manual is available from Help.

Installing Additional Toolboxes

To purchase additional toolboxes, visit the MathWorks Store at (www.mathworks.com/store). Once you purchase a toolbox, it is downloaded to your computer.

When you download a toolbox, you receive an installation program for the toolbox. To install the toolbox, run the installation program by double-clicking on its icon. After you successfully install the toolbox, all of its functionality will be available to you when you start MATLAB.

Note Some toolboxes have ReadMe files associated with them. When you download the toolbox, check to see if there is a ReadMe file. These files contain important information about the toolbox and possibly installation and configuration notes. To view the ReadMe file for a toolbox, use the whatsnew command.

Accessing the Online Documentation (Help)

Access the online documentation (Help) directly from your Documentation CD:

1 Place the Documentation CD in your CD-ROM drive.

2 Select **Full Product Family Help** from the **Help** menu in the MATLAB Command Window. You can also type helpbrowser at the MATLAB prompt.

Mac OS X Documentation

In general, the documentation for MathWorks products is not specific for individual platforms unless the product is available only on a particular platform. For the Macintosh, when you access a product's documentation either in print or online through the Help browser, make sure you refer to the UNIX platform if there is different documentation for different platforms.

For More Information The Installing and Using MATLAB on Mac OS X documentation provides Macintosh-specific information for this release of MATLAB and its related products.

Installing on Linux

System Requirements

Note For the most up-to-date information about system requirements, see the system requirements page, available in the products area at the MathWorks Web site (www.mathworks.com).

MATLAB and Simulink

- Intel-based Pentium, Pentium Pro, Pentium II, Pentium III, Pentium IV, AMD Athlon, Athlon XP-based personal computer
- Linux 2.2.x, 2.4.x kernel; glibc(libc) 2.1.2 required, glibc(libc) 2.2.5 recommended
- X Windows (X11R6)
- 90 MB free disk space for MATLAB only
- 128 MB RAM, additional memory strongly recommended
- 64 MB swap space, 128 MB recommended
- CD-ROM drive for installation, program startup, and online documentation
- Netscape Navigator 4.0 or higher
- Adobe Acrobat Reader 3.0 or higher is required to view and print the MATLAB online documentation that is in PDF format.

MEX-Files

MEX-files are dynamically linked subroutines that MATLAB can automatically load and execute. They provide a mechanism by which you can call your own C and Fortran subroutines from MATLAB as if they were built-in functions.

For More Information "External Interfaces/API" in the MATLAB documentation provides information on how to write MEX-files. "External Interfaces/API Reference" in the MATLAB documentation describes the collection of API functions. Both of these are available from Help.

If you plan to build your own MEX-files, you need an ANSIC C compiler (e.g., the GNU C compiler, gcc).

Note For an up-to-date list of all the compilers supported by MATLAB, see the MathWorks Technical Support Department's Technical Notes at

```
http://www.mathworks.com/support/tech-notes/v5/1600/1601.shtml
```

Installing MATLAB

The following instructions describe how to install the MATLAB Student Version on your computer.

Note On most systems, you will need root privileges to perform certain steps in the installation procedure.

Installing the Software

To install the Student Version:

1 If your CD-ROM drive is not accessible to your operating system, you will need to create a directory to be the mount point for it.

```
mkdir /cdrom
```

2 Place the MathWorks Product CD in the CD-ROM drive.

3 Mount the CD-ROM drive on your system. If your system allows nonroot users to mount a CD-ROM, use the command

```
$ mount /cdrom
```

If your system requires that you have root privileges to mount a CD-ROM drive, this command should work on most systems.

```
# mount -t iso9660 /dev/cdrom /cdrom
```

To enable nonroot users to mount a CD-ROM drive, include the exec option in the entry for CD-ROM drives in your /etc/fstab file, as in the following example.

```
/dev/cdrom /cdrom iso9660 noauto,ro,user,exec 0 0
```

This option is often omitted for security reasons.

4 Move to the installation location using the cd command. For example, if you are going to install into the location /usr/local/matlab6p5, use the commands

```
cd /usr/local
mkdir matlab6p5
cd matlab6p5
```

Subsequent instructions in this section refer to this directory as $MATLAB.

5 Run the CD install script.

```
/cdrom/install_unix.sh
```

The welcome screen appears. Click **OK** to proceed with the installation.

Note If you need additional help on any step during this installation process, click the **Help** button at the bottom of the dialog box.

6 Accept or reject the software licensing agreement displayed. If you accept the terms of the agreement, click **OK** to proceed with the installation.

7 Verify the name of the directory in which you want to install MATLAB in the **MATLAB Root Directory** screen. You can edit the pathname in this dialog box. If the MATLAB root directory is correct, click **OK** to proceed with the installation.

8 View your license file. Click **OK** to proceed with the installation.

9 Select the products you want to install in the **Product Installation Options** dialog box.

The products you are licensed to install are listed in the **Items to install** list box. If you do not want to install a product, select it in the list and click **Remove**. The installer moves the product to the **Items not to install** list.

To install the complete MATLAB Student Version, you must install all the products for which you are licensed (MATLAB, MATLAB Toolbox, MATLAB Kernel, Simulink, and Symbolic Math Toolbox). Click **OK** to proceed with the installation.

10 Specify in the **Installation Data** dialog box the directory in which you want to install symbolic links to the `matlab` and `mex` scripts. Choose a directory that is common to all users path's, such as `/usr/local/bin`. You must be logged in as `root` to do this. Click **OK** to proceed with the installation.

```
┌─────────────────────────────────────────────────────────┐
│                   Installation Data                     │
│                                                         │
│  ☐ Create symbolic links to MATLAB and mex scripts      │
│  Specify directory to put links in:                     │
│  ┌─────────────────────────────────────────────────┐    │
│  │ /usr/local/bin                                  │    │
│  └─────────────────────────────────────────────────┘    │
│                                                         │
│                                                         │
│  Please enter your MATLAB License No.  ┌──────────┐     │
│                                        │ Student  │     │
│                                        └──────────┘     │
│  Press the Help button for more information about these items. │
│  ┌─────────┐      ┌─────────┐        ┌─────────┐        │
│  │   OK    │      │ Cancel  │        │  Help   │        │
│  └─────────┘      └─────────┘        └─────────┘        │
└─────────────────────────────────────────────────────────┘
```

11 Start the installation by clicking **OK** in the **Begin Product Installation** dialog box. The installer displays a dialog box indicating the progress of the installation.

12 After the installation is complete, the installer displays the **Product Installation Complete** dialog box, assuming your installation is successful. Click **Exit** to exit the installer program.

13 Specify the path to the online documentation (Help) by editing the docopt.m M-file, located in the $MATLAB/toolbox/local directory.

For example, if /cdrom is the path to your CD-ROM drive, your documentation path is /cdrom/help. You must specify this path as the value of docpath in the isunix block in the docopt.m file.

```
elseif isunix                 % UNIX
%    doccmd = '';
%    options = '';
     docpath = '/cdrom/help';
```

You can use the docopt.m file to specify several other documentation options, such as the default Web browser. Netscape Navigator is configured as the default browser.

14 If desired, customize any MATLAB environment options. For example, to include default definitions or any MATLAB expressions that you want executed every time MATLAB is invoked, create a file named startup.m in the $MATLAB/toolbox/local directory. MATLAB executes this file each time MATLAB is invoked.

15 Put The MathWorks documentation CD in your CD-ROM drive.

Note To start MATLAB, the MathWorks Documentation CD must be in your CD-ROM drive.

To remove the product CD, you must first unmount it. (You must have root privileges to perform this step.)

```
#umount /cdrom
```

Insert The MathWorks documentation CD into your CD-ROM drive and mount it again, as described in Step 3.

16 Start MATLAB by entering the matlab command. If you did not set up symbolic links in a directory on your path, type $MATLAB/bin/matlab.

Post Installation Procedures

Successful Installation

If you want to use the MATLAB Application Program Interface, you must configure the mex script to work with your compiler. Also, some toolboxes may require some additional configuration. For more information, see "Installing Additional Toolboxes" on page 2-25.

Unsuccessful Installation

If MATLAB does not execute correctly after installation:

1 Check the "MATLAB Release Notes for Release 13" documentation for the latest information concerning installation. This document is accessible from Help.

2 Repeat the installation procedure from the beginning but run the CD install script using the -t option.

```
/cdrom/install_unix.sh -t
```

For More Information The MATLAB Installation Guide for UNIX documentation provides additional installation information. This manual is available from Help.

Installing Additional Toolboxes

To purchase additional toolboxes, visit the MathWorks Store at (www.mathworks.com/store). Once you purchase a toolbox, it is downloaded to your computer. When you download a toolbox on Linux, you receive a tar file (a standard, compressed formatted file).

To install the toolbox, you must

1 Place the tar file in $MATLAB and un-tar it.

```
tar -xf filename
```

2 Run the installation procedure.

```
install
```

After you successfully install the toolbox, all of its functionality will be available to you when you start MATLAB.

Note Some toolboxes have ReadMe files associated with them. When you download the toolbox, check to see if there is a ReadMe file. These files contain important information about the toolbox and possibly installation and configuration notes. To view the ReadMe file for a toolbox, use the whatsnew command.

Accessing the Online Documentation (Help)

Access the online documentation (Help) directly from your Documentation CD:

1 Place the Documentation CD in your CD-ROM drive and mount it.

2 Select **Full Product Family Help** from the **Help** menu in the MATLAB Command Window. You can also type `helpbrowser` at the MATLAB prompt.

Development Environment

This chapter provides a brief introduction to starting and quitting MATLAB, and the tools and functions that help you to work with MATLAB variables and files. For more information about the topics covered here, see the corresponding topics under "Development Environment" in the MATLAB documentation, which is available online.

Starting and Quitting MATLAB (p. 3-2)	Start and quit MATLAB and perform operations upon startup and shutdown.
MATLAB Desktop (p. 3-3)	The graphical user interface to MATLAB
Desktop Tools (p. 3-5)	Use these tools in the desktop:

- Command Window for running functions and entering variables, and Command History for viewing previously run functions

- **Start** button for launching tools, demos, and documentation

- Help browser for accessing documentation

- Current Directory browser for accessing files

- Workspace browser and Array Editor for viewing and editing variables

- Editor/Debugger for modifying MATLAB program files (M-files)

Other Development Environment Features (p. 3-15)	Import and export data including using the Import Wizard, improve M-file performance using the Profiler, interface with source control systems, and access MATLAB from Microsoft Word using the MATLAB Notebook feature.

Starting and Quitting MATLAB

Starting MATLAB

Note The Documentation CD must be in your CD-ROM drive to start MATLAB. To access the online documentation, the Documentation CD must remain in your CD-ROM drive.

Microsoft Windows. Double-click the MATLAB shortcut icon 🔥 on your Windows desktop.

Macintosh OS X. Double-click LaunchMATLAB on the desktop. The LaunchMATLAB application starts X Windows and then runs MATLAB.

Linux. Type matlab at the operating system prompt.

After starting MATLAB, the MATLAB desktop opens — see "MATLAB Desktop" on page 3-3.

You can change the directory in which MATLAB starts, define startup options including running a script upon startup, and reduce startup time in some situations. For more information, refer to "Starting MATLAB" in the MATLAB documentation.

Quitting MATLAB

To end your MATLAB session, select **Exit MATLAB** from the **File** menu in the desktop, or type quit in the Command Window. To execute specified functions each time MATLAB quits, such as saving the workspace, you can create and run a finish.m script.

MATLAB Desktop

When you start MATLAB, the MATLAB desktop appears, containing tools (graphical user interfaces) for managing files, variables, and applications associated with MATLAB.

The first time MATLAB starts, the desktop appears as shown in the following illustration.

Use tab to go to Current Directory browser.   Get help.   Enter MATLAB functions.   View or change current directory.   Click to move window outside of desktop.   Close window.

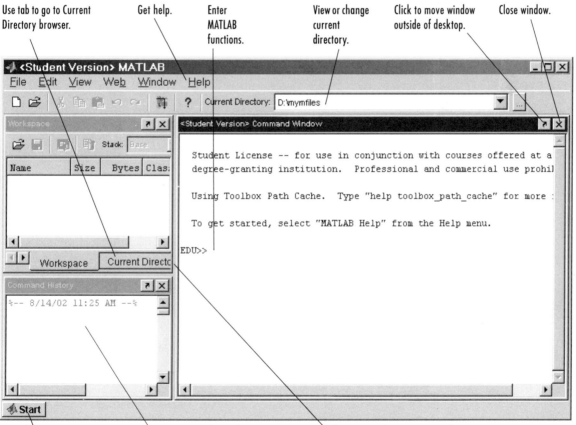

Expand to view documentation, demos, and tools for your products.   View or use previously run functions.   Drag the separator bar to resize windows.

You can change the way your desktop looks by opening, closing, moving, and resizing the tools in it. You can also move tools outside of the desktop (undock) or return them back inside the desktop (dock). All the desktop tools provide common features such as context menus and keyboard shortcuts.

You can specify certain characteristics for the desktop tools by selecting **Preferences** from the **File** menu. For example, you can specify the font characteristics for Command Window text. For more information, click the **Help** button in the **Preferences** dialog box.

Desktop Tools

This section provides an introduction to the MATLAB desktop tools. You can also use MATLAB functions to perform most of the features found in the desktop tools. The tools are

- "Command Window" on page 3-5
- "Command History" on page 3-6
- "Start Button" on page 3-7
- "Help Browser" on page 3-8
- "Current Directory Browser" on page 3-10
- "Workspace Browser" on page 3-12
- "Array Editor" on page 3-12
- "Editor/Debugger" on page 3-14

Command Window

Use the **Command Window** to enter variables and run functions and M-files. For more information on controlling input and output, see "Controlling Command Window Input and Output" on page 4-28.

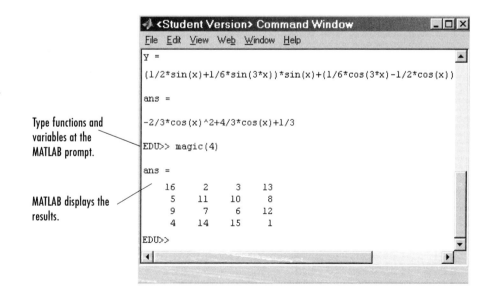

Type functions and variables at the MATLAB prompt.

MATLAB displays the results.

3-5

Command History

Lines you enter in the Command Window are logged in the **Command History** window. In the Command History, you can view previously used functions, and copy and execute selected lines.

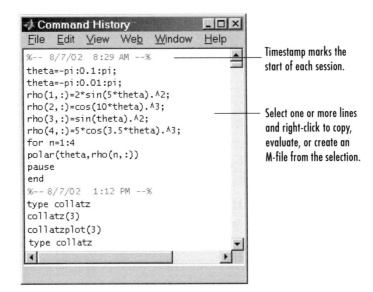

Timestamp marks the start of each session.

Select one or more lines and right-click to copy, evaluate, or create an M-file from the selection.

To save the input and output from a MATLAB session to a file, use the diary function.

Note If other users share the same machine with you, using the same login information, then they will have access to the functions you ran during a session via the Command History. If you do not want other users to have access to the Command History from your session, select **Preferences** from the **File** menu, and for Command History, **Saving**, select **Don't Save History File**. Alternatively, you can clear selected statements from the Command History window before you quit.

Running External Programs

You can run external programs from the MATLAB Command Window. The exclamation point character, !, is a shell escape and indicates that the rest of the input line is a command to the operating system. This is useful for invoking utilities or running other programs without quitting MATLAB. On Linux, for example,

```
!emacs magik.m
```

invokes an editor called emacs for a file named magik.m. When you quit the external program, the operating system returns control to MATLAB.

Start Button

The MATLAB **Start** Button provides easy access to tools, demos, and documentation.

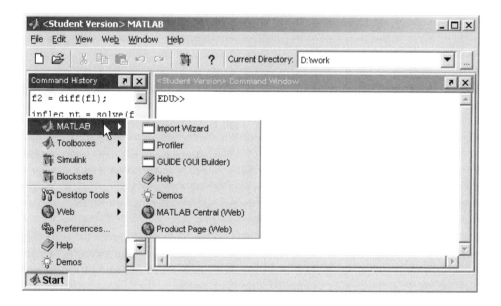

Help Browser

Use the Help browser to search and view documentation and demos for all MathWorks products. The Help browser is a Web browser integrated into the MATLAB desktop that displays HTML documents.

To open the Help browser, click the help button **?** in the toolbar, or type helpbrowser in the Command Window.

Tabs in the Help Navigator pane provide different ways to find documentation.

View documentation in the display pane.

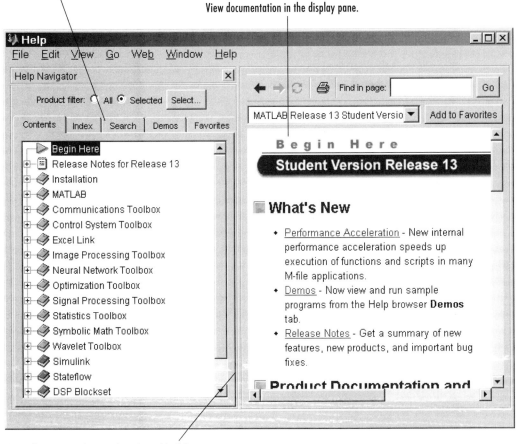

Drag the separator bar to adjust the width of the panes.

The Help browser consists of two panes, the Help Navigator (on the left), which you use to find information, and the display pane (on the right), where you view the information.

Help Navigator

Use the Help Navigator to find information. It includes

- **Product filter** — Set the filter to show documentation only for the products you specify.

Note In the MATLAB Student Version, the product filter is initially set to display a subset of the entire documentation set. You can add or delete which product documentation is displayed by using the product filter.

- **Contents** tab — View the titles and tables of contents for documentation for your products.
- **Index** tab — Find specific index entries (selected keywords) in the MathWorks documentation for your products.
- **Search** tab — Look for a specific phrase in the documentation. To get help for a specific function, set the **Search type** to **Function Name**.
- **Demos** tab — View a listing of and run sample programs.
- **Favorites** tab — View a list of documents you previously designated as favorites.

Display Pane

After finding documentation using the Help Navigator, view it in the display pane. While viewing the documentation, you can

- Browse to other pages — Use the arrows at the tops and bottoms of the pages.
- Bookmark pages — Click the **Add to Favorites** button in the toolbar.
- Print pages — Click the print button in the toolbar.
- Find a term in the page — Type a term in the **Find in page** field in the toolbar, and click **Go**.

Other features available in the display pane are: copying information, evaluating a selection, and viewing Web pages.

For More Help

In addition to the Help browser, you can use help functions. To get help for a specific function, use doc. For example, doc format displays help for the format function in the Help browser. Other means for getting help include contacting Technical Support (http://www.mathworks.com/support) and participating in the newsgroup for MATLAB users, comp.soft-sys.matlab. You can access these from the **Web** menu.

Current Directory Browser

MATLAB file operations use the current directory and the search path as reference points. Any file you want to run must either be in the current directory or on the search path.

A quick way to view or change the current directory is by using the **Current Directory** field in the desktop toolbar as shown below.

Current Directory: D:\mymfiles

To search for, view, open, and make changes to MATLAB related directories and files, use the MATLAB Current Directory browser. Alternatively, you can use the functions dir, cd, and delete.

Use the pathname edit box to view directories and their contents.

Click the find button to search for content within M-files.

Double-click a file to open it in an appropriate tool.

View the help portion of the selected M-file.

```
Current Directory
File  Edit  View  Web  Window  Help
D:\mymfiles

All Files          File Type    Last Modified            Description
results            Folder       22-Feb-2002 11:23 AM
bucky.m            M-file       27-Nov-1997 06:28 AM     BUCKY  Connectivi
caution.mdl        Model        13-Nov-1997 02:43 PM
collatz.m          M-file       07-May-2002 04:00 PM     Collatz problem.
collatz3.fig       FIG-file     17-Jul-2000 05:24 PM
collatzall.asv     ASV File     13-May-2002 07:05 PM
collatzall.m       M-file       13-May-2002 01:05 PM     Plot length of se
collatzplot.m      M-file       08-May-2002 09:38 AM     Plot length of se
diary              File         20-Dec-1999 03:19 PM
falling.m          M-file       10-Dec-1999 04:24 PM

B = BUCKY is the 60-by-60 sparse adjacency matrix of the
connectivity graph of the geodesic dome, the soccer ball,
and the carbon-60 molecule.
[B,V] = BUCKY also returns xyz coordinates of the vertices.
```

Search Path

To determine how to execute functions you call, MATLAB uses a *search path* to find M-files and other MATLAB related files, which are organized in directories on your file system. Any file you want to run in MATLAB must reside in the current directory or in a directory that is on the search path. By default, the files supplied with MATLAB and MathWorks toolboxes are included in the search path.

To see which directories are on the search path or to change the search path, select **Set Path** from the **File** menu in the desktop, and use the **Set Path** dialog box. Alternatively, you can use the path function to view the search path, addpath to add directories to the path, and rmpath to remove directories from the path.

Workspace Browser

The MATLAB workspace consists of the set of variables (named arrays) built up during a MATLAB session and stored in memory. You add variables to the workspace by using functions, running M-files, and loading saved workspaces.

To view the workspace and information about each variable, use the Workspace browser, or use the functions who and whos.

Double-click a variable to see and change its contents in the Array Editor.

Name	Size	Bytes	Class
a	1x10	80	double array
c	1x1	16	double array (complex)
e	1x1	4	cell array
g	1x10	80	double array (global)
i	1x10	10	int8 array
l	1x10	80	double array (logical)
m	1x6	12	char array
n	1x1	822	inline object
p	1x10	164	sparse array
s	1x1	406	struct array
u	1x10	40	uint32 array

To delete variables from the workspace, select the variable and select **Delete** from the **Edit** menu. Alternatively, use the clear function.

The workspace is not maintained after you end the MATLAB session. To save the workspace to a file that can be read during a later MATLAB session, select **Save Workspace As** from the **File** menu, or use the save function. This saves the workspace to a binary file called a MAT-file, which has a .mat extension. There are options for saving to different formats. To read in a MAT-file, select **Import Data** from the **File** menu, or use the load function.

Array Editor

Double-click a variable in the Workspace browser to see it in the Array Editor. Use the Array Editor to view and edit a visual representation of one- or two-dimensional numeric arrays, strings, and cell arrays of strings that are in the workspace.

Change values of array elements.   Change the display format.

	1	2	3	4
1	16	2	3	13
2	5	11	10	8
3	9	7	6	12
4	4	14	15	1

Array Editor: m

File Edit View Web Window Help

Numeric format: shortG   Size: 1   by 10

Array Editor: m   Array Editor: x   Array Editor: theta

Use the tabs to view the variables you have open in the Array Editor.

Editor/Debugger

Use the Editor/Debugger to create and debug M-files, which are programs that run MATLAB functions. The Editor/Debugger provides a graphical user interface for basic text editing, as well as for M-file debugging.

Comment selected lines and specify indenting style using the **Text** menu.　　Find and replace strings.

Set breakpoints where you want to pause execution so you can examine variables.

Hold the cursor over a variable and its current value appears (called a datatip).

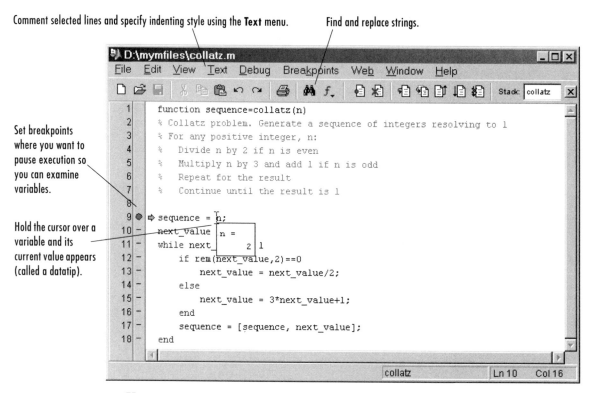

You can use any text editor to create M-files, such as Emacs, and can use preferences (accessible from the desktop **File** menu) to specify that editor as the default. If you use another editor, you can still use the MATLAB Editor/Debugger for debugging, or you can use debugging functions such as dbstop, which sets a breakpoint.

If you only need to view the contents of an M-file, you can display it in the Command Window by using the type function.

Other Development Environment Features

Additional development environment features are

- "Importing and Exporting Data" — Techniques for bringing data created by other applications into the MATLAB workspace, including the Import Wizard, and packaging MATLAB workspace variables for use by other applications.
- "Measuring M-File Performance" — The Profiler is a tool that measures where an M-file is spending its time. Use it to help you make speed improvements.
- "Interfacing with Source Control Systems" — Access your source control system from within MATLAB, Simulink, and Stateflow.
- "Using Notebook" — Access the MATLAB numeric computation and visualization software from within the word processing environment, Microsoft Word.

4

Getting Started

This chapter introduces the basic components of MATLAB and how to work with them.

Matrices and Magic Squares

In MATLAB, a matrix is a rectangular array of numbers. Special meaning is sometimes attached to 1-by-1 matrices, which are scalars, and to matrices with only one row or column, which are vectors. MATLAB has other ways of storing both numeric and nonnumeric data, but in the beginning, it is usually best to think of everything as a matrix. The operations in MATLAB are designed to be as natural as possible. Where other programming languages work with numbers one at a time, MATLAB allows you to work with entire matrices quickly and easily. A good example matrix, used throughout this book, appears in the Renaissance engraving *Melancholia I* by the German artist and amateur mathematician Albrecht Dürer.

This image is filled with mathematical symbolism, and if you look carefully, you will see a matrix in the upper right corner. This matrix is known as a magic square and was believed by many in Dürer's time to have genuinely magical properties. It does turn out to have some fascinating characteristics worth exploring.

Entering Matrices

The best way for you to get started with MATLAB is to learn how to handle matrices. Start MATLAB and follow along with each example.

You can enter matrices into MATLAB in several different ways:

- Enter an explicit list of elements.
- Load matrices from external data files.
- Generate matrices using built-in functions.
- Create matrices with your own functions in M-files.

Start by entering Dürer's matrix as a list of its elements. You have only to follow a few basic conventions:

- Separate the elements of a row with blanks or commas.
- Use a semicolon, ; , to indicate the end of each row.
- Surround the entire list of elements with square brackets, [ ].

To enter Dürer's matrix, simply type in the Command Window

```
A = [16 3 2 13; 5 10 11 8; 9 6 7 12; 4 15 14 1]
```

MATLAB displays the matrix you just entered,

```
A =
    16     3     2    13
     5    10    11     8
     9     6     7    12
     4    15    14     1
```

This exactly matches the numbers in the engraving. Once you have entered the matrix, it is automatically remembered in the MATLAB workspace. You can refer to it simply as A. Now that you have A in the workspace, take a look at what makes it so interesting. Why is it magic?

sum, transpose, and diag

You're probably already aware that the special properties of a magic square have to do with the various ways of summing its elements. If you take the sum along any row or column, or along either of the two main diagonals, you will always get the same number. Let's verify that using MATLAB. The first statement to try is

```
sum(A)
```

MATLAB replies with

```
ans =
    34    34    34    34
```

When you don't specify an output variable, MATLAB uses the variable ans, short for *answer*, to store the results of a calculation. You have computed a row vector containing the sums of the columns of A. Sure enough, each of the columns has the same sum, the *magic* sum, 34.

How about the row sums? MATLAB has a preference for working with the columns of a matrix, so the easiest way to get the row sums is to transpose the matrix, compute the column sums of the transpose, and then transpose the result. The transpose operation is denoted by an apostrophe or single quote, '. It flips a matrix about its main diagonal and it turns a row vector into a column vector. So

```
A'
```
produces

```
ans =
    16     5     9     4
```

```
     3    10     6    15
     2    11     7    14
    13     8    12     1
```

And

```
sum(A')'
```

produces a column vector containing the row sums

```
ans =
    34
    34
    34
    34
```

The sum of the elements on the main diagonal is easily obtained with the help of the diag function, which picks off that diagonal.

```
diag(A)
```

produces

```
ans =
    16
    10
     7
     1
```

and

```
sum(diag(A))
```

produces

```
ans =
    34
```

The other diagonal, the so-called *antidiagonal,* is not so important mathematically, so MATLAB does not have a ready-made function for it. But a function originally intended for use in graphics, fliplr, flips a matrix from left to right.

```
sum(diag(fliplr(A)))
```

```
ans =
      34
```

You have verified that the matrix in Dürer's engraving is indeed a magic square and, in the process, have sampled a few MATLAB matrix operations. The following sections continue to use this matrix to illustrate additional MATLAB capabilities.

Subscripts

The element in row i and column j of A is denoted by $A(i,j)$. For example, $A(4,2)$ is the number in the fourth row and second column. For our magic square, $A(4,2)$ is 15. So it is possible to compute the sum of the elements in the fourth column of A by typing

```
A(1,4) + A(2,4) + A(3,4) + A(4,4)
```

This produces

```
ans =
      34
```

but is not the most elegant way of summing a single column.

It is also possible to refer to the elements of a matrix with a single subscript, $A(k)$. This is the usual way of referencing row and column vectors. But it can also apply to a fully two-dimensional matrix, in which case the array is regarded as one long column vector formed from the columns of the original matrix. So, for our magic square, $A(8)$ is another way of referring to the value 15 stored in $A(4,2)$.

If you try to use the value of an element outside of the matrix, it is an error.

```
t = A(4,5)
Index exceeds matrix dimensions.
```

On the other hand, if you store a value in an element outside of the matrix, the size increases to accommodate the newcomer.

```
X = A;
X(4,5) = 17
```

```
X =
    16     3     2    13     0
     5    10    11     8     0
     9     6     7    12     0
     4    15    14     1    17
```

The Colon Operator

The colon, :, is one of the most important operators in MATLAB. It occurs in several different forms. The expression

    1:10

is a row vector containing the integers from 1 to 10

    1   2   3   4   5   6   7   8   9   10

To obtain nonunit spacing, specify an increment. For example,

    100:-7:50

is

    100   93   86   79   72   65   58   51

and

    0:pi/4:pi

is

    0   0.7854   1.5708   2.3562   3.1416

Subscript expressions involving colons refer to portions of a matrix.

    A(1:k,j)

is the first k elements of the jth column of A. So

    sum(A(1:4,4))

computes the sum of the fourth column. But there is a better way. The colon by itself refers to *all* the elements in a row or column of a matrix and the keyword end refers to the *last* row or column. So

    sum(A(:,end))

computes the sum of the elements in the last column of A.

```
ans =
      34
```

Why is the magic sum for a 4-by-4 square equal to 34? If the integers from 1 to 16 are sorted into four groups with equal sums, that sum must be

```
sum(1:16)/4
```

which, of course, is

```
ans =
      34
```

Using the Symbolic Math Toolbox, you can discover that the magic sum for an n-by-n magic square is $(n^3 + n)/2$.

The magic Function

MATLAB actually has a built-in function that creates magic squares of almost any size. Not surprisingly, this function is named `magic`.

```
B = magic(4)

B =
      16     2     3    13
       5    11    10     8
       9     7     6    12
       4    14    15     1
```

This matrix is almost the same as the one in the Dürer engraving and has all the same "magic" properties; the only difference is that the two middle columns are exchanged. To make this B into Dürer's A, swap the two middle columns.

```
A = B(:,[1 3 2 4])
```

This says "for each of the rows of matrix B, reorder the elements in the order 1, 3, 2, 4." It produces

```
A =
    16     3     2    13
     5    10    11     8
     9     6     7    12
     4    15    14     1
```

Why would Dürer go to the trouble of rearranging the columns when he could have used the MATLAB ordering? No doubt he wanted to include the date of the engraving, 1514, at the bottom of his magic square.

For More Information The MATLAB documentation, which is accessible from Help, provides comprehensive material on the development environment, mathematics, programming and data types, graphics, 3-D visualization, external interfaces/API, and creating graphical user interfaces in MATLAB.

Expressions

Like most other programming languages, MATLAB provides mathematical *expressions*, but unlike most programming languages, these expressions involve entire matrices. The building blocks of expressions are

- Variables
- Numbers
- Operators
- Functions

Variables

MATLAB does not require any type declarations or dimension statements. When MATLAB encounters a new variable name, it automatically creates the variable and allocates the appropriate amount of storage. If the variable already exists, MATLAB changes its contents and, if necessary, allocates new storage. For example,

```
num_students = 25
```

creates a 1-by-1 matrix named `num_students` and stores the value 25 in its single element.

Variable names consist of a letter, followed by any number of letters, digits, or underscores. MATLAB uses only the first 31 characters of a variable name. MATLAB is case sensitive; it distinguishes between uppercase and lowercase letters. A and a are *not* the same variable. To view the matrix assigned to any variable, simply enter the variable name.

Numbers

MATLAB uses conventional decimal notation, with an optional decimal point and leading plus or minus sign, for numbers. *Scientific notation* uses the letter e to specify a power-of-ten scale factor. *Imaginary numbers* use either i or j as a suffix. Some examples of legal numbers are

```
3              -99          0.0001
9.6397238      1.60210e-20  6.02252e23
1i             -3.14159j    3e5i
```

All numbers are stored internally using the *long* format specified by the IEEE floating-point standard. Floating-point numbers have a finite *precision* of roughly 16 significant decimal digits and a finite *range* of roughly 10^{-308} to 10^{+308}.

Operators

Expressions use familiar arithmetic operators and precedence rules.

+	Addition
-	Subtraction
*	Multiplication
/	Division
\	Left division (described in "Matrices and Linear Algebra" in the MATLAB documentation)
^	Power
'	Complex conjugate transpose
( )	Specify evaluation order

Functions

MATLAB provides a large number of standard elementary mathematical functions, including abs, sqrt, exp, and sin. Taking the square root or logarithm of a negative number is not an error; the appropriate complex result is produced automatically. MATLAB also provides many more advanced mathematical functions, including Bessel and gamma functions. Most of these functions accept complex arguments. For a list of the elementary mathematical functions, type

```
help elfun
```

For a list of more advanced mathematical and matrix functions, type

```
help specfun
help elmat
```

For More Information Appendix A, "MATLAB Quick Reference," contains brief descriptions of the MATLAB functions. Use Help to access complete descriptions of all the MATLAB functions using the **Category** or **Alphabetical** option.

Some of the functions, like sqrt and sin, are *built-in*. They are part of the MATLAB core so they are very efficient, but the computational details are not readily accessible. Other functions, like gamma and sinh, are implemented in M-files. You can see the code and even modify it if you want.

Several special functions provide values of useful constants.

pi	3.14159265...
i	Imaginary unit, $\sqrt{-1}$
j	Same as i
eps	Floating-point relative precision, 2^{-52}
realmin	Smallest floating-point number, 2^{-1022}
realmax	Largest floating-point number, $(2 - \varepsilon)2^{1023}$
Inf	Infinity
NaN	Not-a-number

Infinity is generated by dividing a nonzero value by zero, or by evaluating well defined mathematical expressions that *overflow*, i.e., exceed realmax. Not-a-number is generated by trying to evaluate expressions like 0/0 or Inf-Inf that do not have well defined mathematical values.

The function names are not reserved. It is possible to overwrite any of them with a new variable, such as

```
eps = 1.e-6
```

and then use that value in subsequent calculations. The original function can be restored with

```
clear eps
```

Examples of Expressions

You have already seen several examples of MATLAB expressions. Here are a few more examples, and the resulting values.

```
rho = (1+sqrt(5))/2
rho =
    1.6180

a = abs(3+4i)
a =
     5

z = sqrt(besselk(4/3,rho-i))
z =
   0.3730+ 0.3214i

huge = exp(log(realmax))
huge =
  1.7977e+308

toobig = pi*huge
toobig =
    Inf
```

Working with Matrices

This section introduces you to other ways of creating matrices.

Generating Matrices

MATLAB provides four functions that generate basic matrices.

zeros	All zeros
ones	All ones
rand	Uniformly distributed random elements
randn	Normally distributed random elements

Here are some examples.

```
Z = zeros(2,4)
Z =
     0     0     0     0
     0     0     0     0

F = 5*ones(3,3)
F =
     5     5     5
     5     5     5
     5     5     5

N = fix(10*rand(1,10))
N =
     4     9     4     4     8     5     2     6     8     0

R = randn(4,4)
R =
    1.0668    0.2944   -0.6918   -1.4410
    0.0593   -1.3362    0.8580    0.5711
   -0.0956    0.7143    1.2540   -0.3999
   -0.8323    1.6236   -1.5937    0.6900
```

The load Command

The load command reads binary files containing matrices generated by earlier MATLAB sessions, or reads text files containing numeric data. The text file should be organized as a rectangular table of numbers, separated by blanks, with one row per line, and an equal number of elements in each row. For example, outside of MATLAB, create a text file containing these four lines.

```
16.0    3.0    2.0   13.0
 5.0   10.0   11.0    8.0
 9.0    6.0    7.0   12.0
 4.0   15.0   14.0    1.0
```

Store the file under the name magik.dat. Then the command

```
load magik.dat
```

reads the file and creates a variable, magik, containing our example matrix.

An easy way to read data into MATLAB in many text or binary formats is to use the Import Wizard.

M-Files

You can create your own matrices using *M-files*, which are text files containing MATLAB code. Use the MATLAB Editor or another text editor to create a file containing the same statements you would type at the MATLAB command line. Save the file under a name that ends in .m.

For example, create a file containing these five lines.

```
A = [ ...
16.0    3.0    2.0   13.0
 5.0   10.0   11.0    8.0
 9.0    6.0    7.0   12.0
 4.0   15.0   14.0    1.0 ];
```

Store the file under the name magik.m. Then the statement

```
magik
```

reads the file and creates a variable, A, containing our example matrix.

Concatenation

Concatenation is the process of joining small matrices to make bigger ones. In fact, you made your first matrix by concatenating its individual elements. The pair of square brackets, [ ], is the concatenation operator. For an example, start with the 4-by-4 magic square, A, and form

    B = [A A+32; A+48 A+16]

The result is an 8-by-8 matrix, obtained by joining the four submatrices.

    B =

    16   3   2   13   48   35   34   45
     5   10   11   8   37   42   43   40
     9   6   7   12   41   38   39   44
     4   15   14   1   36   47   46   33
    64   51   50   61   32   19   18   29
    53   58   59   56   21   26   27   24
    57   54   55   60   25   22   23   28
    52   63   62   49   20   31   30   17

This matrix is halfway to being another magic square. Its elements are a rearrangement of the integers 1:64. Its column sums are the correct value for an 8-by-8 magic square.

    sum(B)

    ans =
       260   260   260   260   260   260   260   260

But its row sums, sum(B')', are not all the same. Further manipulation is necessary to make this a valid 8-by-8 magic square.

Deleting Rows and Columns

You can delete rows and columns from a matrix using just a pair of square brackets. Start with

    X = A;

Then, to delete the second column of X, use

    X(:,2) = []

This changes X to

```
X =
    16     2    13
     5    11     8
     9     7    12
     4    14     1
```

If you delete a single element from a matrix, the result isn't a matrix anymore. So, expressions like

```
X(1,2) = []
```

result in an error. However, using a single subscript deletes a single element, or sequence of elements, and reshapes the remaining elements into a row vector. So

```
X(2:2:10) = []
```

results in

```
X =
    16     9     2     7    13    12     1
```

More About Matrices and Arrays

This section shows you more about working with matrices and arrays, focusing on

- Linear Algebra
- Arrays
- Multivariate Data

Linear Algebra

Informally, the terms *matrix* and *array* are often used interchangeably. More precisely, a *matrix* is a two-dimensional numeric array that represents a *linear transformation*. The mathematical operations defined on matrices are the subject of *linear algebra*.

Dürer's magic square

```
A =
    16     3     2    13
     5    10    11     8
     9     6     7    12
     4    15    14     1
```

provides several examples that give a taste of MATLAB matrix operations. You've already seen the matrix transpose, A'. Adding a matrix to its transpose produces a *symmetric* matrix.

```
A + A'

ans =
    32     8    11    17
     8    20    17    23
    11    17    14    26
    17    23    26     2
```

The multiplication symbol, *, denotes the *matrix* multiplication involving inner products between rows and columns. Multiplying the transpose of a matrix by the original matrix also produces a symmetric matrix.

```
A'*A
```

```
ans =
      378   212   206   360
      212   370   368   206
      206   368   370   212
      360   206   212   378
```

The determinant of this particular matrix happens to be zero, indicating that the matrix is *singular*.

```
d = det(A)

d =
     0
```

The reduced row echelon form of A is not the identity.

```
R = rref(A)

R =
      1    0    0    1
      0    1    0   -3
      0    0    1    3
      0    0    0    0
```

Since the matrix is singular, it does not have an inverse. If you try to compute the inverse with

```
X = inv(A)
```

you will get a warning message

```
Warning: Matrix is close to singular or badly scaled.
         Results may be inaccurate. RCOND = 9.796086e-018.
```

Roundoff error has prevented the matrix inversion algorithm from detecting exact singularity. But the value of rcond, which stands for *reciprocal condition estimate*, is on the order of eps, the floating-point relative precision, so the computed inverse is unlikely to be of much use.

The eigenvalues of the magic square are interesting.

```
e = eig(A)
```

```
e =
   34.0000
    8.0000
    0.0000
   -8.0000
```

One of the eigenvalues is zero, which is another consequence of singularity. The largest eigenvalue is 34, the magic sum. That's because the vector of all ones is an eigenvector.

```
v = ones(4,1)

v =
     1
     1
     1
     1

A*v

ans =
    34
    34
    34
    34
```

When a magic square is scaled by its magic sum,

```
P = A/34
```

the result is a *doubly stochastic* matrix whose row and column sums are all one.

```
P =
    0.4706    0.0882    0.0588    0.3824
    0.1471    0.2941    0.3235    0.2353
    0.2647    0.1765    0.2059    0.3529
    0.1176    0.4412    0.4118    0.0294
```

Such matrices represent the transition probabilities in a *Markov process*. Repeated powers of the matrix represent repeated steps of the process. For our example, the fifth power

```
P^5
```

is

0.2507	0.2495	0.2494	0.2504
0.2497	0.2501	0.2502	0.2500
0.2500	0.2498	0.2499	0.2503
0.2496	0.2506	0.2505	0.2493

This shows that as k approaches infinity, all the elements in the k th power, p^k, approach $1/4$.

Finally, the coefficients in the characteristic polynomial

```
poly(A)
```

are

1	-34	-64	2176	0

This indicates that the characteristic polynomial

$det(A - \lambda I)$

is

$$\lambda^4 - 34\lambda^3 - 64\lambda^2 + 2176\lambda$$

The constant term is zero, because the matrix is singular, and the coefficient of the cubic term is -34, because the matrix is magic!

For More Information All of the MATLAB math functions are described in the online Help.

Arrays

When matrices are taken away from the world of linear algebra, they become two-dimensional numeric arrays. Arithmetic operations on arrays are done element-by-element. This means that addition and subtraction are the same for arrays and matrices, but that multiplicative operations are different. MATLAB uses a dot, or decimal point, as part of the notation for multiplicative array operations.

The list of operators includes

+	Addition
-	Subtraction
.*	Element-by-element multiplication
./	Element-by-element division
.\	Element-by-element left division
.^	Element-by-element power
.'	Unconjugated array transpose

If the Dürer magic square is multiplied by itself with array multiplication

```
A.*A
```

the result is an array containing the squares of the integers from 1 to 16, in an unusual order.

```
ans =
     256      9      4    169
      25    100    121     64
      81     36     49    144
      16    225    196      1
```

Building Tables

Array operations are useful for building tables. Suppose n is the column vector

```
n = (0:9)';
```

Then

```
pows = [n   n.^2   2.^n]
```

builds a table of squares and powers of two.

```
pows =
     0      0      1
     1      1      2
     2      4      4
     3      9      8
     4     16     16
     5     25     32
     6     36     64
     7     49    128
     8     64    256
     9     81    512
```

The elementary math functions operate on arrays element by element. So

```
format short g
x = (1:0.1:2)';
logs = [x log10(x)]
```

builds a table of logarithms.

```
logs =
       1.0            0
       1.1      0.04139
       1.2      0.07918
       1.3      0.11394
       1.4      0.14613
       1.5      0.17609
       1.6      0.20412
       1.7      0.23045
       1.8      0.25527
       1.9      0.27875
       2.0      0.30103
```

Multivariate Data

MATLAB uses column-oriented analysis for multivariate statistical data. Each column in a data set represents a variable and each row an observation. The (i,j)th element is the ith observation of the jth variable.

As an example, consider a data set with three variables:

- Heart rate
- Weight
- Hours of exercise per week

For five observations, the resulting array might look like

```
D =
        72            134           3.2
        81            201           3.5
        69            156           7.1
        82            148           2.4
        75            170           1.2
```

The first row contains the heart rate, weight, and exercise hours for patient 1, the second row contains the data for patient 2, and so on. Now you can apply many of MATLAB data analysis functions to this data set. For example, to obtain the mean and standard deviation of each column:

```
mu = mean(D), sigma = std(D)

mu =
      75.8          161.8           3.48

sigma =
       5.6303        25.499         2.2107
```

For a list of the data analysis functions available in MATLAB, type

```
help datafun
```

If you have access to the Statistics Toolbox, type

```
help stats
```

Scalar Expansion

Matrices and scalars can be combined in several different ways. For example, a scalar is subtracted from a matrix by subtracting it from each element. The average value of the elements in our magic square is 8.5, so

```
B = A - 8.5
```

forms a matrix whose column sums are zero.

```
B =
       7.5      -5.5      -6.5       4.5
      -3.5       1.5       2.5      -0.5
       0.5      -2.5      -1.5       3.5
      -4.5       6.5       5.5      -7.5

sum(B)

ans =
       0        0        0        0
```

With scalar expansion, MATLAB assigns a specified scalar to all indices in a range. For example,

```
B(1:2,2:3) = 0
```

zeros out a portion of B

```
B =
       7.5        0         0       4.5
      -3.5        0         0      -0.5
       0.5      -2.5      -1.5       3.5
      -4.5       6.5       5.5      -7.5
```

Logical Subscripting

The logical vectors created from logical and relational operations can be used to reference subarrays. Suppose X is an ordinary matrix and L is a matrix of the same size that is the result of some logical operation. Then X(L) specifies the elements of X where the elements of L are nonzero.

This kind of subscripting can be done in one step by specifying the logical operation as the subscripting expression. Suppose you have the following set of data.

```
x =
  2.1 1.7 1.6 1.5 NaN 1.9 1.8 1.5 5.1 1.8 1.4 2.2 1.6 1.8
```

The NaN is a marker for a missing observation, such as a failure to respond to an item on a questionnaire. To remove the missing data with logical indexing, use finite(x), which is true for all finite numerical values and false for NaN and Inf.

```
x = x(finite(x))
x =
   2.1 1.7 1.6 1.5 1.9 1.8 1.5 5.1 1.8 1.4 2.2 1.6 1.8
```

Now there is one observation, 5.1, which seems to be very different from the others. It is an *outlier*. The following statement removes outliers, in this case those elements more than three standard deviations from the mean.

```
x = x(abs(x-mean(x)) <= 3*std(x))
x =
   2.1 1.7 1.6 1.5 1.9 1.8 1.5 1.8 1.4 2.2 1.6 1.8
```

For another example, highlight the location of the prime numbers in Dürer's magic square by using logical indexing and scalar expansion to set the nonprimes to 0.

```
A(~isprime(A)) = 0

A =
     0     3     2    13
     5     0    11     0
     0     0     7     0
     0     0     0     0
```

The find Function

The find function determines the indices of array elements that meet a given logical condition. In its simplest form, find returns a column vector of indices. Transpose that vector to obtain a row vector of indices. For example, start again with Dürer's magic square. (See "The magic Function" on page 4-8.)

```
k = find(isprime(A))'
```

picks out the locations, using one-dimensional indexing, of the primes in the magic square.

```
k =
     2     5     9    10    11    13
```

Display those primes, as a row vector in the order determined by k, with

```
A(k)

ans =
     5     3     2    11     7    13
```

When you use k as a left-side index in an assignment statement, the matrix structure is preserved.

```
A(k) = NaN

A =
    16   NaN   NaN   NaN
   NaN    10   NaN     8
     9     6   NaN    12
     4    15    14     1
```

Controlling Command Window Input and Output

So far, you have been using the MATLAB command line, typing commands and expressions, and seeing the results printed in the Command Window. This section describes how to

- Control the appearance of the output values
- Suppress output from MATLAB commands
- Enter long commands at the command line
- Edit the command line

The format Command

The format command controls the numeric format of the values displayed by MATLAB. The command affects only how numbers are displayed, not how MATLAB computes or saves them. Here are the different formats, together with the resulting output produced from a vector x with components of different magnitudes.

Note To ensure proper spacing, use a fixed-width font, such as Fixedsys or Courier.

```
x = [4/3 1.2345e-6]

format short

    1.3333    0.0000

format short e

    1.3333e+000   1.2345e-006

format short g

    1.3333   1.2345e-006

format long
```

```
     1.33333333333333     0.00000123450000

format long e

     1.333333333333333e+000     1.234500000000000e-006

format long g

     1.33333333333333                    1.2345e-006

format bank

     1.33           0.00

format rat

     4/3            1/810045

format hex

     3ff5555555555555     3eb4b6231abfd271
```

If the largest element of a matrix is larger than 10^3 or smaller than 10^{-3}, MATLAB applies a common scale factor for the short and long formats.

In addition to the `format` commands shown above

```
format compact
```

suppresses many of the blank lines that appear in the output. This lets you view more information on a screen or window. If you want more control over the output format, use the `sprintf` and `fprintf` functions.

Suppressing Output

If you simply type a statement and press **Return** or **Enter**, MATLAB automatically displays the results on screen. However, if you end the line with a semicolon, MATLAB performs the computation but does not display any output. This is particularly useful when you generate large matrices. For example,

```
A = magic(100);
```

Entering Long Command Lines

If a statement does not fit on one line, use three periods, . . ., followed by **Return** or **Enter** to indicate that the statement continues on the next line. For example:

```
s = 1 -1/2 + 1/3 -1/4 + 1/5 - 1/6 + 1/7 ...
    - 1/8 + 1/9 - 1/10 + 1/11 - 1/12;
```

Blank spaces around the =, +, and - signs are optional, but they improve readability.

Command Line Editing

Various arrow and control keys on your keyboard allow you to recall, edit, and reuse commands you have typed earlier. For example, suppose you mistakenly enter

```
rho = (1 + sqt(5))/2
```

You have misspelled sqrt. MATLAB responds with

```
Undefined function or variable 'sqt'.
```

Instead of retyping the entire line, simply press the ↑ key. The misspelled command is redisplayed. Use the ← key to move the cursor over and insert the missing r. Repeated use of the ↑ key recalls earlier lines. Typing a few characters and then the ↑ key finds a previous line that begins with those characters. You can also copy previously executed commands from the Command History. For more information, see "Command History" on page 3-6.

The list of available command line editing keys is different on different computers. Experiment to see which of the following keys is available on your machine. (Many of these keys will be familiar to users of the Emacs editor.)

↑	**Ctrl+p**	Recall previous line
↓	**Ctrl+n**	Recall next line
←	**Ctrl+b**	Move back one character
→	**Ctrl+f**	Move forward one character
Ctrl+→	**Ctrl+r**	Move right one word
Ctrl+←	**Ctrl+l**	Move left one word
Home	**Ctrl+a**	Move to beginning of line
End	**Ctrl+e**	Move to end of line
Esc	**Ctrl+u**	Clear line
Del	**Ctrl+d**	Delete character at cursor
Backspace	**Ctrl+h**	Delete character before cursor
	Ctrl+k	Delete to end of line

Tab Completion

MATLAB completes the name of a function, variable, filename, or handle graphics property if you type the first few letters and then press the **Tab** key. If there is a unique name, the name is automatically completed. If there is more than one name that starts with the letters you typed, press the **Tab** key again to see a list of the possibilities.

5

Graphics

This chapter provides an overview of graphing in MATLAB.

Basic Plotting

MATLAB has extensive facilities for displaying vectors and matrices as graphs, as well as annotating and printing these graphs. This section describes a few of the most important graphics functions and provides examples of some typical applications.

For More Information "Graphics" and "3-D Visualization" in the MATLAB documentation provide in-depth coverage of MATLAB graphics and visualization tools. Access these from Help.

Creating a Plot

The plot function has different forms, depending on the input arguments. If y is a vector, plot(y) produces a piecewise linear graph of the elements of y versus the index of the elements of y. If you specify two vectors as arguments, plot(x,y) produces a graph of y versus x.

For example, these statements use the colon operator to create a vector of x values ranging from zero to 2π, compute the sine of these values, and plot the result.

```
x = 0:pi/100:2*pi;
y = sin(x);
plot(x,y)
```

Now label the axes and add a title. The characters \pi create the symbol π.

```
xlabel('x = 0:2\pi')
ylabel('Sine of x')
title('Plot of the Sine Function','FontSize',12)
```

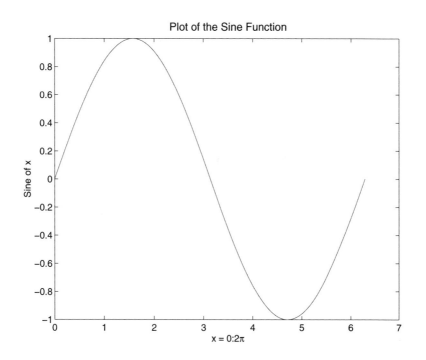

Multiple Data Sets in One Graph

Multiple x-y pair arguments create multiple graphs with a single call to plot. MATLAB automatically cycles through a predefined (but user settable) list of colors to allow discrimination between each set of data. For example, these statements plot three related functions of x, each curve in a separate distinguishing color.

```
y2 = sin(x-.25);
y3 = sin(x-.5);
plot(x,y,x,y2,x,y3)
```

The legend command provides an easy way to identify the individual plots.

```
legend('sin(x)','sin(x-.25)','sin(x-.5)')
```

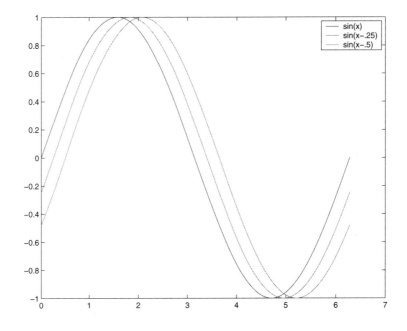

For More Information See "Defining the Color of Lines for Plotting" in "Axes Properties" in the MATLAB documentation.

Specifying Line Styles and Colors

It is possible to specify color, line styles, and markers (such as plus signs or circles) when you plot your data using the plot command.

```
plot(x,y,'color_style_marker')
```

color_style_marker is a string containing from one to four characters (enclosed in single quotation marks) constructed from a color, a line style, and a marker type:

- Color strings are 'c', 'm', 'y', 'r', 'g', 'b', 'w', and 'k'. These correspond to cyan, magenta, yellow, red, green, blue, white, and black.

- Linestyle strings are '-' for solid, '--' for dashed, ':' for dotted, '-.' for dash-dot, and 'none' for no line.
- The marker types are '+', 'o', '*', and 'x' and the filled marker types 's' for square, 'd' for diamond, '^' for up triangle, 'v' for down triangle, '>' for right triangle, '<' for left triangle, 'p' for pentagram, 'h' for hexagram, and none for no marker.

You can also edit color, line style, and markers interactively. See "Editing Plots" on page 5-14 for more information.

Plotting Lines and Markers

If you specify a marker type but not a linestyle, MATLAB draws only the marker. For example,

```
plot(x,y,'ks')
```

plots black squares at each data point, but does not connect the markers with a line.

The statement

```
plot(x,y,'r:+')
```

plots a red dotted line and places plus sign markers at each data point. You may want to use fewer data points to plot the markers than you use to plot the lines. This example plots the data twice using a different number of points for the dotted line and marker plots.

```
x1 = 0:pi/100:2*pi;
x2 = 0:pi/10:2*pi;
plot(x1,sin(x1),'r:',x2,sin(x2),'r+')
```

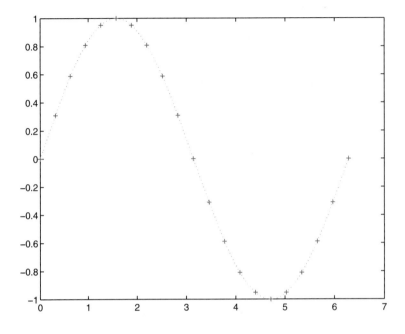

For More Information See "Basic Plotting" in the MATLAB documentation for more examples of plotting options.

Imaginary and Complex Data

When the arguments to plot are complex, the imaginary part is ignored *except* when plot is given a single complex argument. For this special case, the command is a shortcut for a plot of the real part versus the imaginary part. Therefore,

```
plot(Z)
```

where Z is a complex vector or matrix, is equivalent to

```
plot(real(Z),imag(Z))
```

For example,

```
t = 0:pi/10:2*pi;
plot(exp(i*t),'-o')
axis equal
```

draws a 20-sided polygon with little circles at the vertices. The command, axis equal, makes the individual tick mark increments on the *x*- and *y*-axes the same length, which makes this plot more circular in appearance.

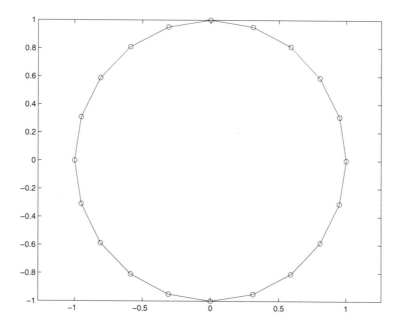

Adding Plots to an Existing Graph

The hold command enables you to add plots to an existing graph. When you type

```
hold on
```

MATLAB does not replace the existing graph when you issue another plotting command; it adds the new data to the current graph, rescaling the axes if necessary.

For example, these statements first create a contour plot of the peaks function, then superimpose a pseudocolor plot of the same function.

```
[x,y,z] = peaks;
contour(x,y,z,20,'k')
hold on
pcolor(x,y,z)
shading interp
hold off
```

The hold on command causes the pcolor plot to be combined with the contour plot in one figure.

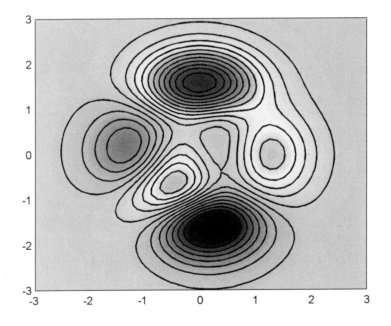

For More Information See "Creating Specialized Plots" in the MATLAB documentation for information on a variety of graph types.

Figure Windows

Graphing functions automatically open a new figure window if there are no figure windows already on the screen. If a figure window exists, MATLAB uses that window for graphics output. If there are multiple figure windows open, MATLAB targets the one that is designated the "current figure" (the last figure used or clicked in).

To make an existing figure window the current figure, you can click the mouse while the pointer is in that window or you can type

```
figure(n)
```

where n is the number in the figure title bar. The results of subsequent graphics commands are displayed in this window.

To open a new figure window and make it the current figure, type

```
figure
```

Clearing the Figure for a New Plot

When a figure already exists, most plotting commands clear the axes and use this figure to create the new plot. However, these commands do not reset figure properties, such as the background color or the colormap. If you have set any figure properties in the previous plot, you may want to use the clf command with the reset option,

```
clf reset
```

before creating your new plot to set the figure's properties to their defaults.

For More Information   See "Figure Properties" and the reference page for the figure command in the MATLAB documentation. See "Controlling Graphics Output" in the MATLAB documentation for information on how to control property resetting in your graphics programs.

Multiple Plots in One Figure

The subplot command enables you to display multiple plots in the same window or print them on the same piece of paper. Typing

```
subplot(m,n,p)
```

partitions the figure window into an m-by-n matrix of small subplots and selects the pth subplot for the current plot. The plots are numbered along first the top row of the figure window, then the second row, and so on. For example, these statements plot data in four different subregions of the figure window.

```
t = 0:pi/10:2*pi;
[X,Y,Z] = cylinder(4*cos(t));
subplot(2,2,1); mesh(X)
subplot(2,2,2); mesh(Y)
subplot(2,2,3); mesh(Z)
subplot(2,2,4); mesh(X,Y,Z)
```

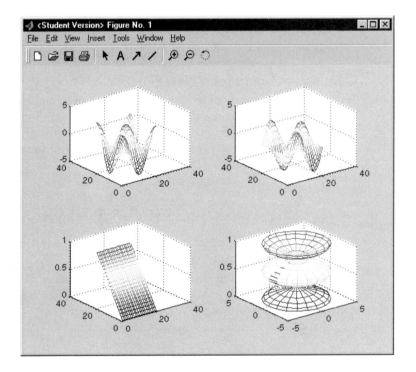

Controlling the Axes

The axis command supports a number of options for setting the scaling, orientation, and aspect ratio of plots. You can also set these options interactively. See "Editing Plots" on page 5-14 for more information.

Setting Axis Limits

By default, MATLAB finds the maxima and minima of the data to choose the axis limits to span this range. The axis command enables you to specify your own limits

```
axis([xmin xmax ymin ymax])
```

or for three-dimensional graphs,

```
axis([xmin xmax ymin ymax zmin zmax])
```

Use the command

```
axis auto
```

to reenable MATLAB automatic limit selection.

Setting Axis Aspect Ratio

axis also enables you to specify a number of predefined modes. For example,

```
axis square
```

makes the x-axes and y-axes the same length.

```
axis equal
```

makes the individual tick mark increments on the x- and y-axes the same length. This means

```
plot(exp(i*[0:pi/10:2*pi]))
```

followed by either axis square or axis equal turns the oval into a proper circle.

```
axis auto normal
```

returns the axis scaling to its default, automatic mode.

Setting Axis Visibility

You can use the `axis` command to make the axis visible or invisible.

```
axis on
```

makes the axis visible. This is the default.

```
axis off
```

makes the axis invisible.

Setting Grid Lines

The `grid` command toggles grid lines on and off. The statement

```
grid on
```

turns the grid lines on and

```
grid off
```

turns them back off again.

For More Information See the `axis` and `axes` reference pages and "Axes Properties" in the MATLAB documentation.

Axis Labels and Titles

The `xlabel`, `ylabel`, and `zlabel` commands add x-, y-, and z-axis labels. The `title` command adds a title at the top of the figure and the `text` function inserts text anywhere in the figure. A subset of TeX notation produces Greek letters. You can also set these options interactively. See "Editing Plots" on page 5-14 for more information.

```
t = -pi:pi/100:pi;
y = sin(t);
plot(t,y)
axis([-pi pi -1 1])
xlabel('-\pi \leq {\itt} \leq \pi')
ylabel('sin(t)')
title('Graph of the sine function')
text(1,-1/3,'{\itNote the odd symmetry.}')
```

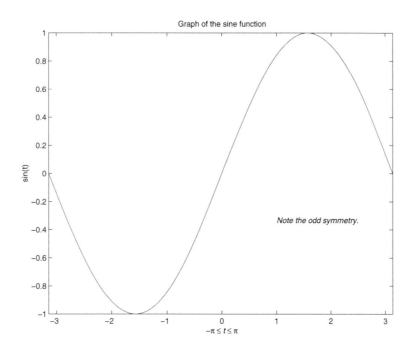

For More Information See "Formatting Graphs" in the MATLAB documentation for additional information on adding labels and annotations to your graphs.

Saving a Figure

To save a figure, select **Save** from the **File** menu. The figure is saved as a FIG-file, which you can load using the open or hgload commands.

Formats for Importing into Other Applications

You can export the figure as a standard graphics format, such as TIFF, for use with other applications. To do this, select **Export** from the **File** menu. You can also export figures from the command line using the saveas and print commands.

Editing Plots

MATLAB formats a graph to provide readability, setting the scale of axes, including tick marks on the axes, and using color and line style to distinguish the plots in the graph. However, if you are creating presentation graphics, you may want to change this default formatting or add descriptive labels, titles, legends and other annotations to help explain your data.

MATLAB supports two ways to edit the plots you create:

- Using the mouse to select and edit objects interactively
- Using MATLAB functions at the command line or in an M-file

Interactive Plot Editing

If you enable plot editing mode in the MATLAB figure window, you can perform point-and-click editing of the objects in your graph. In this mode, you select the object (or objects) you want to edit by double-clicking on it. This starts the Property Editor, which provides access to properties of the object that control its appearance and behavior.

For more information about interactive editing, see "Using Plot Editing Mode" on page 5-15. For information about editing object properties in plot editing mode, see "Using the Property Editor" on page 5-15.

Note Plot editing mode provides an alternative way to access the properties of MATLAB graphic objects. However, you can only access a subset of object properties through this mechanism. You may need to use a combination of interactive editing and command line editing to achieve the effect you desire.

Using Functions to Edit Graphs

If you prefer to work from the MATLAB command line or if you are creating an M-file, you can use MATLAB commands to edit the graphs you create. Taking advantage of MATLAB Handle Graphics system, you can use the set and get commands to change the properties of the objects in a graph. For more information about using command line, see "Handle Graphics" on page 5-28.

Using Plot Editing Mode

The MATLAB figure window supports a point-and-click style editing mode that you can use to customize the appearance of your graph. The following illustration shows a figure window with plot editing mode enabled and labels the main plot editing mode features.

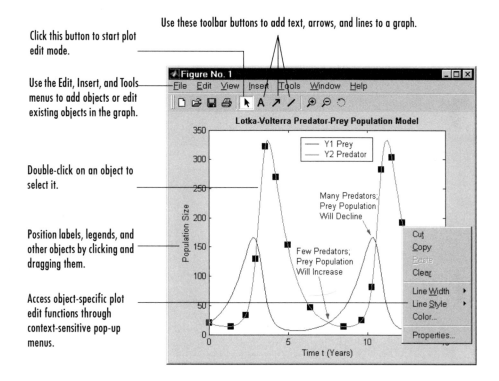

Use these toolbar buttons to add text, arrows, and lines to a graph.

Click this button to start plot edit mode.

Use the Edit, Insert, and Tools menus to add objects or edit existing objects in the graph.

Double-click on an object to select it.

Position labels, legends, and other objects by clicking and dragging them.

Access object-specific plot edit functions through context-sensitive pop-up menus.

Using the Property Editor

In plot editing mode, you can use a graphical user interface, called the Property Editor, to edit the properties of objects in the graph. The Property Editor provides access to many properties of the root, figure, axes, line, light, patch, image, surfaces rectangle, and text objects. For example, using the Property Editor, you can change the thickness of a line, add titles and axes labels, add lights, and perform many other plot editing tasks.

This figure shows the components of the Property Editor interface.

Click on a tab to view a category of properties.

Use these buttons to move back and forth among the graphics objects you have edited.

Use the navigation bar to select the object you want to edit.

Property Editor - Line

Edit Properties for line:

Data   Style   Info

Line Properties
Line style: Solid line (-)
Line width: 0.5
Line color: Blue   Custom color...

Click here to define a custom color.

Marker Properties
Style: No marker (none)
Size: 6.0
Edge color: Inherited (auto)   Custom color...
Face color: No color (none)   Custom color...

Click here to view a list of values for this field.

Example

Click OK to apply your changes and dismiss the Property Editor.

Click Cancel to dismiss the Property Editor without applying your changes.

Click Apply to apply your changes without dismissing the Property Editor.

OK   Cancel   Apply   Help

☑ Immediate apply

Check this check box to see the effect of your changes as you make them.

Click Help to get information about particular properties.

Starting the Property Editor

When in plot editing mode, start the Property Editor by double-clicking on an object in a graph, such as a line, or by right-clicking on an object and selecting the **Properties** option from the object's context menu.

You can also start the Property Editor by selecting either the **Figure Properties**, **Axes Properties**, or **Current Object Properties** from the figure window **Edit** menu. These options automatically enable plot editing mode, if it is not already enabled.

Once you start the Property Editor, keep it open throughout an editing session. It provides access to all the objects in the graph. If you click on another object in the graph, the Property Editor displays the set of panels associated with that object type. You can also use the Property Editor's navigation bar to select an object in the graph to edit.

Saving a Figure

To save a figure, select **Save** from the **File** menu. To save it using a graphics format, such as TIFF, for use with other applications, select **Export** from the **File** menu. You can also save from the command line — use the saveas command, including any options to save the figure in a different format.

Mesh and Surface Plots

MATLAB defines a surface by the z-coordinates of points above a grid in the x-y plane, using straight lines to connect adjacent points. The mesh and surf plotting functions display surfaces in three dimensions. mesh produces wireframe surfaces that color only the lines connecting the defining points. surf displays both the connecting lines and the faces of the surface in color.

Visualizing Functions of Two Variables

To display a function of two variables, $z = f(x,y)$:

• Generate X and Y matrices consisting of repeated rows and columns, respectively, over the domain of the function.

• Use X and Y to evaluate and graph the function.

The meshgrid function transforms the domain specified by a single vector or two vectors x and y into matrices X and Y for use in evaluating functions of two variables. The rows of X are copies of the vector x and the columns of Y are copies of the vector y.

Example — Graphing the sinc Function

This example evaluates and graphs the two-dimensional *sinc* function, $\sin(r)/r$, between the x and y directions. R is the distance from origin, which is at the center of the matrix. Adding eps (a MATLAB command that returns the smallest floating-point number on your system) avoids the indeterminate 0/0 at the origin.

```
[X,Y] = meshgrid(-8:.5:8);
R = sqrt(X.^2 + Y.^2) + eps;
Z = sin(R)./R;
mesh(X,Y,Z,'EdgeColor','black')
```

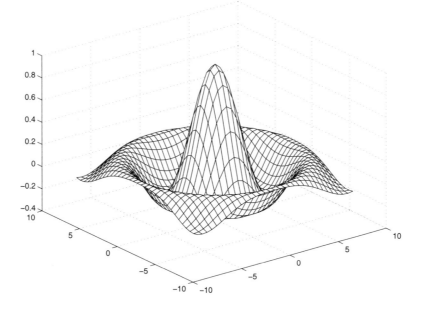

By default, MATLAB colors the mesh using the current colormap. However, this example uses a single-colored mesh by specifying the EdgeColor surface property. See the surface reference page for a list of all surface properties.

You can create a transparent mesh by disabling hidden line removal.

```
hidden off
```

See the hidden reference page for more information on this option.

Example — Colored Surface Plots

A surface plot is similar to a mesh plot except the rectangular faces of the surface are colored. The color of the faces is determined by the values of Z and the colormap (a colormap is an ordered list of colors). These statements graph the *sinc* function as a surface plot, select a colormap, and add a color bar to show the mapping of data to color.

```
surf(X,Y,Z)
colormap hsv
colorbar
```

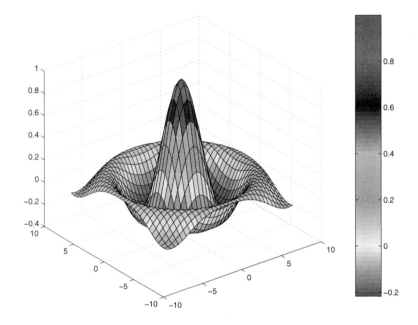

See the `colormap` reference page for information on colormaps.

For More Information See "Creating 3-D Graphs" in the MATLAB documentation for more information on surface plots.

Transparent Surfaces

You can make the faces of a surface transparent to a varying degree. Transparency (referred to as the alpha value) can be specified for the whole object or can be based on an alphamap, which behaves in a way analogous to colormaps. For example,

```
surf(X,Y,Z)
colormap hsv
alpha(.4)
```

produces a surface with a face alpha value of 0.4. Alpha values range from 0 (completely transparent) to 1 (not transparent).

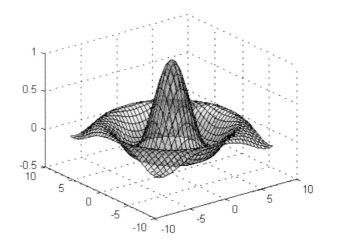

For More Information See "Transparency" in the MATLAB documentation for more information on using this feature.

Surface Plots with Lighting

Lighting is the technique of illuminating an object with a directional light source. In certain cases, this technique can make subtle differences in surface shape easier to see. Lighting can also be used to add realism to three-dimensional graphs.

This example uses the same surface as the previous examples, but colors it red and removes the mesh lines. A light object is then added to the left of the "camera" (that is the location in space from where you are viewing the surface).

```
surf(X,Y,Z,'FaceColor','red','EdgeColor','none')
camlight left; lighting phong
```

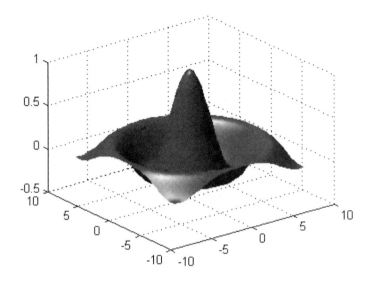

Manipulating the Surface

The Camera Toolbar provides a way to interactively explore 3-D graphics. Display the toolbar by selecting **Camera Toolbar** from the figure window's **View** menu. Here is the toolbar with the orbit camera tool selected.

The Camera Toolbar enables you to move the camera around the surface object, zoom, add a light, and perform other viewing operations without issuing commands. The following picture shows the surface viewed by orbiting the camera toward the bottom. A scene light has been added to illuminate the underside of the surface, which is not lit by the light added in the previous section.

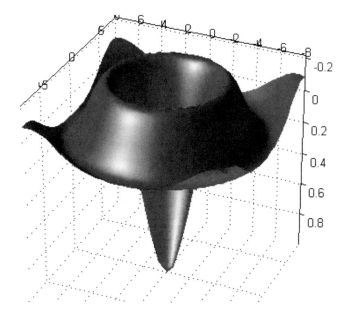

For More Information See the "Lighting as a Visualization Tool" and "View Control with the Camera Toolbar" in the MATLAB documentation for information on these techniques.

Images

Two-dimensional arrays can be displayed as *images*, where the array elements determine brightness or color of the images. For example, the statements

```
load durer
whos
Name          Size         Bytes   Class

    X         648x509     2638656   double array
    caption   2x28            112   char array
    map       128x3          3072   double array
```

load the file durer.mat, adding three variables to the workspace. The matrix X is a 648-by-509 matrix and map is a 128-by-3 matrix that is the colormap for this image.

Note MAT-files, such as durer.mat, are binary files that can be created on one platform and later read by MATLAB on a different platform.

The elements of X are integers between 1 and 128, which serve as indices into the colormap, map. Then

```
image(X)
colormap(map)
axis image
```

reproduces Dürer's etching shown at the beginning of this book. A high-resolution scan of the magic square in the upper right corner is available in another file. Type

```
load detail
```

and then use the up arrow key on your keyboard to reexecute the image, colormap, and axis commands. The statement

```
colormap(hot)
```

adds some unusual coloring to the sixteenth century etching. The function hot generates a colormap containing shades of reds, oranges, and yellows.

Typically a given image matrix has a specific colormap associated with it. See the `colormap` reference page for a list of other predefined colormaps.

For More Information See "Displaying Bit-Mapped Images" in the MATLAB documentation for information on the image processing capabilities of MATLAB.

Printing Graphics

You can print a MATLAB figure directly on a printer connected to your computer or you can export the figure to one of the standard graphic file formats supported by MATLAB. There are two ways to print and export figures:

- Using the **Print** option under the **File** menu
- Using the print command

Printing from the Menu

There are four menu options under the **File** menu that pertain to printing:

- The **Page Setup** option displays a dialog box that enables you to adjust characteristics of the figure on the printed page.
- The **Print Setup** option displays a dialog box that sets printing defaults, but does not actually print the figure.
- The **Print Preview** option enables you to view the figure the way it will look on the printed page.
- The **Print** option displays a dialog box that lets you select standard printing options and print the figure.

Generally, use **Print Preview** to determine whether the printed output is what you want. If not, use the **Page Setup** dialog box to change the output settings. Select the **Page Setup** dialog box **Help** button to display information on how to set up the page.

Exporting Figure to Graphics Files

The **Export** option under the **File** menu enables you to export the figure to a variety of standard graphics file formats.

Using the Print Command

The print command provides more flexibility in the type of output sent to the printer and allows you to control printing from M-files. The result can be sent directly to your default printer or stored in a specified file. A wide variety of output formats, including TIFF, JPEG, and PostScript, is available.

For example, this statement saves the contents of the current figure window as color Encapsulated Level 2 PostScript in the file called magicsquare.eps. It also includes a TIFF preview, which enables most word processors to display the picture

```
print -depsc2 -tiff magicsquare.eps
```

To save the same figure as a TIFF file with a resolution of 200 dpi, use the command

```
print -dtiff -r200 magicsquare.tiff
```

If you type print on the command line,

```
print
```

MATLAB prints the current figure on your default printer.

For More Information   See the print command reference page and "Printing and Exporting" in the MATLAB documentation for more information on printing.

Handle Graphics

When you use a plotting command, MATLAB creates the graph using various graphics objects, such as lines, text, and surfaces (see "Graphics Objects" on page 5-28 for a complete list). All graphics objects have properties that control the appearance and behavior of the object. MATLAB enables you to query the value of each property and set the values of most properties.

Whenever MATLAB creates a graphics object, it assigns an identifier (called a handle) to the object. You can use this handle to access the object's properties. Handle Graphics is useful if you want to

- Modify the appearance of graphs.
- Create custom plotting commands by writing M-files that create and manipulate objects directly.

Graphics Objects

Graphics objects are the basic elements used to display graphics and user interface elements. This table lists the graphics objects.

Object	Description
Root	Top of the hierarchy corresponding to the computer screen
Figure	Window used to display graphics and user interfaces
Axes	Axes for displaying graphs in a figure
Uicontrol	User interface control that executes a function in response to user interaction
Uimenu	User-defined figure window menu
Uicontextmenu	Pop-up menu invoked by right clicking on a graphics object
Image	Two-dimensional pixel-based picture

Object	Description
Light	Light sources that affect the coloring of patch and surface objects
Line	Line used by functions such as `plot`, `plot3`, `semilogx`
Patch	Filled polygon with edges
Rectangle	Two-dimensional shape varying from rectangles to ovals
Surface	Three-dimensional representation of matrix data created by plotting the value of the data as heights above the x-y plane
Text	Character string

Object Hierarchy

The objects are organized in a tree structured hierarchy reflecting their interdependence. For example, line objects require axes objects as a frame of reference. In turn, axes objects exist only within figure objects. This diagram illustrates the tree structure.

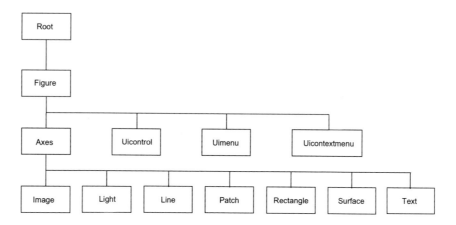

Creating Objects

Each object has an associated function that creates the object. These functions have the same name as the objects they create. For example, the text function creates text objects, the figure function creates figure objects, and so on. MATLAB high-level graphics functions (like plot and surf) call the appropriate low-level function to draw their respective graphics. For more information about an object and a description of its properties, see the reference page for the object's creation function. Object creation functions have the same name as the object. For example, the object creation function for axes objects is called axes.

Commands for Working with Objects

This table lists commands commonly used when working with objects.

Function	Purpose
copyobj	Copy graphics object
delete	Delete an object
findobj	Find the handle of objects having specified property values
gca	Return the handle of the current axes
gcf	Return the handle of the current figure
gco	Return the handle of the current object
get	Query the value of an objects properties
set	Set the value of an objects properties

For More Information See the "MATLAB Function Reference" in the MATLAB documentation for a description of each of these functions.

Setting Object Properties

All object properties have default values. However, you may find it useful to change the settings of some properties to customize your graph. There are two ways to set object properties:

- Specify values for properties when you create the object.
- Set the property value on an object that already exists.

For More Information See "Handle Graphics Objects" in the MATLAB documentation for information on graphics objects.

Setting Properties from Plotting Commands

You can specify object property values as arguments to object creation functions as well as with plotting function, such as plot, mesh, and surf.

For example, plotting commands that create lines or surfaces enable you to specify property name/property value pairs as arguments. The command

```
plot(x,y,'LineWidth',1.5)
```

plots the data in the variables x and y using lines having a LineWidth property set to 1.5 points (one point = 1/72 inch). You can set any line object property this way.

Setting Properties of Existing Objects

To modify the property values of existing objects, you can use the set command or, if plot editing mode is enabled, the Property Editor. The Property Editor provides a graphical user interface to many object properties. This section describes how to use the set command. See "Using the Property Editor" on page 5-15 for more information.

Many plotting commands can return the handles of the objects created so you can modify the objects using the set command. For example, these statements plot a five-by-five matrix (creating five lines, one per column) and then set the Marker to a square and the MarkerFaceColor to green.

```
h = plot(magic(5));
set(h,'Marker','s',MarkerFaceColor','g')
```

In this case, h is a vector containing five handles, one for each of the five lines in the plot. The set statement sets the Marker and MarkerFaceColor properties of all lines to the same values.

Setting Multiple Property Values

If you want to set the properties of each line to a different value, you can use cell arrays to store all the data and pass it to the set command. For example, create a plot and save the line handles.

```
h = plot(magic(5));
```

Suppose you want to add different markers to each line and color the marker's face color to the same color as the line. You need to define two cell arrays — one containing the property names and the other containing the desired values of the properties.

The prop_name cell array contains two elements.

```
prop_name(1) = {'Marker'};
prop_name(2) = {'MarkerFaceColor'};
```

The prop_values cell array contains 10 values — five values for the Marker property and five values for the MarkerFaceColor property. Notice that prop_values is a two-dimensional cell array. The first dimension indicates which handle in h the values apply to and the second dimension indicates which property the value is assigned to.

```
prop_values(1,1) = {'s'};
prop_values(1,2) = {get(h(1),'Color')};
prop_values(2,1) = {'d'};
prop_values(2,2) = {get(h(2),'Color')};
prop_values(3,1) = {'o'};
prop_values(3,2) = {get(h(3),'Color')};
prop_values(4,1) = {'p'};
prop_values(4,2) = {get(h(4),'Color')};
prop_values(5,1) = {'h'};
prop_values(5,2) = {get(h(5),'Color')};
```

The MarkerFaceColor is always assigned the value of the corresponding line's color (obtained by getting the line's Color property with the get command).

After defining the cell arrays, call set to specify the new property values.

```
set(h,prop_name,prop_values)
```

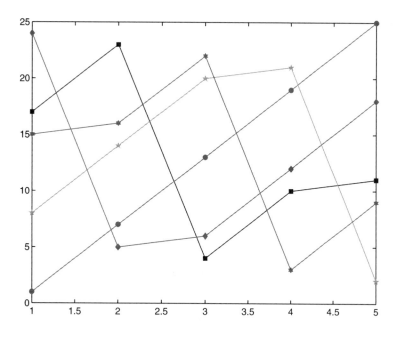

For More Information See "Structures and Cell Arrays" in the MATLAB documentation for information on cell arrays.

Finding the Handles of Existing Objects

The findobj command enables you to obtain the handles of graphics objects by searching for objects with particular property values. With findobj you can specify the value of any combination of properties, which makes it easy to pick one object out of many. For example, you may want to find the blue line with square marker having blue face color.

You can also specify which figures or axes to search, if there is more than one. The following sections provide examples illustrating how to use findobj.

Finding All Objects of a Certain Type

Since all objects have a Type property that identifies the type of object, you can find the handles of all occurrences of a particular type of object. For example,

```
h = findobj('Type','line');
```

finds the handles of all line objects.

Finding Objects with a Particular Property

You can specify multiple properties to narrow the search. For example,

```
h = findobj('Type','line','Color','r','LineStyle',':');
```

finds the handles of all red, dotted lines.

Limiting the Scope of the Search

You can specify the starting point in the object hierarchy by passing the handle of the starting figure or axes as the first argument. For example,

```
h = findobj(gca,'Type','text','String','\pi/2');
```

finds the string $\pi/2$ only within the current axes.

Using findobj as an Argument

Since findobj returns the handles it finds, you can use it in place of the handle argument. For example,

```
set(findobj('Type','line','Color','red'),'LineStyle',':')
```

finds all red lines and sets their line style to dotted.

For More Information See "Accessing Object Handles" in the MATLAB documentation for more information.

Graphics User Interfaces

Here is a simple example illustrating how to use Handle Graphics to build user interfaces. The statement

```
b = uicontrol('Style','pushbutton', ...
        'Units','normalized', ...
        'Position',[.5 .5 .2 .1], ...
        'String','click here');
```

creates a pushbutton in the center of a figure window and returns a handle to the new object. But, so far, clicking on the button does nothing. The statement

```
s = 'set(b,''Position'',[.8*rand .9*rand .2 .1])';
```

creates a string containing a command that alters the pushbutton's position. Repeated execution of

```
eval(s)
```

moves the button to random positions. Finally,

```
set(b,'Callback',s)
```

installs s as the button's callback action, so every time you click on the button, it moves to a new position.

Graphical User Interface Design Tools

MATLAB includes a set of layout tools that simplify the process of creating graphical user interfaces (GUIs). These tools include

- Layout Editor — Add and arrange objects in the figure window.
- Alignment Tool — Align objects with respect to each other.
- Property Inspector — Inspect and set property values.
- Object Browser — Observe a hierarchical list of the Handle Graphics objects in the current MATLAB session.
- Menu Editor — Create window menus and context menus.

Access these tools from the Layout Editor. To start the Layout Editor, use the guide command. For example,

```
guide
```

displays an empty layout.

To load an existing GUI for editing, use the syntax (the .fig is not required)

```
guide mygui.fig
```

or use **Open...** from the **File** menu on the Layout Editor.

For More Information See "Creating Graphical User Interfaces" in the MATLAB documentation for more information.

Animations

MATLAB provides two ways of generating moving, animated graphics:

- Continually erase and then redraw the objects on the screen, making incremental changes with each redraw.
- Save a number of different pictures and then play them back as a movie.

Erase Mode Method

Using the EraseMode property is appropriate for long sequences of simple plots where the change from frame to frame is minimal. Here is an example showing simulated Brownian motion. Specify a number of points, such as

```
n = 20
```

and a temperature or velocity, such as

```
s = .02
```

The best values for these two parameters depend upon the speed of your particular computer. Generate n random points with (x,y) coordinates between $-1/2$ and $+1/2$.

```
x = rand(n,1)-0.5;
y = rand(n,1)-0.5;
```

Plot the points in a square with sides at -1 and +1. Save the handle for the vector of points and set its EraseMode to xor. This tells the MATLAB graphics system not to redraw the entire plot when the coordinates of one point are changed, but to restore the background color in the vicinity of the point using an "exclusive or" operation.

```
h = plot(x,y,'.');
axis([-1 1 -1 1])
axis square
grid off
set(h,'EraseMode','xor','MarkerSize',18)
```

Now begin the animation. Here is an infinite while loop, which you can eventually exit by typing **Ctrl+c**. Each time through the loop, add a small amount of normally distributed random noise to the coordinates of the points.

Then, instead of creating an entirely new plot, simply change the XData and YData properties of the original plot.

```
while 1
    drawnow
    x = x + s*randn(n,1);
    y = y + s*randn(n,1);
    set(h,'XData',x,'YData',y)
end
```

How long does it take for one of the points to get outside of the square? How long before all of the points are outside the square?

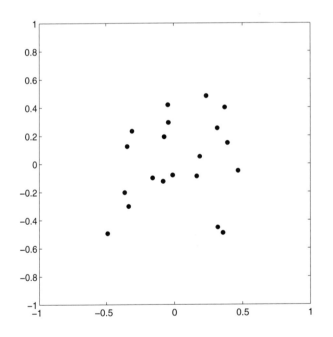

Creating Movies

If you increase the number of points in the Brownian motion example to something like n = 300 and s = .02, the motion is no longer very fluid; it takes too much time to draw each time step. It becomes more effective to save a predetermined number of frames as bitmaps and to play them back as a *movie*.

First, decide on the number of frames, for example,

```
nframes = 50;
```

Next, set up the first plot as before, except using the default EraseMode (normal).

```
x = rand(n,1)-0.5;
y = rand(n,1)-0.5;
h = plot(x,y,'.');
set(h,'MarkerSize',18);
axis([-1 1 -1 1])
axis square
grid off
```

Generate the movie and use getframe to capture each frame.

```
for k = 1:nframes
    x = x + s*randn(n,1);
    y = y + s*randn(n,1);
    set(h,'XData',x,'YData',y)
    M(k) = getframe;
end
```

Finally, play the movie 30 times.

```
movie(M,30)
```

Programming with MATLAB

This chapter introduces programming in MATLAB, data structures, and functions.

Flow Control (p. 6-2)

Use flow control constructs including `if`, `switch` and `case`, `for`, `while`, `continue`, and `break`.

Other Data Structures (p. 6-8)

Work with multidimensional arrays, cell arrays, character and text data, and structures.

Scripts and Functions (p. 6-18)

Write scripts and functions, use global variables, pass string arguments to functions, use `eval` to evaluate text expressions, vectorize code, preallocate arrays, reference functions using handles, and use functions that operate on functions.

Flow Control

MATLAB has several flow control constructs:

- `if` statements
- `switch` statements
- `for` loops
- `while` loops
- `continue` statements
- `break` statements
- `try-catch` statements
- `return` statements

For More Information See "Programming and Data Types" in the MATLAB documentation for a complete discussion about programming in MATLAB.

---

if

The `if` statement evaluates a logical expression and executes a group of statements when the expression is *true*. The optional `elseif` and `else` keywords provide for the execution of alternate groups of statements. An `end` keyword, which matches the `if`, terminates the last group of statements. The groups of statements are delineated by the four keywords — no braces or brackets are involved.

The MATLAB algorithm for generating a magic square of order n involves three different cases: when n is odd, when n is even but not divisible by 4, or when n is divisible by 4. This is described by

```
if rem(n,2) ~= 0
   M = odd_magic(n)
elseif rem(n,4) ~= 0
   M = single_even_magic(n)
else
   M = double_even_magic(n)
end
```

In this example, the three cases are mutually exclusive, but if they weren't, the first *true* condition would be executed.

It is important to understand how relational operators and `if` statements work with matrices. When you want to check for equality between two variables, you might use

```
if A == B, ...
```

This is legal MATLAB code, and does what you expect when A and B are scalars. But when A and B are matrices, A == B does not test *if* they are equal, it tests *where* they are equal; the result is another matrix of 0's and 1's showing element-by-element equality. In fact, if A and B are not the same size, then A == B is an error.

The proper way to check for equality between two variables is to use the `isequal` function,

```
if isequal(A,B), ...
```

Here is another example to emphasize this point. If A and B are scalars, the following program will never reach the unexpected situation. But for most pairs of matrices, including our magic squares with interchanged columns, none of the matrix conditions A > B, A < B or A == B is true for *all* elements and so the `else` clause is executed.

```
if A > B
    'greater'
elseif A < B
    'less'
elseif A == B
    'equal'
else
    error('Unexpected situation')
end
```

Several functions are helpful for reducing the results of matrix comparisons to scalar conditions for use with `if`, including

```
isequal
isempty
all
any
```

switch and case

The switch statement executes groups of statements based on the value of a variable or expression. The keywords case and otherwise delineate the groups. Only the first matching case is executed. There must always be an end to match the switch.

The logic of the magic squares algorithm can also be described by

```
switch (rem(n,4)==0) + (rem(n,2)==0)
   case 0
      M = odd_magic(n)
   case 1
      M = single_even_magic(n)
   case 2
      M = double_even_magic(n)
   otherwise
      error('This is impossible')
end
```

Note Unlike the C language switch statement, MATLAB switch does not fall through. If the first case statement is *true*, the other case statements do not execute. So, break statements are not required.

for

The for loop repeats a group of statements a fixed, predetermined number of times. A matching end delineates the statements.

```
for n = 3:32
   r(n) = rank(magic(n));
end
r
```

The semicolon terminating the inner statement suppresses repeated printing, and the r after the loop displays the final result.

It is a good idea to indent the loops for readability, especially when they are nested.

```
for i = 1:m
    for j = 1:n
        H(i,j) = 1/(i+j);
    end
end
```

while

The while loop repeats a group of statements an indefinite number of times under control of a logical condition. A matching end delineates the statements.

Here is a complete program, illustrating while, if, else, and end, that uses interval bisection to find a zero of a polynomial.

```
a = 0; fa = -Inf;
b = 3; fb = Inf;
while b-a > eps*b
    x = (a+b)/2;
    fx = x^3-2*x-5;
    if sign(fx) == sign(fa)
        a = x; fa = fx;
    else
        b = x; fb = fx;
    end
end
x
```

The result is a root of the polynomial $x^3 - 2x - 5$, namely

```
x =
    2.09455148154233
```

The cautions involving matrix comparisons that are discussed in the section on the if statement also apply to the while statement.

continue

The continue statement passes control to the next iteration of the for or while loop in which it appears, skipping any remaining statements in the body of the loop. In nested loops, continue passes control to the next iteration of the for or while loop enclosing it.

The example below shows a continue loop that counts the lines of code in the file, magic.m, skipping all blank lines and comments. A continue statement is used to advance to the next line in magic.m without incrementing the count whenever a blank line or comment line is encountered.

```
fid = fopen('magic.m','r');
count = 0;
while ~feof(fid)
    line = fgetl(fid);
    if isempty(line) | strncmp(line,'%',1)
        continue
    end
    count = count + 1;
end
disp(sprintf('%d lines',count));
```

break

The break statement lets you exit early from a for- or while-loop. In nested loops, break exits from the innermost loop only.

Here is an improvement on the example from the previous section. Why is this use of break a good idea?

```
a = 0; fa = -Inf;
b = 3; fb = Inf;
while b-a > eps*b
  x = (a+b)/2;
  fx = x^3-2*x-5;
  if fx == 0
     break
  elseif sign(fx) == sign(fa)
     a = x; fa = fx;
  else
     b = x; fb = fx;
  end
end
x
```

try-catch

The general form of a try-catch statement sequence is

```
try
    statement
    ...
    statement
catch
    statement
    ...
    statement
end
```

In this sequence the statements between try and catch are executed until an error occurs. The statements between catch and end are then executed. Use lasterr to see the cause of the error. If an error occurs between catch and end, MATLAB terminates execution unless another try-catch sequence has been established.

return

return terminates the current sequence of commands and returns control to the invoking function or to the keyboard. return is also used to terminate keyboard mode. A called function normally transfers control to the function that invoked it when it reaches the end of the function. return may be inserted within the called function to force an early termination and to transfer control to the invoking function.

Other Data Structures

This section introduces you to some other data structures in MATLAB, including

- Multidimensional arrays
- Cell arrays
- Characters and text
- Structures

For More Information For a complete discussion of MATLAB data structures, see "Programming and Data Types" in the MATLAB documentation.

Multidimensional Arrays

Multidimensional arrays in MATLAB are arrays with more than two subscripts. They can be created by calling zeros, ones, rand, or randn with more than two arguments. For example,

```
R = randn(3,4,5);
```

creates a 3-by-4-by-5 array with a total of 3x4x5 = 60 normally distributed random elements.

A three-dimensional array might represent three-dimensional physical data, perhaps the temperature in a room, sampled on a rectangular grid. Or, it might represent a sequence of matrices, $A^{(k)}$, or samples of a time-dependent matrix, $A(t)$. In these latter cases, the (i, j)th element of the kth matrix, or the t_k th matrix, is denoted by A(i,j,k).

MATLAB and Dürer's versions of the magic square of order 4 differ by an interchange of two columns. Many different magic squares can be generated by interchanging columns. The statement

```
p = perms(1:4);
```

generates the 4! = 24 permutations of 1:4. The kth permutation is the row vector, p(k,:). Then

```
A = magic(4);
M = zeros(4,4,24);
for k = 1:24
    M(:,:,k) = A(:,p(k,:));
end
```

stores the sequence of 24 magic squares in a three-dimensional array, M. The size of M is

```
size(M)

ans =
        4       4      24
```

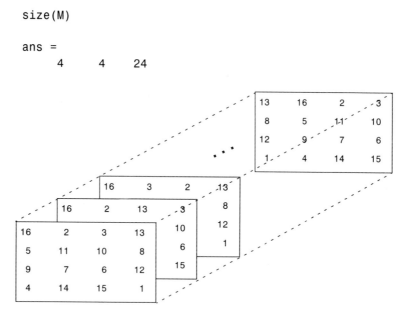

Note The order of the matrices shown in this illustration may differ from your results. The perms function always returns all permutations of the input vector, but the order of the permutations may be different for different MATLAB versions.

The statement

```
sum(M,d)
```

computes sums by varying the dth subscript. So

```
sum(M,1)
```

is a 1-by-4-by-24 array containing 24 copies of the row vector

```
34     34     34     34
```

and

```
sum(M,2)
```

is a 4-by-1-by-24 array containing 24 copies of the column vector

```
34
34
34
34
```

Finally,

```
S = sum(M,3)
```

adds the 24 matrices in the sequence. The result has size 4-by-4-by-1, so it looks like a 4-by-4 array.

```
S =
   204    204    204    204
   204    204    204    204
   204    204    204    204
   204    204    204    204
```

Cell Arrays

Cell arrays in MATLAB are multidimensional arrays whose elements are copies of other arrays. A cell array of empty matrices can be created with the cell function. But, more often, cell arrays are created by enclosing a miscellaneous collection of things in curly braces, {}. The curly braces are also used with subscripts to access the contents of various cells. For example,

```
C = {A sum(A) prod(prod(A))}
```

produces a 1-by-3 cell array. The three cells contain the magic square, the row vector of column sums, and the product of all its elements. When C is displayed, you see

```
C =
    [4x4 double]    [1x4 double]    [20922789888000]
```

This is because the first two cells are too large to print in this limited space, but the third cell contains only a single number, 16!, so there is room to print it.

Here are two important points to remember. First, to retrieve the contents of one of the cells, use subscripts in curly braces. For example, C{1} retrieves the magic square and C{3} is 16!. Second, cell arrays contain *copies* of other arrays, not *pointers* to those arrays. If you subsequently change A, nothing happens to C.

Three-dimensional arrays can be used to store a sequence of matrices of the *same* size. Cell arrays can be used to store a sequence of matrices of *different* sizes. For example,

```
M = cell(8,1);
for n = 1:8
    M{n} = magic(n);
end
M
```

produces a sequence of magic squares of different order.

```
M =
    [         1]
    [ 2x2  double]
    [ 3x3  double]
    [ 4x4  double]
    [ 5x5  double]
    [ 6x6  double]
    [ 7x7  double]
    [ 8x8  double]
```

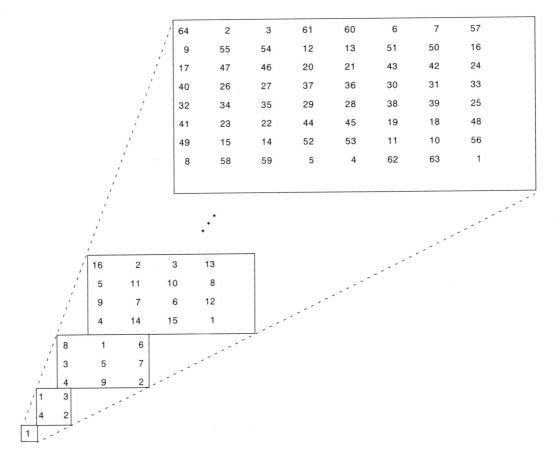

You can retrieve our old friend with

```
M{4}
```

Characters and Text

Enter text into MATLAB using single quotes. For example:

```
s = 'Hello'
```

The result is not the same kind of numeric matrix or array we have been dealing with up to now. It is a 1-by-5 character array.

Internally, the characters are stored as numbers, but not in floating-point format. The statement

```
a = double(s)
```

converts the character array to a numeric matrix containing floating-point representations of the ASCII codes for each character. The result is

```
a =
    72    101    108    108    111
```

The statement

```
s = char(a)
```

reverses the conversion.

Converting numbers to characters makes it possible to investigate the various fonts available on your computer. The printable characters in the basic ASCII character set are represented by the integers 32:127. (The integers less than 32 represent nonprintable control characters.) These integers are arranged in an appropriate 6-by-16 array with

```
F = reshape(32:127,16,6)';
```

The printable characters in the extended ASCII character set are represented by F+128. When these integers are interpreted as characters, the result depends on the font currently being used. Type the statements

```
char(F)
char(F+128)
```

and then vary the font being used for the Command Window. Select **Preferences** from the **File** menu to change the font. If you include tabs in lines of code, use a fixed-width font, such as Monospaced, to align the tab positions on different lines.

Concatenation with square brackets joins text variables together into larger strings. The statement

```
h = [s, ' world']
```

joins the strings horizontally and produces

```
h =
    Hello world
```

The statement

```
v = [s; 'world']
```

joins the strings vertically and produces

```
v =
   Hello
   world
```

Note that a blank has to be inserted before the 'w' in h and that both words in v have to have the same length. The resulting arrays are both character arrays; h is 1-by-11 and v is 2-by-5.

To manipulate a body of text containing lines of different lengths, you have two choices — a padded character array or a cell array of strings. When creating a character array, you must make each row of the array the same length. (Pad the ends of the shorter rows with spaces.) The char function does this padding for you. For example,

```
S = char('A','rolling','stone','gathers','momentum.')
```

produces a 5-by-9 character array.

```
S =
A
rolling
stone
gathers
momentum.
```

Alternatively, you can store the text in a cell array. For example,

```
C = {'A';'rolling';'stone';'gathers';'momentum.'}
```

creates a 5-by-1 cell array that requires no padding because each row of the array can have a different length.

```
C =
    'A'
    'rolling'
    'stone'
    'gathers'
    'momentum.'
```

You can convert a padded character array to a cell array of strings with

```
C = cellstr(S)
```

and reverse the process with

```
S = char(C)
```

For More Information MATLAB also supports regular expression operations on character arrays. See "Regular Expressions" in the MATLAB documentation.

Structures

Structures are multidimensional MATLAB arrays with elements accessed by textual *field designators*. For example,

```
S.name = 'Ed Plum';
S.score = 83;
S.grade = 'B+'
```

creates a scalar structure with three fields.

```
S =
     name: 'Ed Plum'
    score: 83
    grade: 'B+'
```

Like everything else in MATLAB, structures are arrays, so you can insert additional elements. In this case, each element of the array is a structure with several fields. The fields can be added one at a time,

```
S(2).name = 'Toni Miller';
S(2).score = 91;
S(2).grade = 'A-';
```

or, an entire element can be added with a single statement.

```
S(3) = struct('name','Jerry Garcia',...
              'score',70,'grade','C')
```

Now the structure is large enough that only a summary is printed.

```
S =
1x3 struct array with fields:
    name
    score
    grade
```

There are several ways to reassemble the various fields into other MATLAB arrays. They are all based on the notation of a *comma separated list*. If you type

```
S.score
```

it is the same as typing

```
S(1).score, S(2).score, S(3).score
```

This is a comma separated list. Without any other punctuation, it is not very useful. It assigns the three scores, one at a time, to the default variable ans and dutifully prints out the result of each assignment. But when you enclose the expression in square brackets,

```
[S.score]
```

it is the same as

```
[S(1).score, S(2).score, S(3).score]
```

which produces a numeric row vector containing all of the scores.

```
ans =
    83    91    70
```

Similarly, typing

```
S.name
```

just assigns the names, one at time, to ans. But enclosing the expression in curly braces,

```
{S.name}
```

creates a 1-by-3 cell array containing the three names.

```
ans =
    'Ed Plum'    'Toni Miller'    'Jerry Garcia'
```

And

```
char(S.name)
```

calls the char function with three arguments to create a character array from the name fields,

```
ans =
Ed Plum
Toni Miller
Jerry Garcia
```

Scripts and Functions

MATLAB is a powerful programming language as well as an interactive computational environment. Files that contain code in the MATLAB language are called M-files. You create M-files using a text editor, then use them as you would any other MATLAB function or command.

There are two kinds of M-files:

- Scripts, which do not accept input arguments or return output arguments. They operate on data in the workspace.
- Functions, which can accept input arguments and return output arguments. Internal variables are local to the function.

If you're a new MATLAB programmer, just create the M-files that you want to try out in the current directory. As you develop more of your own M-files, you will want to organize them into other directories and personal toolboxes that you can add to MATLAB search path.

If you duplicate function names, MATLAB executes the one that occurs first in the search path.

To view the contents of an M-file, for example, `myfunction.m`, use

```
type myfunction
```

Scripts

When you invoke a *script*, MATLAB simply executes the commands found in the file. Scripts can operate on existing data in the workspace, or they can create new data on which to operate. Although scripts do not return output arguments, any variables that they create remain in the workspace, to be used in subsequent computations. In addition, scripts can produce graphical output using functions like `plot`.

For example, create a file called `magicrank.m` that contains these MATLAB commands.

```
% Investigate the rank of magic squares
r = zeros(1,32);
for n = 3:32
    r(n) = rank(magic(n));
end
```

```
r
bar(r)
```

Typing the statement

```
magicrank
```

causes MATLAB to execute the commands, compute the rank of the first 30 magic squares, and plot a bar graph of the result. After execution of the file is complete, the variables n and r remain in the workspace.

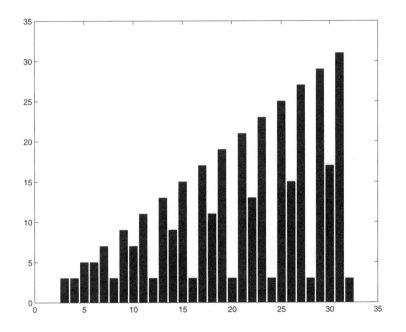

Functions

Functions are M-files that can accept input arguments and return output arguments. The name of the M-file and of the function should be the same. Functions operate on variables within their own workspace, separate from the workspace you access at the MATLAB command prompt.

A good example is provided by rank. The M-file rank.m is available in the directory

```
toolbox/matlab/matfun
```

You can see the file with

```
type rank
```

Here is the file.

```
function r = rank(A,tol)
%    RANK Matrix rank.
%    RANK(A) provides an estimate of the number of linearly
%    independent rows or columns of a matrix A.
%    RANK(A,tol) is the number of singular values of A
%    that are larger than tol.
%    RANK(A) uses the default tol = max(size(A)) * norm(A) * eps.

s = svd(A);
if nargin==1
   tol = max(size(A)') * max(s) * eps;
end
r = sum(s > tol);
```

The first line of a function M-file starts with the keyword `function`. It gives the function name and order of arguments. In this case, there are up to two input arguments and one output argument.

The next several lines, up to the first blank or executable line, are comment lines that provide the help text. These lines are printed when you type

```
help rank
```

The first line of the help text is the H1 line, which MATLAB displays when you use the `lookfor` command or request `help` on a directory.

The rest of the file is the executable MATLAB code defining the function. The variable s introduced in the body of the function, as well as the variables on the first line, r, A and tol, are all *local* to the function; they are separate from any variables in the MATLAB workspace.

This example illustrates one aspect of MATLAB functions that is not ordinarily found in other programming languages — a variable number of arguments. The rank function can be used in several different ways.

```
rank(A)
r = rank(A)
r = rank(A,1.e-6)
```

Many M-files work this way. If no output argument is supplied, the result is stored in `ans`. If the second input argument is not supplied, the function computes a default value. Within the body of the function, two quantities named `nargin` and `nargout` are available which tell you the number of input and output arguments involved in each particular use of the function. The `rank` function uses `nargin`, but does not need to use `nargout`.

Global Variables

If you want more than one function to share a single copy of a variable, simply declare the variable as `global` in all the functions. Do the same thing at the command line if you want the base workspace to access the variable. The global declaration must occur before the variable is actually used in a function. Although it is not required, using capital letters for the names of global variables helps distinguish them from other variables. For example, create an M-file called `falling.m`.

```
function h = falling(t)
global GRAVITY
h = 1/2*GRAVITY*t.^2;
```

Then interactively enter the statements

```
global GRAVITY
GRAVITY = 32;
y = falling((0:.1:5)');
```

The two global statements make the value assigned to `GRAVITY` at the command prompt available inside the function. You can then modify `GRAVITY` interactively and obtain new solutions without editing any files.

Passing String Arguments to Functions

You can write MATLAB functions that accept string arguments without the parentheses and quotes. That is, MATLAB interprets

```
foo a b c
```

as

```
foo('a','b','c')
```

However, when using the unquoted form, MATLAB cannot return output arguments. For example,

```
legend apples oranges
```

creates a legend on a plot using the strings apples and oranges as labels. If you want the legend command to return its output arguments, then you must use the quoted form.

```
[legh,objh] = legend('apples','oranges');
```

In addition, you cannot use the unquoted form if any of the arguments are not strings.

Constructing String Arguments in Code

The quoted form enables you to construct string arguments within the code. The following example processes multiple data files, August1.dat, August2.dat, and so on. It uses the function int2str, which converts an integer to a character, to build the filename.

```
for d = 1:31
    s = ['August' int2str(d) '.dat'];
    load(s)
    % Code to process the contents of the d-th file
end
```

A Cautionary Note

While the unquoted syntax is convenient, it can be used incorrectly without causing MATLAB to generate an error. For example, given a matrix A:

```
A =
     0    -6    -1
     6     2   -16
    -5    20   -10
```

The eig command returns the eigenvalues of A.

```
eig(A)
ans =
  -3.0710
  -2.4645+17.6008i
  -2.4645-17.6008i
```

The following statement is not allowed because A is not a string, however MATLAB does not generate an error.

```
eig A
ans =
    65
```

MATLAB actually takes the eigenvalues of ASCII numeric equivalent of the letter A (which is the number 65).

The eval Function

The eval function works with text variables to implement a powerful text macro facility. The expression or statement

```
eval(s)
```

uses the MATLAB interpreter to evaluate the expression or execute the statement contained in the text string s.

The example of the previous section could also be done with the following code, although this would be somewhat less efficient because it involves the full interpreter, not just a function call.

```
for d = 1:31
    s = ['load August' int2str(d) '.dat'];
    eval(s)
    % Process the contents of the d-th file
end
```

Function Handles

You can create a handle to any MATLAB function and then use that handle as a means of referencing the function. A function handle is typically passed in an argument list to other functions, which can then execute, or *evaluate*, the function using the handle.

Construct a function handle in MATLAB using the *at* sign, @, before the function name. The following example creates a function handle for the sin function and assigns it to the variable fhandle.

```
fhandle = @sin;
```

Evaluate a function handle using the MATLAB `feval` function. The function `plot_fhandle`, shown below, receives a function handle and data, and then performs an evaluation of the function handle on that data using `feval`.

```
function x = plot_fhandle(fhandle, data)
plot(data, feval(fhandle, data))
```

When you call `plot_fhandle` with a handle to the `sin` function and the argument shown below, the resulting evaluation produces a sine wave plot.

```
plot_fhandle(@sin, -pi:0.01:pi)
```

Function Functions

A class of functions, called "function functions," works with nonlinear functions of a scalar variable. That is, one function works on another function. The function functions include

- Zero finding
- Optimization
- Quadrature
- Ordinary differential equations

MATLAB represents the nonlinear function by a function M-file. For example, here is a simplified version of the function `humps` from the `matlab/demos` directory.

```
function y = humps(x)
y = 1./((x-.3).^2 + .01) + 1./((x-.9).^2 + .04) - 6;
```

Evaluate this function at a set of points in the interval $0 \leq x \leq 1$ with

```
x = 0:.002:1;
y = humps(x);
```

Then plot the function with

```
plot(x,y)
```

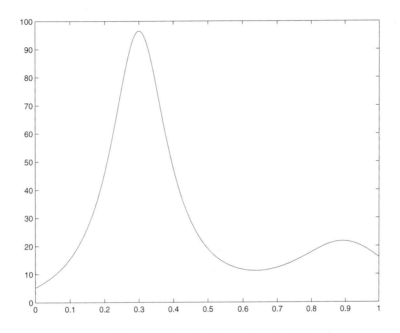

The graph shows that the function has a local minimum near $x = 0.6$. The function fminsearch finds the *minimizer*, the value of x where the function takes on this minimum. The first argument to fminsearch is a function handle to the function being minimized and the second argument is a rough guess at the location of the minimum.

```
p = fminsearch(@humps,.5)
p =
    0.6370
```

To evaluate the function at the minimizer,

```
humps(p)

ans =
    11.2528
```

Numerical analysts use the terms *quadrature* and *integration* to distinguish between numerical approximation of definite integrals and numerical integration of ordinary differential equations. MATLAB quadrature routines are quad and quadl. The statement

```
Q = quadl(@humps,0,1)
```

computes the area under the curve in the graph and produces

```
Q =
   29.8583
```

Finally, the graph shows that the function is never zero on this interval. So, if you search for a zero with

```
z = fzero(@humps,.5)
```

you will find one outside of the interval

```
z =
   -0.1316
```

Vectorization

One way to make your MATLAB programs run faster is to vectorize the algorithms you use in constructing the programs. Where other programming languages might use for or DO loops, MATLAB can use vector or matrix operations. A simple example involves creating a table of logarithms.

```
x = .01;
for k = 1:1001
    y(k) = log10(x);
    x = x + .01;
end
```

A vectorized version of the same code is

```
x = .01:.01:10;
y = log10(x);
```

For more complicated code, vectorization options are not always so obvious. See "Maximizing MATLAB Performance" in the MATLAB documentation for other techniques that you can use.

Preallocation

If you can't vectorize a piece of code, you can make your for loops go faster by preallocating any vectors or arrays in which output results are stored. For example, this code uses the function zeros to preallocate the vector created in the for-loop. This makes the for-loop execute significantly faster.

```
r = zeros(32,1);
for n = 1:32
    r(n) = rank(magic(n));
end
```

Without the preallocation in the previous example, the MATLAB interpreter enlarges the r vector by one element each time through the loop. Vector preallocation eliminates this step and results in faster execution.

MATLAB Programming Tips

This chapter is a categorized compilation of tips for the MATLAB programmer. Each item is relatively brief to help you to browse through them and find information that is useful. Many of the tips include a link to specific MATLAB documentation that gives you more complete coverage of the topic. You can find information on the following topics:

Command and Function Syntax

This section covers the following topics:

- "Syntax Help" on page 7-3
- "Command and Function Syntaxes" on page 7-3
- "Command Line Continuation" on page 7-3
- "Completing Commands Using the Tab Key" on page 7-4
- "Recalling Commands" on page 7-5
- "Clearing Commands" on page 7-5
- "Suppressing Output to the Screen" on page 7-5

Syntax Help

For help about the general syntax of MATLAB functions and commands, type

```
help syntax
```

Command and Function Syntaxes

You can enter MATLAB commands using either a *command* or *function* syntax. It is important to learn the restrictions and interpretation rules for both.

```
functionname arg1 arg2 arg3              % Command syntax
functionname('arg1','arg2','arg3')       % Function syntax
```

For More Information See "Calling Functions" in the MATLAB "Programming and Data Types" documentation.

Command Line Continuation

You can continue most statements to one or more additional lines by terminating each incomplete line with an ellipsis (...). Breaking down a statement into a number of lines can sometimes result in a clearer programming style.

```
sprintf ('Example %d shows a command coded on %d lines.\n', ...
         example_number, ...
         number_of_lines)
```

Note that you cannot continue an incomplete string to another line.

```
disp 'This statement attempts to continue a string ...
      to another line, resulting in an error.'
```

For More Information See "Entering Long Lines" in the MATLAB "Development Environment" documentation.

Completing Commands Using the Tab Key

You can save some typing when entering commands by entering only the first few letters of the command, variable, property, etc. followed by the **Tab** key. Typing the second line below (with **T** representing **Tab**) yields the expanded, full command shown in the third line.

```
f = figure;
set(f, 'papTuT,'cT)                  % Type this line.
set(f, 'paperunits','centimeters')   % This is what you get.
```

If there are too many matches for the string you are trying to complete, you will get no response from the first **Tab**. Press **Tab** again to see all possible choices.

```
set(f, 'paTT
PaperOrientation    PaperPositionMode  PaperType        Parent
PaperPosition       PaperSize          PaperUnits
```

For More Information See "Tab Completion" in the MATLAB "Development Environment" documentation.

Recalling Commands

Use any of the following methods to simplify recalling previous commands to the screen:

- To recall an earlier command to the screen, press the up arrow key one or more times, until you see the command you want. If you want to modify the recalled command, you can edit its text before pressing **Enter** or **Return** to execute it.
- To recall a specific command by name without having to scroll through your earlier commands one by one, type the starting letters of the command, followed by the up arrow key.
- Open the Command History window (**View -> Command History**) to see all previous commands. Double-click on the one you want to execute.

For More Information See "Recalling Previous Lines" and "Command History" in the MATLAB "Development Environment" documentation.

Clearing Commands

If you have typed a command that you then decide not to execute, you can clear it from the Command Window by pressing the Escape (**Esc**) key.

Suppressing Output to the Screen

To suppress output to the screen, end statements with a semicolon. This can be particularly useful when generating large matrices.

```
A = magic(100);     % Create matrix A, but do not display it.
```

Help

This section covers the following topics:

- "Using the Help Browser" on page 7-6
- "Help on Functions from the Help Browser" on page 7-7
- "Help on Functions from the Command Window" on page 7-7
- "Topical Help" on page 7-8
- "Paged Output" on page 7-8
- "Writing Your Own Help" on page 7-9
- "Help for Subfunctions and Private Functions" on page 7-9
- "Help for Methods and Overloaded Functions" on page 7-9

Using the Help Browser

Open the Help browser from the MATLAB Command Window using one of the following means:

- Click on the blue question mark symbol in the toolbar.
- Select **Help -> MATLAB Help** from the menu.
- Type the word doc at the command prompt.

Some of the features of the Help browser are listed below.

Feature	Description
Product Filter	Establish which products to find help on
Contents	Look up topics in the Table of Contents
Index	Look up help using the documentation Index
Search	Search the documentation for one or more words
Demos	See what demos are available; run selected demos
Favorites	Save bookmarks for frequently used Help pages

For More Information See "Finding Information with the Help Browser" in the MATLAB "Development Environment" documentation.

Help on Functions from the Help Browser

To find help on any function from the Help browser, do either of the following:

- Select the **Contents** tab of the Help browser, open the **Contents** entry labeled MATLAB, and find the two subentries shown below. Use one of these to look up the function you want help on.
  - Functions — By Category
  - Functions — Alphabetical List

- Use the syntax doc *functionname* at the command line.

Help on Functions from the Command Window

Several types of help on functions are available from the Command Window:

- To list all categories that you can request help on from the Command Window, just type

      help

- To see a list of functions for one of these categories, along with a brief description of each function, use the syntax help *category*. For example,

      help datafun

- To get help on a particular function, use the syntax help *functionname*. For example,

      help sortrows

Topical Help

In addition to the help on individual functions, you can get help on any of the following topics by using the syntax help *topicname* at the command line.

Topic Name	Description
arith	Arithmetic operators
relop	Relational and logical operators
punct	Special character operators
slash	Arithmetic division operators
paren	Parentheses, braces, and bracket operators
precedence	Operator precedence
lists	Comma separated lists
strings	Character strings
function_handle	Function handles and the @ operator
debug	Debugging functions
java	Using Java from within MATLAB
fileformats	A list of readable file formats
change_notification	Windows directory change notification

Paged Output

Before displaying a lengthy section of help text or code, put MATLAB into its paged output mode by typing more on. This breaks up any ensuing display into pages for easier viewing. Turn off paged output with more off.

Page through the displayed text using the space bar key. Or step through line by line using **Enter** or **Return**. Discontinue the display by pressing the **Q** key or **Ctrl+C**.

Writing Your Own Help

Start each program you write with a section of text providing help on how and when to use the function. If formatted properly, the MATLAB `help` function displays this text when you use the syntax

```
help functionname
```

MATLAB considers the first group of consecutive lines immediately following the function definition line that begin with % to be the help section for the function. The first line without % as the leftmost character ends the help.

For More Information See "Help Text" in the MATLAB "Development Environment" documentation.

Help for Subfunctions and Private Functions

You can write help for subfunctions using the same rules that apply to main functions. To display the help for the subfunction `mysubfun` in file `myfun.m`, type

```
help myfun/mysubfun
```

To display the help for a private function, precede the function name with `private/`. To get help on private function `myprivfun`, type

```
help private/myprivfun
```

Help for Methods and Overloaded Functions

You can write help text for object-oriented class methods implemented with M-files. Display help for the method by typing

```
help classname/methodname
```

where the file `methodname.m` resides in subdirectory `@classname`.

For example, if you write a `plot` method for a class named `polynom`, (where the `plot` method is defined in the file `@polynom/plot.m`), you can display this help by typing

```
help polynom/plot
```

You can get help on overloaded MATLAB functions in the same way. To display the help text for the eq function as implemented in matlab/iofun/@serial, type

```
help serial/eq
```

Development Environment

This section covers the following topics:

- "Workspace Browser" on page 7-11
- "Using the Find and Replace Utility" on page 7-11
- "Commenting Out a Block of Code" on page 7-12
- "Creating M-Files from Command History" on page 7-12
- "Editing M-Files in EMACS" on page 7-12

Workspace Browser

The Workspace Browser is a graphical interface to the variables stored in the MATLAB base and function workspaces. You can view, modify, save, load, and create graphics from workspace data using the browser. Select **View -> Workspace** to open the browser.

To view function workspaces, you need to be in debug mode.

For More Information See "MATLAB Workspace" in the MATLAB "Development Environment" documentation.

Using the Find and Replace Utility

Find any word or phrase in a group of files using the Find and Replace utility. Click on **View -> Current Directory**, and then click on the binoculars icon at the top of the **Current Directory** window.

When entering search text, you don't need to put quotes around a phrase. In fact, parts of words, such as win for windows, will not be found if enclosed in quotes.

For More Information See "Finding and Replacing a String" in the MATLAB "Development Environment" documentation.

Commenting Out a Block of Code

To comment out a block of text or code within the MATLAB editor,

1 Highlight the block of text you would like to comment out.

2 Holding the mouse over the highlighted text, select **Text -> Comment** (or **Uncomment**, to do the reverse) from the toolbar. (You can also get these options by right-clicking the mouse.)

For More Information See "Commenting" in the MATLAB "Development Environment" documentation.

Creating M-Files from Command History

If there is part of your current MATLAB session that you would like to put into an M-file, this is easily done using the Command History window:

1 Open this window by selecting **View -> Command History**.

2 Use **Shift+Click** or **Ctrl+Click** to select the lines you want to use. MATLAB highlights the selected lines.

3 Right-click once, and select **Create M-File** from the menu that appears. MATLAB creates a new Editor window displaying the selected code.

Editing M-Files in EMACS

If you use Emacs, you can download editing modes for editing M-files with GNU-Emacs or with early versions of Emacs from the MATLAB Central Web site.

```
http://www.mathworks.com/matlabcentral/
```

At this Web site, select **File Exchange**, and then **Utilities -> Emacs**.

For More Information See "General Preferences for the Editor/Debugger" in the MATLAB "Development Environment" documentation.

M-File Functions

This section covers the following topics:

- "M-File Structure" on page 7-14
- "Using Lowercase for Function Names" on page 7-14
- "Getting a Function's Name and Path" on page 7-15
- "What M-Files Does a Function Use?" in Chapter 7
- "Dependent Functions, Built-Ins, Classes" on page 7-16

M-File Structure

An M-file consists of the components shown here:

```
function [x, y] = myfun(a, b, c)        Function definition line
% H1 Line   A one-line summary of the function's purpose.
% Help Text   One or more lines of help text that explain
%   how to use the function. This text is displayed when
%   the user types "help functionname".

% The Function Body normally starts after the first blank line.
% Comments   Description (for internal use) of what the function
%   does, what inputs are expected, what outputs are generated.
%   Typing "help functionname" does not display this text.

x = prod(a, b);                 % Start of Function Code
```

For More Information See "Basic Parts of a Function M-file" in the MATLAB "Programming and Data Types" documentation.

Using Lowercase for Function Names

Function names appear in uppercase in MATLAB help text only to make the help easier to read. In practice, however, it is usually best to use lowercase when calling functions.

Specifically, MATLAB requires that you use lowercase when calling any built-in function. For M-file functions, case requirements depend on the case sensitivity of the operating system you are using. As a rule, naming and calling functions using lowercase generally makes your M-files more portable from one operating system to another.

Getting a Function's Name and Path

To obtain the name of an M-file that is currently being executed, use the following function in your M-file code.

```
mfilename
```

To include the path along with the M-file name, use

```
mfilename('fullpath')
```

For More Information   See the `mfilename` function reference page.

What M-Files Does a Function Use?

For a simple display of all M-files referenced by a particular function, follow the steps below:

1 Type `clear functions` to clear all functions from memory (see Note below).

2 Execute the function you want to check. Note that the function arguments you choose to use in this step are important, since you can get different results when calling the same function with different arguments.

3 Type `inmem` to display all M-Files that were used when the function ran. If you want to see what MEX-files were used as well, specify an additional output, as shown here.

```
[mfiles, mexfiles] = inmem
```

Note `clear functions` does not clear functions locked by `mlock`. If you have locked functions, (which you can check using `inmem`), unlock them with `munlock`, and then repeat step 1.

Dependent Functions, Built-Ins, Classes

For a much more detailed display of dependent function information, use the `depfun` function. In addition to M-files, `depfun` shows which built-ins and classes a particular function depends on.

Function Arguments

This section covers the following topics:

- "Getting the Input and Output Arguments" on page 7-17
- "Variable Numbers of Arguments" on page 7-17
- "String or Numeric Arguments" on page 7-18
- "Passing Arguments in a Structure" on page 7-18
- "Passing Arguments in a Cell Array" on page 7-19

Getting the Input and Output Arguments

Use `nargin` and `nargout` to determine the number of input and output arguments in a particular function call. Use `nargchk` and `nargoutchk` to verify that your function is called with the required number of input and output arguments.

```
function [x, y] = myplot(a, b, c, d)
disp(nargchk(2, 4, nargin))        % Allow 2 to 4 inputs
disp(nargoutchk(0, 2, nargout))    % Allow 0 to 2 outputs

x = plot(a, b);
if nargin == 4
   y = myfun(c, d);
end
```

Variable Numbers of Arguments

You can call functions with fewer input and output arguments than you have specified in the function definition, but not more. If you want to call a function with a variable number of arguments, use the `varargin` and `varargout` function parameters in the function definition.

This function returns the size vector and, optionally, individual dimensions.

```
function [s, varargout] = mysize(x)
nout = max(nargout, 1) - 1;
s = size(x);
for k = 1:nout
   varargout(k) = {s(k)};
end
```

Try calling it with

```
[s, rows, cols] = mysize(rand(4, 5))
```

String or Numeric Arguments

If you are passing only string arguments into a function, you can use MATLAB command syntax. All arguments entered in command syntax are interpreted as strings.

```
strcmp string1 string1
ans =
     1
```

When passing numeric arguments, it is best to use function syntax unless you want the number passed as a string. The right-hand example below passes the number 75 as the string, '75'.

```
isnumeric(75)              isnumeric 75
ans =                      ans =
     1                          0
```

For More Information See "Passing Arguments" in the MATLAB "Programming and Data Types" documentation.

Passing Arguments in a Structure

Instead of requiring an additional argument for every value you want to pass in a function call, you can package them in a MATLAB structure and pass the structure. Make each input you want to pass a separate field in the structure argument, using descriptive names for the fields.

Structures allow you to change the number, contents, or order of the arguments without having to modify the function. They can also be useful when you have a number of functions that need similar information.

Passing Arguments in a Cell Array

You can also group arguments into cell arrays. The disadvantage over structures is that you don't have field names to describe each variable. The advantage is that cell arrays are referenced by index, allowing you to loop through a cell array and access each argument passed in or out of the function.

Program Development

This section covers the following topics:

- "Planning the Program" on page 7-20
- "Using Pseudocode" on page 7-20
- "Selecting the Right Data Structures" on page 7-20
- "General Coding Practices" on page 7-21
- "Naming a Function Uniquely" on page 7-21
- "The Importance of Comments" on page 7-21
- "Coding in Steps" on page 7-22
- "Making Modifications in Steps" in Chapter 7
- "Functions with One Calling Function" on page 7-22
- "Testing the Final Program" on page 7-22

Planning the Program

When planning how to write a program, take the problem you are trying to solve and break it down into a series of smaller, independent tasks. Implement each task as a separate function. Try to keep functions fairly short, each having a single purpose.

Using Pseudocode

You may find it helpful to write the initial draft of your program in a structured format using your own natural language. This *pseudocode* is often easier to think through, review, and modify than using a formal programming language, yet it is easily translated into a programming language in the next stage of development.

Selecting the Right Data Structures

Look at what data types and data structures are available to you in MATLAB and determine which of those best fit your needs in storing and passing your data.

For More Information See "Data Types" in the MATLAB "Programming and Data Types" documentation.

General Coding Practices

A few suggested programming practices:

- Use descriptive function and variable names to make your code easier to understand.
- Order subfunctions alphabetically in an M-file to make them easier to find.
- Precede each subfunction with a block of help text describing what that subfunction does. This not only explains the subfunctions, but also helps to visually separate them.
- Don't extend lines of code beyond the 80th column. Otherwise, it will be hard to read when you print it out.
- Use full Handle Graphics™ property and value names. Abbreviated names are often allowed, but can make your code unreadable. They also could be incompatible in future releases of MATLAB.

Naming a Function Uniquely

To avoid choosing a name for a new function that might conflict with a name already in use, check for any occurrences of the name using this syntax:

```
which -all functionname
```

For More Information See the which function reference page.

The Importance of Comments

Be sure to document your programs well to make it easier for you or someone else to maintain them. Add comments generously, explaining each major section and any smaller segments of code that are not obvious. You can add a block of comments as shown here.

```
%-----------------------------------------------------------
% This function computes the ... <and so on>
%-----------------------------------------------------------
```

For More Information See "Comments" in the MATLAB "Programming and Data Types" documentation.

Coding in Steps

Don't try to write the entire program all at once. Write a portion of it, and then test that piece out. When you have that part working the way you want, then write the next piece, and so on. It's much easier to find programming errors in a small piece of code than in a large program.

Making Modifications in Steps

When making modifications to a working program, don't make widespread changes all at one time. It's better to make a few small changes, test and debug, make a few more changes, and so on. Tracking down a difficult bug in the small section that you've changed is much easier than trying to find it in a huge block of new code.

Functions with One Calling Function

If you have a function that is called by only one other function, put it in the same M-file as the calling function, making it a subfunction.

For More Information See "Subfunctions" in the MATLAB "Programming and Data Types" documentation.

Testing the Final Program

One suggested practice for testing a new program is to step through the program in the MATLAB debugger while keeping a record of each line that gets executed on a printed copy of the program. Use different combinations of inputs until you have observed that every line of code is executed at least once.

Debugging

This section covers the following topics:

- "The MATLAB Debug Functions" on page 7-23
- "More Debug Functions" on page 7-23
- "The MATLAB Graphical Debugger" on page 7-24
- "A Quick Way to Examine Variables" on page 7-25
- "Setting Breakpoints from the Command Line" on page 7-25
- "Finding Line Numbers to Set Breakpoints" on page 7-25
- "Stopping Execution on an Error or Warning" on page 7-25
- "Locating an Error from the Error Message" on page 7-26
- "Using Warnings to Help Debug" on page 7-26
- "Making Code Execution Visible" on page 7-26
- "Debugging Scripts" on page 7-27

The MATLAB Debug Functions

For a brief description of the main debug functions in MATLAB, type

```
help debug
```

For More Information See "Debugging M-Files" in the MATLAB "Development Environment" documentation.

More Debug Functions

Other functions you may find useful in debugging are listed below.

Function	Description
echo	Display function or script code as it executes.
disp	Display specified values or messages.

Function	Description
sprintf, fprintf	Display formatted data of different types.
whos	List variables in the workspace.
size	Show array dimensions.
keyboard	Interrupt program execution and allow input from keyboard.
return	Resume execution following a keyboard interruption.
warning	Display specified warning message.
error	Display specified error message.
lasterr	Return error message that was last issued.
lasterror	Return last error message and related information.
lastwarn	Return warning message that was last issued.

The MATLAB Graphical Debugger

Learn to use the MATLAB graphical debugger. You can view the function and its calling functions as you debug, set and clear breakpoints, single-step through the program, step into or over called functions, control visibility into all workspaces, and find and replace strings in your files.

Start out by opening the file you want to debug using **File -> Open** or the open function. Use the debugging functions available on the toolbar and pull-down menus to set breakpoints, run or step through the program, and examine variables.

For More Information See "Debugging M-Files" and "Using Debugging Features" in the MATLAB "Development Environment" documentation.

A Quick Way to Examine Variables

To see the value of a variable from the Editor/Debugger window, hold the mouse cursor over the variable name for a second or two. You will see the value of the selected variable displayed.

Setting Breakpoints from the Command Line

You can set breakpoints with dbstop in any of the following ways:

- Break at a specific M-file line number.
- Break at the beginning of a specific subfunction.
- Break at the first executable line in an M-file.
- Break when a warning, or error, is generated.
- Break if any infinite or NaN values are encountered.

For More Information See "Setting Breakpoints" in the MATLAB "Development Environment" documentation.

Finding Line Numbers to Set Breakpoints

When debugging from the command line, a quick way to find line numbers for setting breakpoints is to use dbtype. The dbtype function displays all or part of an M-file, also numbering each line. To display copyfile.m, use

```
dbtype copyfile
```

To display only lines 70 through 90, use

```
dbtype copyfile 70:90
```

Stopping Execution on an Error or Warning

Use dbstop if error to stop program execution on any error and enter debug mode. Use warning debug to stop execution on any warning and enter debug mode.

For More Information See "Debug, Backtrace, and Verbose Modes" in the MATLAB "Programming and Data Types" documentation.

Locating an Error from the Error Message

Click on the underlined text in an error message, and MATLAB opens the M-file being executed in its editor and places the cursor at the point of error.

For More Information See "Types of Errors" in the MATLAB "Development Environment" documentation.

Using Warnings to Help Debug

You can detect erroneous or unexpected behavior in your programs by inserting warning messages that MATLAB will display under the conditions you specify. See the section on "Warning Control" in the MATLAB "Programming and Data Types" documentation to find out how to selectively enable warnings.

For More Information See the warning function reference page.

Making Code Execution Visible

An easy way to see the end result of a particular line of code is to edit the program and temporarily remove the terminating semicolon from that line. Then, run your program and the evaluation of that statement is displayed on the screen.

For More Information See "Finding Errors" in the MATLAB "Development Environment" documentation.

Debugging Scripts

Scripts store their variables in a workspace that is shared with the caller of the script. So, when you debug a script from the command line, the script uses variables from the base workspace. To avoid errors caused by workspace sharing, type `clear all` before starting to debug your script to clear the base workspace.

Variables

This section covers the following topics:

- "Rules for Variable Names" on page 7-28
- "Making Sure Variable Names Are Valid" on page 7-28
- "Don't Use Function Names for Variables" on page 7-29
- "Checking for Reserved Keywords" on page 7-29
- "Avoid Using i and j for Variables" on page 7-30
- "Avoid Overwriting Variables in Scripts" on page 7-30
- "Persistent Variables" on page 7-30
- "Protecting Persistent Variables" on page 7-30
- "Global Variables" on page 7-31

Rules for Variable Names

Although variable names can be of any length, MATLAB uses only the first N characters of the name, (where N is the number returned by the function `namelengthmax`), and ignores the rest. Hence, it is important to make each variable name unique in the first N characters to enable MATLAB to distinguish variables. Also note that variable names are case sensitive.

```
N = namelengthmax
N =
    63
```

For More Information See "Naming Variables" in the MATLAB "Programming and Data Types" documentation.

Making Sure Variable Names Are Valid

Before using a new variable name, you can check to see if it is valid with the `isvarname` function. Note that `isvarname` does not consider names longer than `namelengthmax` characters to be valid.

For example, the following name cannot be used for a variable since it begins with a number.

```
isvarname 8th_column
ans =
     0
```

For More Information See "Naming Variables" in the MATLAB "Programming and Data Types" documentation.

Don't Use Function Names for Variables

When naming a variable, make sure you are not using a name that is already used as a function name. If you do define a variable with a function name, you won't be able to call that function until you clear the variable from memory. (If it's a MATLAB built-in function, then you will still be able to call that function, but you must do so using builtin.)

To test whether a proposed variable name is already used as a function name, use the syntax

```
which -all name
```

Checking for Reserved Keywords

MATLAB reserves certain keywords for its own use and does not allow you to override them. Attempts to use these words may result in any one of a number of error messages, some of which are shown here.

```
Error: Expected a variable, function, or constant, found "=".
Error: "End of Input" expected, "case" found.
Error: Missing operator, comma, or semicolon.
Error: "identifier" expected, "=" found.
```

Use the iskeyword function with no input arguments to list all reserved words.

Avoid Using i and j for Variables

MATLAB uses the characters i and j to represent imaginary units. Avoid using i and j for variable names if you intend to use them in complex arithmetic.

If you want to create a complex number without using i and j, you can use the complex function.

Avoid Overwriting Variables in Scripts

MATLAB scripts store their variables in a workspace that is shared with the caller of the script. When called from the command line, they share the base workspace. When called from a function, they share that function's workspace. If you run a script that alters a variable that already exists in the caller's workspace, that variable is overwritten by the script.

For More Information See "Scripts" in the MATLAB "Programming and Data Types" documentation.

Persistent Variables

To get the equivalent of a static variable in MATLAB, use persistent. When you declare a variable to be persistent within a function, its value is retained in memory between calls to that function. Unlike global variables, persistent variables are known only to the function in which they are declared.

For More Information See "Persistent Variables" in the MATLAB "Programming and Data Types" documentation.

Protecting Persistent Variables

You can inadvertently clear persistent variables from memory by either modifying the function in which the variables are defined, or by clearing the function with one of the following commands.

```
clear all
```

```
clear functions
```

Locking the M-file in memory with `mlock` prevents any `persistent` variables defined in the file from being reinitialized.

Global Variables

Use global variables sparingly. The global workspace is shared by all of your functions and also by your interactive MATLAB session. The more global variables you use, the greater the chances of unintentionally reusing a variable name, thus leaving yourself open to having those variables change in value unexpectedly. This can be a difficult bug to track down.

For More Information See "Global Variables" in the MATLAB "Programming and Data Types" documentation.

Strings

This section covers the following topics:

- "Creating Strings with Concatenation" on page 7-32
- "Comparing Methods of Concatenation" on page 7-32
- "Store Arrays of Strings in a Cell Array" on page 7-33
- "Search and Replace Using Regular Expressions" on page 7-33
- "Converting Between Strings and Cell Arrays" on page 7-34

Creating Strings with Concatenation

Strings are often created by concatenating smaller elements together (e.g., strings, values, etc.). Two common methods of concatenating are to use the MATLAB concatenation operator ([ ]) or the sprintf function. The second and third lines below illustrate both of these methods. Both lines give the same result.

```
num_chars = 28;
s = ['There are ' int2str(num_chars) ' characters here']
s = sprintf('There are %d characters here\n', num_chars)
```

For More Information See "Creating Character Arrays" and "Numeric/String Conversion" in the MATLAB "Programming and Data Types" documentation.

Comparing Methods of Concatenation

When building strings with concatenation, sprintf is often preferable to [ ] because

- It is easier to read, especially when forming complicated expressions.
- It gives you more control over the output format.
- It often executes more quickly.

You can also concatenate using the strcat function, However, for simple concatenations, sprintf and [ ] are faster.

Store Arrays of Strings in a Cell Array

It is usually best to store an array of strings in a cell array instead of a character array, especially if the strings are of different lengths. Strings in a character array must be of equal length, which often requires padding the strings with blanks. This is not necessary when using a cell array of strings that has no such requirement.

The cellRecord below does not require padding the strings with spaces.

```
charRecord  = ['Allison Jones'; 'Development  '; 'Phoenix     '];
cellRecord  = {'Allison Jones'; 'Development'; 'Phoenix'};
```

For More Information See "Cell Arrays of Strings" in the MATLAB "Programming and Data Types" documentation.

Search and Replace Using Regular Expressions

Using regular expressions in MATLAB offers a very versatile way of searching for and replacing characters or phrases within a string. See the help on these functions for more information.

Function	Description
regexp	Match regular expression
regexpi	Match regular expression, ignoring case
regexprep	Replace string using regular expression

For More Information See "Regular Expressions" in the MATLAB "Programming and Data Types" documentation.

Converting Between Strings and Cell Arrays

You can convert between standard character arrays and cell arrays of strings using the cellstr and char functions.

```
charRecord = ['Allison Jones'; 'Development  '; 'Phoenix      '];
cellRecord = cellstr(charRecord);
```

Also, a number of the MATLAB string operations can be used with either character arrays, or cell arrays, or both.

```
cellRecord2 = {'Brian Lewis'; 'Development'; 'Albuquerque'};
strcmp(charRecord, cellRecord2)
ans =
     0
     1
     0
```

For More Information See "Converting to a Cell Array of Strings", and "String Comparisons" in the MATLAB Programming and Data Types documentation.

Evaluating Expressions

This section covers the following topics:

- "Find Alternatives to Using eval" on page 7-35
- "Assigning to a Series of Variables" on page 7-35
- "Short-Circuit Logical Operators" on page 7-36
- "Changing the Counter Variable Within a for Loop" on page 7-36

Find Alternatives to Using eval

While the eval function can provide a convenient solution to certain programming challenges, it is best to limit its use. The main reason is that code that uses eval is often difficult to read and hard to debug. A second reason is that eval statements cannot always be translated into C or C++ code by the MATLAB Compiler.

If you are evaluating a function, it is more efficient to use feval than eval. The feval function is made specifically for this purpose and is optimized to provide better performance.

For More Information See MATLAB Technical Note 1103, "What Is the EVAL Function, When Should I Use It, and How Can I Avoid It?" at URL http://www.mathworks.com/support/tech-notes/1100/1103.shtml.

Assigning to a Series of Variables

One common pattern for creating variables is to use a variable name suffixed with a number (e.g., phase1, phase2, phase3, etc.). We recommend using a cell array to build this type of variable name series, as it makes code more readable and executes more quickly than some other methods. For example,

```
for k = 1:800
    phase{k} = expression;
end
```

Short-Circuit Logical Operators

MATLAB has logical AND and OR operators (&& and ||) that enable you to partially evaluate, or *short-circuit*, logical expressions. Short-circuit operators are useful when you want to evaluate a statement only when certain conditions are satisfied.

In this example, MATLAB does not execute the function myfun unless its M-file exists on the current path.

```
comp = (exist('myfun.m') == 2) && (myfun(x) >= y)
```

For More Information See "Short-Circuit Operators" in the MATLAB "Programming and Data Types" documentation.

Changing the Counter Variable Within a for Loop

You cannot change the value of the loop counter variable (e.g., the variable k in the example below) in the body of a for loop. For example, this loop executes just 10 times, even though k is set back to 1 on each iteration.

```
for k = 1:10
   disp(sprintf('Pass %d', k))
   k = 1;
end
```

Although MATLAB does allow you to use a variable of the same name as the loop counter within a loop, this is not a recommended practice.

MATLAB Path

This section covers the following topics:

Precedence Rules

When MATLAB is given a name to interpret, it determines its usage by checking the name against each of the entities listed below, and in the order shown:

1 Variable

2 Built-in function

3 Subfunction

4 Private function

5 Class constructor

6 Overloaded method

7 M-file in the current directory

8 M-file on the path

If the name is found to be an M-file on the path (No. 8 in the list), and there is more than one M-file on the path with the same name, MATLAB uses the one in the directory that is closest to the beginning of the path string.

For More Information See "Function Precedence Order" in the MATLAB "Programming and Data Types" documentation.

File Precedence

If you refer to a file by its filename only (leaving out the file extension), and there is more than one file of this name in the directory, MATLAB selects the file to use according to the following precedence:

1 MEX-file

2 MDL-file (Simulink model)

3 P-Code file

4 M-file

For More Information See "Selecting Methods from Multiple Implementation Types" in the MATLAB "Programming and Data Types" documentation.

Adding a Directory to the Search Path

To add a directory to the search path, use either of the following:

- At the toolbar, select **File -> Set Path**.
- At the command line, use the addpath function.

You can also add a directory and all of its subdirectories in one operation by either of these means. To do this from the command line, use genpath together with addpath. The online help for the genpath function shows how to do this.

This example adds /control and all of its subdirectories to the MATLAB path:

```
addpath(genpath('K:/toolbox/control'))
```

For More Information See "Search Path" in the MATLAB "Development Environment" documentation.

Handles to Functions Not on the Path

You cannot create function handles to functions that are not on the MATLAB path. But you can achieve essentially the same thing by creating the handles through a script file placed in the same off-path directory as the functions. If you then run the script, using run *path/script*, you will have created the handles that you need.

For example,

1 Create a script in this off-path directory that constructs function handles and assigns them to variables. That script might look something like this.

```
File E:/testdir/create_fhandles.m
    fhset = @set_items
    fhsort = @sort_items
    fhdel = @delete_item
```

2 Run the script from your current directory to create the function handles.

```
run E:/testdir/create_fhandles
```

3 You can now execute one of the functions through its handle using `feval`.

```
feval(fhset, item, value)
```

Making Toolbox File Changes Visible to MATLAB

Unlike functions in user-supplied directories, M-files (and MEX-files) in the $MATLAB/toolbox directories are not timestamp checked, so MATLAB does not automatically see changes to them. If you modify one of these files, and then rerun it, you may find that the behavior does not reflect the changes that you made. This is most likely because MATLAB is still using the previously loaded version of the file.

To force MATLAB to reload a function from disk, you need to explicitly clear the function from memory using `clear` *functionname*. Note that there are rare cases where clear will not have the desired effect, (for example, if the file is locked, or if it is a class constructor and objects of the given class exist in memory).

Similarly, MATLAB does not automatically detect the presence of new files in $MATLAB/toolbox directories. If you add (or remove) files from these directories, use rehash toolbox to force MATLAB to see your changes. Note that if you use the MATLAB Editor to create files, these steps are unnecessary, as the Editor automatically informs MATLAB of such changes.

Making Nontoolbox File Changes Visible to MATLAB

For M-files outside of the toolbox directories, MATLAB sees the changes made to these files by comparing timestamps and reloads any file that has changed the next time you execute the corresponding function.

If MATLAB does not see the changes you make to one of these files, try clearing the old copy of the function from memory using clear *functionname*. You can verify that MATLAB has cleared the function using inmem to list all functions currently loaded into memory.

Change Notification on Windows

If MATLAB, running on Windows, is unable to see new files or changes you have made to an existing file, the problem may be related to operating system change notification handles.

Type the following for more information.

```
help change_notification
help change_notification_advanced
```

Program Control

This section covers the following topics:

- "Using break, continue, and return" on page 7-41
- "Using switch Versus if" on page 7-42
- "MATLAB case Evaluates Strings" on page 7-42
- "Multiple Conditions in a case Statement" on page 7-42
- "Implicit Break in switch-case" on page 7-43
- "Variable Scope in a switch" on page 7-43
- "Catching Errors with try-catch" on page 7-43
- "Nested try-catch Blocks" on page 7-44
- "Forcing an Early Return from a Function" on page 7-44

Using break, continue, and return

It's easy to confuse the break, continue, and return functions, as they are similar in some ways. Make sure you use these functions appropriately.

Function	Where to Use It	Description
break	for or while loops	Exits the loop in which it appears. In nested loops, control passes to the next outer loop.
continue	for or while loops	Skips any remaining statements in the current loop. Control passes to the next iteration of the same loop.
return	Anywhere	Immediately exits the function in which it appears. Control passes to the caller of the function.

Using switch Versus if

It is possible, but usually not advantageous, to implement switch-case statements using if-elseif instead. See pros and cons in the table.

switch-case Statements	if-elseif Statements
Easier to read	Can be difficult to read
Can compare strings of different lengths	You need strcmp to compare strings of different lengths
Test for equality only	Test for equality or inequality

MATLAB case Evaluates Strings

A useful difference between switch-case statements in MATLAB and C is that you can specify string values in MATLAB case statements, which you cannot do in C.

```
switch(method)
   case 'linear'
      disp('Method is linear')
   case 'cubic'
      disp('Method is cubic')
end
```

Multiple Conditions in a case Statement

You can test against more than one condition with switch. The first case below tests for either a linear or bilinear method by using a cell array in the case statement.

```
switch(method)
   case {'linear', 'bilinear'}
      disp('Method is linear or bilinear')
   case (<and so on>)
end
```

Implicit Break in switch-case

In C, if you don't end each case with a break statement, code execution falls through to the following case. In MATLAB, case statements do not fall through; only one case may execute. Using break within a case statement is not only unnecessary, it is also invalid and generates a warning.

In this example, if result is 52, only the first disp statement executes, even though the second is also a valid match:

```
switch(result)
   case 52
      disp('result is 52')
   case {52, 78}
      disp('result is 52 or 78')
end
```

Variable Scope in a switch

Since MATLAB executes only one case of any switch statement, variables defined within one case are not known in the other cases of that switch statement. The same holds true for if-ifelse statements.

In these examples, you get an error when choice equals 2, because x is undefined.

```
      SWITCH-CASE                        IF-ELSEIF
switch choice
   case 1                      if choice == 1
      x = -pi:0.01:pi;             x = -pi:0.01:pi;
   case 2                      elseif choice == 2
      plot(x, sin(x));            plot(x, sin(x));
end                            end
```

Catching Errors with try-catch

When you have statements in your code that could possibly generate unwanted results, put those statements into a try-catch block that will catch any errors and handle them appropriately.

The example below shows a try-catch block within a function that multiplies two matrices. If a statement in the try segment of the block fails, control passes to the catch segment. In this case, the catch statements check the error message that was issued (returned by lasterr) and respond appropriately.

```
try
   X = A * B
catch
   errmsg = lasterr;
   if(strfind(errmsg, 'Inner matrix dimensions'))
       disp('** Wrong dimensions for matrix multiply')
end
```

For More Information See "Checking for Errors with try-catch" in the MATLAB "Programming and Data Types" documentation.

Nested try-catch Blocks

You can also nest try-catch blocks, as shown here. You can use this to attempt to recover from an error caught in the first try section.

```
try
   statement1              % Try to execute statement1
catch
   try
       statement2          % Attempt to recover from error
   catch
       disp 'Operation failed'   % Handle the error
   end
end
```

Forcing an Early Return from a Function

To force an early return from a function, place a return statement in the function at the point where you want to exit. For example,

```
if <done>
   return
end
```

Save and Load

This section covers the following topics:

- "Saving Data from the Workspace" on page 7-45
- "Loading Data into the Workspace" on page 7-45
- "Viewing Variables in a MAT-File" on page 7-46
- "Appending to a MAT-File" on page 7-46
- "Save and Load on Startup or Quit" on page 7-47
- "Saving to an ASCII File" on page 7-47

Saving Data from the Workspace

To save data from your workspace, you can do any of the following:

- Copy from the MATLAB Command Window and paste into a text file.
- Record part of your session in a `diary` file, and then edit the file in a text editor.
- Save to a binary or ASCII file using the `save` function.
- Save spreadsheet, scientific, image, or audio data with appropriate function.
- Save to a file using low-level file I/O functions (`fwrite`, `fprintf`, ...).

For More Information See "Using the diary Command to Export Data," "Saving the Current Workspace," and "Using Low-Level File I/O Functions" in the MATLAB "Development Environment" documentation.

Loading Data into the Workspace

Similarly, to load new or saved data into the workspace, you can do any of the following:

- Enter or paste data at the command line.
- Create a script file to initialize large matrices or data structures.
- Read a binary or ASCII file using `load`.
- Load spreadsheet, scientific, image, or audio data with appropriate function.

• Load from a file using low-level file I/O functions (`fread`, `fscanf`, ...).

For More Information See "Loading a Saved Workspace and Importing Data" and "Using Low-Level File I/O Functions" in the MATLAB "Development Environment" documentation.

Viewing Variables in a MAT-File

To see what variables are saved in a MAT-file, use `who` or `whos` as shown here (the `.mat` extension is not required). `who` returns a cell array and `whos` returns a structure array.

```
mydata_variables = who('-file', 'mydata.mat');
```

Appending to a MAT-File

To save additional variables to an existing MAT-file, use the syntax

```
save matfilename -append
```

Any variables you save that do not yet exist in the MAT-file are added to the file. Any variables you save that already exist in the MAT-file overwrite the old values.

Note Saving with the `-append` switch does not append additional elements to an array that is already saved in a MAT-file. See example below.

In this example, the second `save` operation does not concatenate new elements to vector A, (making A equal to [1 2 3 4 5 6 7 8]) in the MAT-file. Instead, it replaces the 5 element vector, A, with a 3 element vector, also retaining all other variables that were stored on the first `save` operation.

```
A = [1 2 3 4 5];  B = 12.5;  C = rand(4);
save savefile;
A = [6 7 8];
save savefile A -append;
```

Save and Load on Startup or Quit

You can automatically save your variables at the end of each MATLAB session by creating a finish.m file to save the contents of your base workspace every time you quit MATLAB. Load these variables back into your workspace at the beginning of each session by creating a startup.m file that uses the load function to load variables from your MAT-file.

For More Information See the startup and finish function reference pages.

Saving to an ASCII File

When you save matrix data to an ASCII file using save -ascii, MATLAB combines the individual matrices into one collection of numbers. Variable names are not saved. If this is not acceptable for your application, use fprintf to store your data instead.

For More Information See "Exporting ASCII Data" in the MATLAB "Development Environment" documentation.

Files and Filenames

This section covers the following topics:

- "Naming M-Files" on page 7-48
- "Naming Other Files" on page 7-48
- "Passing Filenames as Arguments" on page 7-49
- "Passing Filenames to ASCII Files" on page 7-49
- "Determining Filenames at Run-Time" on page 7-49
- "Returning the Size of a File" on page 7-50

Naming M-Files

M-file names must start with an alphabetic character, may contain any alphanumeric characters or underscores, and must be no longer than the maximum allowed M-file name length (returned by the function namelengthmax).

```
N = namelengthmax
N =
    63
```

Since variables must obey similar rules, you can use the isvarname function to check whether a filename (minus its .m file extension) is valid for an M-file.

```
isvarname mfilename
```

Naming Other Files

The names of other files that MATLAB interacts with (e.g., MAT-, MEX-, and MDL-files) follow the same rules as M-files, but may be of any length.

Depending on your operating system, you may be able to include certain non-alphanumeric characters in your filenames. Check your operating system manual for information on valid filename restrictions.

Passing Filenames as Arguments

In MATLAB commands, you can specify a filename argument using the MATLAB command or function syntax. For example, either of the following are acceptable. (The .mat file extension is optional for save and load.)

```
load mydata.mat            % Command syntax
load('mydata.mat')         % Function syntax
```

If you assign the output to a variable, you must use the function syntax.

```
saved_data = load('mydata.mat')
```

Passing Filenames to ASCII Files

ASCII files are specified as follows. Here, the file extension is required.

```
load mydata.dat -ascii             % Command syntax
load('mydata.dat','-ascii')        % Function syntax
```

Determining Filenames at Run-Time

There are several ways that your function code can work on specific files without you having to hard-code their filenames into the program. You can

- Pass the filename in as an argument

```
function myfun(datafile)
```

- Prompt for the filename using the input function

```
filename = input('Enter name of file:  ', 's');
```

- Browse for the file using the uigetfile function

```
[filename, pathname] = uigetfile('*.mat', 'Select MAT-file');
```

For More Information See "Obtaining User Input" in the MATLAB "Programming and Data Types" documentation, and the input and uigetfile function reference pages.

Returning the Size of a File

Two ways to have your program determine the size of a file are shown here.

METHOD #1	METHOD #2
``` s = dir('myfile.dat'); filesize = s.bytes ```	``` fid = fopen('myfile.dat'); fseek(fid, 0, 'eof'); filesize = ftell(fid) fclose(fid); ```

The dir function also returns the filename (s.name), last modification date (s.date), and whether or not it's a directory (s.isdir).

(The second method requires read access to the file.)

For More Information See the fopen, fseek, ftell, and fclose function reference pages.

Input/Output

This section covers the following topics:

- "File I/O Function Overview" on page 7-51
- "Common I/O Functions" on page 7-51
- "Readable File Formats" on page 7-51
- "Using the Import Wizard" on page 7-52
- "Loading Mixed Format Data" on page 7-52
- "Reading Files with Different Formats" on page 7-53
- "Reading ASCII Data into a Cell Array" on page 7-53
- "Interactive Input into Your Program" on page 7-53

File I/O Function Overview

For a good overview of MATLAB file I/O functions, use the online Functions by Category reference. In the Help browser **Contents**, click on **MATLAB -> Functions — By Category**, and then click on **File I/O**.

Common I/O Functions

The most commonly used, high-level, file I/O functions in MATLAB are `save` and `load`. For help on these, type `doc save` or `doc load`.

Functions for I/O to text files with delimited values are `textread`, `dlmread`, `dlmwrite`. Functions for I/O to text files with comma-separated values are `csvread`, `csvwrite`.

For More Information See "Text Files" in the MATLAB "Functions — By Category" reference documentation.

Readable File Formats

Type `doc fileformats` to see a list of file formats that MATLAB can read, along with the associated MATLAB functions.

Using the Import Wizard

A quick method of importing text or binary data from a file (e.g., Excel files) is to use the MATLAB Import Wizard. Open the Import Wizard with the command uiimport *filename* or by selecting **File -> Import Data** at the Command Window.

Specify or browse for the file containing the data you want to import and you will see a preview of what the file contains. Select the data you want and click **Finish**.

For More Information See "Using the Import Wizard with Text Data" and "Using the Import Wizard with Binary Data Files" in the MATLAB Development Environment documentation.

Loading Mixed Format Data

To load data that is in mixed formats, use textread instead of load. The textread function lets you specify the format of each piece of data.

If the first line of file mydata.dat is

```
Sally    12.34 45
```

Read the first line of the file as a free format file using the % format.

```
[names, x, y] = textread('mydata.dat', '%s %f %d', 1)
```

returns

```
names =
    'Sally'
x =
  12.34000000000000
y =
    45
```

Reading Files with Different Formats

Attempting to read data from a file that was generated on a different platform may result in an error because the binary formats of the platforms may differ. Using the fopen function, you can specify a machine format when you open the file to avoid these errors.

Reading ASCII Data into a Cell Array

A common technique used to read an ASCII data file into a cell array is

```
[a,b,c,d] = textread('data.txt', '%s %s %s %s');
mydata = cellstr([a b c d]);
```

For More Information See the textread and cellstr function reference pages.

Interactive Input into Your Program

Your program can accept interactive input from users during execution. Use the input function to prompt the user for input, and then read in a response. When executed, input causes the program to display your prompt, pause while a response is entered, and then resume when the **Enter** key is pressed.

For More Information See "Obtaining User Input" in the MATLAB "Programming and Data Types" documentation.

Managing Memory

This section covers the following topics:

For More Information See "Making Efficient Use of Memory" in the MATLAB "Programming and Data Types" documentation.

Useful Functions for Managing Memory

Several functions that are useful in managing memory are listed below.

Function	Description
clear	Remove variables from memory.
pack	Save existing variables to disk, and then reload them contiguously.
save	Selectively store variables to disk.
load	Reload a data file saved with the save function.
quit	Exit MATLAB and return all allocated memory to the system.

Compressing Data in Memory

Since MATLAB uses a heap method of memory management, extended MATLAB sessions may cause memory to become fragmented. When memory is fragmented, there may be plenty of free space, but not enough contiguous memory to store a new large variable. If you get the Out of Memory message from MATLAB, the pack function may be able to compress some of your data in memory, thus freeing up larger contiguous blocks.

For More Information See "Ways to Conserve Memory" in the MATLAB "Programming and Data Types" documentation.

Clearing Unused Variables from Memory

If you use pack and there is still not enough free memory to proceed, you probably need to remove some of the variables you are no longer using from memory. Use clear to do this.

Conserving Memory with Large Amounts of Data

If your program generates very large amounts of data, consider writing the data to disk periodically. After saving that portion of the data, clear the variable from memory and continue with the data generation.

Matrix Manipulation with Sparse Matrices

Matrices with values that are mostly zero are best stored in sparse format. Sparse matrices can use less memory and may also be faster to manipulate than full matrices. You can convert a full matrix to sparse using the sparse function.

For More Information See "Converting Full Matrices into Sparse" in the MATLAB "Programming and Data Types" documentation, and the sparse function reference page.

Structure of Arrays Rather Than Array of Structures

If your MATLAB application needs to store a large amount of data, and the definition of that data lends itself to being stored in either a structure of arrays or an array of structures, the former is preferable. A structure of arrays requires significantly less memory than an array of structures, and also has a corresponding speed benefit.

Preallocating Is Better Than Growing an Array

for and while loops that incrementally increase, or *grow*, the size of a data structure each time through the loop can adversely affect memory usage and performance. On each iteration, MATLAB has to allocate more memory for the growing matrix and also move data in memory whenever it cannot allocate a contiguous block. This can also result in fragmentation or in used memory not being returned to the operating system.

To avoid this, preallocate a block of memory large enough to hold the matrix at its final size. For example,

```
zeros(10000, 10000)        % Preallocate a 10000 x 10000 matrix
```

For More Information See "Preallocating Arrays" in the MATLAB "Programming and Data Types" documentation.

Use repmat When You Need to Grow Arrays

If you do need to grow an array, see if you can do it using the repmat function. repmat gets you a contiguous block of memory for your expanding array.

Preallocating a Nondouble Matrix

When you preallocate a block of memory to hold a matrix of some type other than double, it is more memory efficient and sometimes faster to use the repmat function for this.

The statement below uses zeros to preallocate a 100-by-100 matrix of uint8. It does this by first creating a full matrix of doubles, and then converting the matrix to uint8. This costs time and uses memory unnecessarily.

```
A = int8(zeros(100));
```

Using repmat, you create only one double, thus reducing your memory needs.

```
A = repmat(int8(0), 100, 100);
```

For More Information See "Preallocating Arrays" in the MATLAB "Programming and Data Types" documentation.

System-Specific Ways to Use Less Memory

If you run out of memory often, you can allocate your larger matrices earlier in the MATLAB session and also use these system-specific tips:

- UNIX: Ask your system manager to increase your swap space.
- Windows: Increase virtual memory using the Windows Control Panel.

For UNIX systems, we recommend that your machine be configured with twice as much swap space as you have RAM. The UNIX command pstat -s lets you know how much swap space you have.

For More Information See "Platform-Specific Memory Topics" in the MATLAB "Programming and Data Types" documentation.

Out of Memory Errors on UNIX

On UNIX systems, you may get Out of Memory errors when executing an operating system command from within MATLAB (using the shell escape (!) operator). This is because, when a process shells out to a subprocess, UNIX allocates as much memory for the subprocess as has been allocated for the parent process.

For More Information See "Running External Programs" in the MATLAB "Development Environment" documentation.

Reclaiming Memory on UNIX

On UNIX systems, MATLAB does not return memory to the operating system even after variables have been cleared. This is due to the manner in which UNIX manages memory. UNIX does not accept memory back from a program until the program has terminated. So, the amount of memory used in a MATLAB session is not returned to the operating system until you exit MATLAB.

To free up the memory used in your MATLAB session, save your workspace variables, exit MATLAB, and then load your variables back in.

Out of Memory Errors and the JVM

You are more likely to encounter Out of Memory errors when using MATLAB 6.0 or greater, due to the use of the Java virtual machine within MATLAB. On UNIX systems, you can reduce the amount of memory MATLAB uses by starting MATLAB with the -nojvm option. When you use this option, you cannot use the desktop or any of the MATLAB tools that require Java.

Type the following at the UNIX prompt:

```
matlab -nojvm
```

For More Information See "Running MATLAB without the Java Virtual Machine" in the MATLAB "Programming and Data Types" documentation.

Memory Requirements for Cell Arrays

The memory requirement for an M-by-N cell array containing the same type of data is

```
memreq = M*N*(100 + (num. of elements in cell)*bytes per element)
```

So a 5-by-6 cell array that contains a 10-by-10 real matrix in each cell takes up 27,000 bytes.

Memory Required for Cell Arrays and Structures

Contiguous memory is not required for an entire cell array or structure array. Since each of these is actually an array of pointers to other arrays, the memory for each array needs to be contiguous, but the entire memory collection does not need to be.

Preallocating Cell Arrays to Save Memory

Preallocation of cell arrays is recommended if you know the data type of your cells' components. This makes it unnecessary for MATLAB to grow the cell array each time you assign values.

For example, to preallocate a 1000-by-200 cell array of empty arrays, use

```
A = cell(1000, 200);
```

For More Information See "Preallocating Arrays" in the MATLAB "Programming and Data Types" documentation.

Optimizing for Speed

This section covers the following topics:

- "Finding Bottlenecks with the Profiler" on page 7-61
- "Measuring Execution Time with tic and toc" on page 7-62
- "Measuring Smaller Programs" on page 7-62
- "Speeding Up MATLAB Performance" on page 7-62
- "Vectorizing Your Code" on page 7-63
- "Functions Used in Vectorizing" on page 7-63
- "Coding Loops in a MEX-File for Speed" on page 7-63
- "Preallocate to Improve Performance" on page 7-64
- "Functions Are Faster Than Scripts" on page 7-64
- "Avoid Large Background Processes" on page 7-65
- "Load and Save Are Faster Than File I/O Functions" on page 7-65
- "Conserving Both Time and Memory" on page 7-65

For More Information See "Maximizing MATLAB Performance" in the MATLAB "Programming and Data Types" documentation.

Finding Bottlenecks with the Profiler

A good first step to speeding up your programs is to use the MATLAB Profiler to find out where the bottlenecks are. This is where you need to concentrate your attention to optimize your code.

To start the Profiler, type `profile viewer` or select **View -> Profiler** in the MATLAB desktop.

For More Information See "Measuring Performance" in the MATLAB "Programming and Data Types" documentation, and the `profile` function reference page.

Measuring Execution Time with tic and toc

The functions tic and toc help you to measure the execution time of a piece of code. You may want to test different algorithms to see how they compare in execution time.

Use tic and toc as shown here.

```
tic
    - run the program section to be timed -
toc
```

For More Information See "Techniques for Improving Performance" in the MATLAB "Programming and Data Types" documentation, and the tic/toc function reference page.

Measuring Smaller Programs

Programs can sometimes run too fast to get useful data from tic and toc. When this is the case, try measuring the program running repeatedly in a loop, and then average to find the time for a single run.

```
tic;
    for k=1:100
        - run the program -
    end;
toc
```

Speeding Up MATLAB Performance

MATLAB internally processes much of the code in M-file functions and scripts to run at an accelerated speed. The effects of performance acceleration can be particularly noticeable when you use for loops and, in some cases, the accelerated loops run as fast as vectorized code.

Implementing performance acceleration in MATLAB is a work in progress, and not all components of the MATLAB language can be accelerated at this time.

For More Information Read "Performance Acceleration" in the MATLAB "Programming and Data Types" documentation to see how you can make the best use of this feature.

Vectorizing Your Code

It's best to avoid the use of for loops in programs that cannot benefit from performance acceleration. Unlike compiled languages, MATLAB interprets each line in a for loop on each iteration of the loop. Most loops can be eliminated by performing an equivalent operation using MATLAB vectors instead. In many cases, this is fairly easy to do and is well worth the effort required to convert from using a loop.

For More Information See "Vectorizing Loops" in the MATLAB "Programming and Data Types" documentation.

Functions Used in Vectorizing

Some of the most commonly used functions for vectorizing are

all	end	logical	repmat	squeeze
any	find	ndgrid	reshape	sub2ind
cumsum	ind2sub	permute	shiftdim	sum
diff	ipermute	prod	sort	

Coding Loops in a MEX-File for Speed

If there are instances where you must use a for loop, consider coding the loop in a MEX-file. In this way, the loop executes much more quickly since the instructions in the loop do not have to be interpreted each time they execute.

For More Information See "Introducing MEX-Files" in the External Interfaces/API documentation.

Preallocate to Improve Performance

MATLAB allows you to increase the size of an existing matrix incrementally, usually within a `for` or `while` loop. However, this can slow a program down considerably, as MATLAB must continually allocate more memory for the growing matrix and also move data in memory whenever a contiguous block cannot be allocated.

It is much faster to preallocate a block of memory large enough to hold the matrix at its final size. For example, to preallocate a 10000-by-10000 matrix, use

```
zeros(10000, 10000)        % Preallocate a 10000 x 10000 matrix
```

For More Information See "Preallocating Arrays" in the MATLAB "Programming and Data Types" documentation.

Functions Are Faster Than Scripts

Your code executes more quickly if it is implemented in a function rather than a script. Every time a script is used in MATLAB, it is loaded into memory and evaluated one line at a time. Functions, on the other hand, are compiled into pseudocode and loaded into memory once. Therefore, additional calls to the function are faster.

For More Information See "Techniques for Improving Performance" in the MATLAB "Programming and Data Types" documentation.

Avoid Large Background Processes

Avoid running large processes in the background at the same time you are executing your program in MATLAB. This frees more CPU time for your MATLAB session.

Load and Save Are Faster Than File I/O Functions

If you have a choice of whether to use load and save instead of the MATLAB file I/O routines, choose the former. load and save have been optimized to run faster and reduce memory fragmentation.

Conserving Both Time and Memory

The following tips have already been mentioned under "Managing Memory" on page 7-54, but apply to optimizing for speed as well:

- "Conserving Memory with Large Amounts of Data" on page 7-56
- "Matrix Manipulation with Sparse Matrices" on page 7-56
- "Structure of Arrays Rather Than Array of Structures" on page 7-56
- "Preallocating Is Better Than Growing an Array" on page 7-56
- "Preallocating a Nondouble Matrix" on page 7-57

Starting MATLAB

Getting MATLAB to Start Up Faster

Here are some things that you can do to make MATLAB start up faster:

- Make sure toolbox path caching is enabled.
- Make sure that the system on which MATLAB is running has enough RAM.
- Choose only the windows you need in the MATLAB desktop.
- Close the Help browser before exiting MATLAB. When you start your next session, MATLAB will not open the Help browser, and thus will start faster.
- If disconnected from the network, check the `LM_LICENSE_FILE` variable. See `http://www.mathworks.com/support/solutions/data/25731.shtml` for a more detailed explanation.

For More Information See "Reduced Startup Time with Toolbox Path Caching" in the MATLAB "Development Environment" documentation.

Operating System Compatibility

This section covers the following topics:

- "Executing OS Commands from MATLAB" on page 7-67
- "Searching Text with grep" on page 7-67
- "Constructing Path and File Names" on page 7-68
- "Finding the MATLAB Root Directory" on page 7-68
- "Temporary Directories and Filenames" on page 7-68

Executing OS Commands from MATLAB

To execute a command from your operating system prompt without having to exit MATLAB, precede the command with the MATLAB ! operator.

On Windows, you can add an ampersand (&) to the end of the line to make the output appear in a separate window.

For More Information See "Running External Programs" in the MATLAB "Development Environment" documentation, and the system and dos function reference pages.

Searching Text with grep

grep is a powerful tool for performing text searches in files on UNIX systems. To grep from within MATLAB, precede the command with an exclamation point (!grep).

For example, to search for the word warning, ignoring case, in all M-files of the current directory, you would use

```
!grep -i 'warning' *.m
```

Constructing Path and File Names

Use the fullfile function to construct path names and filenames rather than entering them as strings into your programs. In this way, you always get the correct path specification, regardless of which operating system you are using at the time.

Finding the MATLAB Root Directory

The matlabroot function returns the location of the MATLAB installation on your system. Use matlabroot to create a path to MATLAB and toolbox directories that does not depend on a specific platform or MATLAB version.

The following example uses matlabroot with fullfile to return a platform-independent path to the general toolbox directory.

```
fullfile(matlabroot,'toolbox','matlab','general')
```

Temporary Directories and Filenames

If you need to locate the directory on your system that has been designated to hold temporary files, use the tempdir function. tempdir returns a string that specifies the path to this directory.

To create a new file in this directory, use the tempname function. tempname returns a string that specifies the path to the temporary file directory, plus a unique filename.

For example, to store some data in a temporary file, you might issue the following command first.

```
fid = fopen(tempname, 'w');
```

Demos

Demos Available with MATLAB

MATLAB comes with a wide array of visual demonstrations to help you see the extent of what you can do with the product. To start running any of the demos, simply type demo at the MATLAB command prompt. Demos cover the following major areas:

- MATLAB
- Toolboxes
- Simulink
- Blocksets
- Real-Time Workshop
- Stateflow

For More Information See "Running Demonstrations" in the MATLAB "Development Environment" documentation, and the demo function reference page.

For More Information

Current CSSM
```
news:comp.soft-sys.matlab
```

Archived CSSM
```
http://mathforum.org/epigone/comp.soft-sys.matlab/
```

MATLAB Technical Support
```
http://www.mathworks.com/support/
```

Search Selected Online Resources
```
http://www.mathworks.com/search/
```

Tech Notes
```
http://www.mathworks.com/support/tech-notes/1100/index.shtml
```

MATLAB Central
```
http://www.mathworks.com/matlabcentral/
```

MATLAB Tips
```
http://www.mathworks.com/products/gallery/tips/
```

MATLAB Digest
```
http://www.mathworks.com/company/digest/index.shtml
```

MATLAB News & Notes
```
http://www.mathworks.com/company/newsletter/index.shtml
```

MATLAB Documentation
```
http://www.mathworks.com/access/helpdesk/help/helpdesk.shtml
```

MATLAB Index of Examples
```
http://www.mathworks.com/access/helpdesk/help/techdoc/
   demo_example.shtml
```

Introducing the
Symbolic Math Toolbox

This chapter introduces the Symbolic Math Toolbox and how to create and work with symbolic objects.

Introduction

The Symbolic Math Toolbox incorporates symbolic computation into the numeric environment of MATLAB. This toolbox supplements the numeric and graphical facilities of MATLAB with several other types of mathematical computation, which are summarized in the following table.

Facility	Covers
Calculus	Differentiation, integration, limits, summation, and Taylor series
Linear Algebra	Inverses, determinants, eigenvalues, singular value decomposition, and canonical forms of symbolic matrices
Simplification	Methods of simplifying algebraic expressions
Solution of Equations	Symbolic and numerical solutions to algebraic and differential equations
Variable-Precision Arithmetic	Numerical evaluation of mathematical expressions to any specified accuracy
Transforms	Fourier, Laplace, z-transform, and corresponding inverse transforms

The computational engine underlying this toolbox is the kernel of Maple®, a system developed primarily at the University of Waterloo, Canada, and, more recently, at the Eidgenössiche Technische Hochschule, Zürich, Switzerland. Maple is marketed and supported by Waterloo Maple, Inc.

This version of the Symbolic Math Toolbox is designed to work with MATLAB 6 or greater and Maple 8.

The Symbolic Math Toolbox

The Symbolic Math Toolbox is a collection of more than 100 MATLAB functions that provide access to the Maple kernel using a syntax and style that is a natural extension of the MATLAB language. The toolbox also allows you to access functions in the Maple linear algebra package.

Learning About the Symbolic Math Toolbox

This tutorial provide explanation and examples on how to use the toolbox. It is divided into the following sections.

"Getting Started" on page 8-6	An introduction to the toolbox for new users
"Using the Symbolic Math Toolbox" on page 9-1	A detailed description of how to use the toolbox
"Symbolic Math Toolbox Quick Reference" on page B-1	Reference pages for the functions in the toolbox

If you are new to the Symbolic Math Toolbox, you should begin by reading "Getting Started" on page 8-6. If you are already familiar with the functionality of the toolbox, you can proceed to "Using the Symbolic Math Toolbox" on page 9-1.

Finding Help for Specific Topics

The are several ways to find help for specific features of the Symbolic Math Toolbox:

- Enter doc function at the MATLAB prompt, where function is the name of the function you want help for. This opens the reference page for the function in the Help browser.

- Click the **Search** tab in the Help Navigator and enter the text you want to search for in the **Search for** field.

- Click the **Index** tab and enter the text you want to search for in the **Search index for** field.

Note To restrict the search or index topics to the Symbolic Math Toolbox documentation, click the **Select** button next to **Product filter** and clear the check boxes next to all products except **Symbolic Math Toolbox**.

Using Command-Line Help

As a supplement to this guide, you can find information on Symbolic Math Toolbox functions using the MATLAB command line help system. You can obtain help for any MATLAB function by typing

```
help function
```

where `function` is the name of the function for which you need help.

The Symbolic Math Toolbox "overloads" many of the numeric functions of MATLAB with symbolic-specific implementations of those functions, using the same function name. To obtain help for the symbolic version of an overloaded function, type

```
help sym/function
```

where `function` is the overloaded function's name. For example, to obtain help on the symbolic version of the overloaded function `diff`, type

```
help sym/diff
```

Demos

To get a quick online introduction to the Symbolic Math Toolbox, type `demos` at the MATLAB command line. MATLAB displays the Demos pane in the Help browser. To run the demos,

1 Click the **+** sign next to **Toolboxes** in the left pane.

2 Click the **+** sign next to **Symbolic Math**.

3 Select **Introduction**.

4 Click **Run this demo** in the right pane, as shown in the following figure.

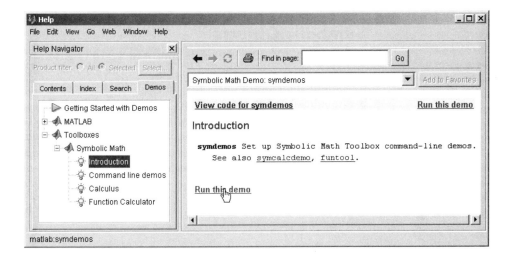

For More Information You can access complete reference information for the Symbolic Math Toolbox functions from Help. Also, you can print the PDF version of the complete Symbolic Math Toolbox User's Guide (tutorial and reference information) from the Symbolic Math Toolbox Roadmap page in Help.

Getting Started

Symbolic Objects

The Symbolic Math Toolbox defines a new MATLAB data type called a *symbolic object*. (See "Programming and Data Types" in the MATLAB documentation for an introduction to MATLAB classes and objects.) Internally, a symbolic object is a data structure that stores a string representation of the symbol. The Symbolic Math Toolbox uses symbolic objects to represent symbolic variables, expressions, and matrices. The actual computations involving symbolic objects are performed primarily by Maple, mathematical software developed by Waterloo Maple, Inc.

The following example illustrates the difference between a standard MATLAB data type, such as double, and the corresponding symbolic object. The MATLAB command

```
sqrt(2)
```

returns a floating-point decimal number.

```
ans =
    1.4142
```

However, if you convert 2 to a symbolic object using the sym command, and then take its square root by entering

```
a = sqrt(sym(2))
```

the result is

```
a =
2^(1/2)
```

MATLAB gives the result 2^(1/2), which means $2^{1/2}$, using symbolic notation for the square root operation, without actually calculating a numerical value. MATLAB records this symbolic expression in the string that represents 2^(1/2). You can always obtain the numerical value of a symbolic object with the double command.

```
double(a)
ans =
    1.4142
```

Notice that the result is indented, which tells you it has data type `double`. Symbolic results are not indented.

When you create a fraction involving symbolic objects, MATLAB records the numerator and denominator. For example:

```
sym(2)/sym(5)
ans =
2/5
```

MATLAB performs arithmetic on symbolic objects differently than it does on standard data types. If you add two fractions that are of data type `double`, MATLAB gives the answer as a decimal fraction. For example:

```
2/5 + 1/3
ans =
0.7333
```

If you add the same fractions as symbolic objects, MATLAB finds their common denominator and combines them by the usual procedure for adding rational numbers.

```
sym(2)/sym(5) + sym(1)/sym(3)
ans =
11/15
```

The Symbolic Math Toolbox enables you to perform a variety of symbolic calculations that arise in mathematics and science. These are described in detail in Chapter 9, "Using the Symbolic Math Toolbox."

Creating Symbolic Variables and Expressions

The `sym` command lets you construct symbolic variables and expressions. For example, the commands

```
x = sym('x')
a = sym('alpha')
```

create a symbolic variable x that prints as x and a symbolic variable a that prints as `alpha`.

Suppose you want to use a symbolic variable to represent the golden ratio

$$\rho = \frac{1 + \sqrt{5}}{2}$$

The command

```
rho = sym('(1 + sqrt(5))/2')
```

achieves this goal. Now you can perform various mathematical operations on rho. For example,

```
f = rho^2 - rho - 1
```

returns

```
f =

(1/2+1/2*5^(1/2))^2-3/2-1/2*5^(1/2)
```

You can simplify this answer by entering

```
simplify(f)
```

which returns

```
ans =
0
```

Now suppose you want to study the quadratic function $f = ax^2 + bx + c$. One approach is to enter the command

```
f = sym('a*x^2 + b*x + c')
```

which assigns the symbolic expression $ax^2 + bx + c$ to the variable f. However, in this case, the Symbolic Math Toolbox does not create variables corresponding to the terms of the expression, a, b, c, and x. To perform symbolic math operations (e.g., integration, differentiation, substitution, and so on) on f, you need to create the variables explicitly. A better alternative is to enter the commands

```
a = sym('a')
b = sym('b')
c = sym('c')
x = sym('x')
```

or simply

```
syms a b c x
```

Then enter

```
f = sym('a*x^2 + b*x + c')
```

In general, you can use sym or syms to create symbolic variables. We recommend you use syms because it requires less typing.

Note To create a symbolic expression that is a constant, you must use the sym command. For example, to create the expression whose value is 5, enter f = sym('5'). Note that the command f = 5 does *not* define f as a symbolic expression.

If you set a variable equal to a symbolic expression, and then apply the syms command to the variable, MATLAB removes the previously defined expression from the variable. For example,

```
syms a b
f = a + b
```

returns

```
f =
a+b
```

If you then enter

```
syms f
f
```

MATLAB returns

```
f =
f
```

You can use the syms command to clear variables of definitions that you assigned to them previously in your MATLAB session. However, syms does not clear the properties of the variables in the Maple workspace. See "Clearing Variables in the Maple Workspace" on page 8-14 for more information.

The findsym Command

To determine what symbolic variables are present in an expression, use the findsym command. For example, given the symbolic expressions f and g defined by

```
syms a b n t x z
f = x^n; g = sin(a*t + b);
```

you can find the symbolic variables in f by entering

```
findsym(f)
ans =
n, x
```

Similarly, you can find the symbolic variables in g by entering

```
findsym(g)
ans =
a, b, t
```

The subs Command

You can substitute a numerical value for a symbolic variable using the subs command. For example, to substitute the value $x = 2$ in the symbolic expression

```
f = 2*x^2 - 3*x + 1
```

enter the command

```
subs(f,2)
```

This returns $f(2)$:

```
ans =
    3
```

When your expression contains more than one variable, you can specify the variable for which you want to make the substitution. For example, to substitute the value $x = 3$ in the symbolic expression

```
syms x y
f = x^2*y + 5*x*sqrt(y)
```

enter the command

```
subs(f, x, 3)
```

This returns

```
ans =
9*y+15*y^(1/2)
```

On the other hand, to substitute $y = 3$, enter

```
subs(f, y, 3)
ans =
3*x^2+5*x*3^(1/2)
```

If you do not specify a variable to substitute for, MATLAB chooses a default variable according to the following rule. For one-letter variables, MATLAB chooses the letter closest to x in the alphabet. If there are two letters equally close to x, MATLAB chooses the one that comes later in the alphabet. In the preceding function, subs(f, 3) returns the same answer as subs(f, x, 3).

You can use the findsym command to determine the default variable. For example,

```
syms s t
g = s + t;
findsym(g,1)
```

returns the default variable:

```
ans =
t
```

See "Substitutions" on page 9-49 to learn more about substituting for variables.

Symbolic and Numeric Conversions

Consider the ordinary MATLAB quantity

```
t = 0.1
```

The sym function has four options for returning a symbolic representation of the numeric value stored in t. The 'f' option

```
sym(t,'f')
```

returns a symbolic floating-point representation

```
'1.999999999999a'*2^(-4)
```

The 'r' option

```
sym(t,'r')
```

returns the rational form

```
1/10
```

This is the default setting for sym. That is, calling sym without a second argument is the same as using sym with the 'r' option:

```
sym(t)

ans =
1/10
```

The third option 'e' returns the rational form of t plus the difference between the theoretical rational expression for t and its actual (machine) floating-point value in terms of eps (the floating-point relative accuracy).

```
sym(t,'e')

ans =
1/10+eps/40
```

The fourth option 'd' returns the decimal expansion of t up to the number of significant digits specified by digits.

```
sym(t,'d')

ans =
.10000000000000000555111512312578
```

The default value of digits is 32 (hence, sym(t,'d') returns a number with 32 significant digits), but if you prefer a shorter representation, use the digits command as follows.

```
digits(7)
sym(t,'d')
```

```
ans =
.1000000
```

A particularly effective use of sym is to convert a matrix from numeric to symbolic form. The command

```
A = hilb(3)
```

generates the 3-by-3 Hilbert matrix.

```
A =

        1.0000    0.5000    0.3333
        0.5000    0.3333    0.2500
        0.3333    0.2500    0.2000
```

By applying sym to A

```
A = sym(A)
```

you can obtain the symbolic (infinitely precise) form of the 3-by-3 Hilbert matrix.

```
A =

[   1, 1/2, 1/3]
[ 1/2, 1/3, 1/4]
[ 1/3, 1/4, 1/5]
```

Constructing Real and Complex Variables

The sym command allows you to specify the mathematical properties of symbolic variables by using the 'real' option. That is, the statements

```
x = sym('x','real'); y = sym('y','real');
```

or more efficiently

```
syms x y real
z = x + i*y
```

create symbolic variables x and y that have the added mathematical property of being real variables. Specifically this means that the expression

```
f = x^2 + y^2
```

is strictly nonnegative. Hence, z is a complex variable and can be manipulated as such. Thus, the commands

```
conj(x), conj(z), expand(z*conj(z))
```

return

```
x, x-i*y, x^2+y^2
```

respectively. The conj command is the complex conjugate operator for the toolbox. If conj(x) == x returns 1, then x is a real variable.

Clearing Variables in the Maple Workspace

When you declare x to be real with the command

```
syms x real
```

a becomes a symbolic object in the MATLAB workspace and a positive real variable in the Maple kernel workspace. If you later want to remove the real property from x, enter

```
syms a unreal
```

Note that entering

```
clear x
```

only clears x in the MATLAB workspace. If you then enter syms x, MATLAB still treats x as a positive real number.

Creating Abstract Functions

If you want to create an abstract (i.e., indeterminant) function $f(x)$, type

```
f = sym('f(x)')
```

Then f acts like $f(x)$ and can be manipulated by the toolbox commands. For example, to construct the first difference ratio, type

```
df = (subs(f,'x','x+h') - f)/'h'
```

or

```
syms x h
df = (subs(f,x,x+h)-f)/h
```

which returns

```
df =
(f(x+h)-f(x))/h
```

This application of sym is useful when computing Fourier, Laplace, and z-transforms.

Using sym to Access Maple Functions

Similarly, you can access the Maple factorial function k! using sym.

```
kfac = sym('k!')
```

To compute 6! or n!, type

```
syms k n
subs(kfac,k,6), subs(kfac,k,n)

ans =
720

ans =
n!
```

Example: Creating a Symbolic Matrix

A circulant matrix has the property that each row is obtained from the previous one by cyclically permuting the entries one step forward. You can create the circulant matrix A whose elements are a, b, and c, using the commands

```
syms a b c
A = [a b c; b c a; c a b]
```

which return

```
A =
[ a, b, c ]
[ b, c, a ]
[ c, a, b ]
```

Since A is circulant, the sum over each row and column is the same. To check this for the first row and second column, enter the command

```
sum(A(1,:))
```

which returns

```
ans =
a+b+c
```

The command

```
sum(A(1,:)) == sum(A(:,2)) % This is a logical test.
```

returns

```
ans =
     1
```

Now replace the (2,3) entry of A with `beta` and the variable `b` with `alpha`. The commands

```
syms alpha beta;
A(2,3) = beta;
A = subs(A,b,alpha)
```

return

```
A =
[     a, alpha,     c]
[ alpha,     c, beta]
[     c,     a, alpha]
```

From this example, you can see that using symbolic objects is very similar to using regular MATLAB numeric objects.

Creating Symbolic Math Functions

There are two ways to create functions:

- Use symbolic expressions
- Create an M-file

Using Symbolic Expressions

The sequence of commands

```
syms x y z
r = sqrt(x^2 + y^2 + z^2)
t = atan(y/x)
f = sin(x*y)/(x*y)
```

generates the symbolic expressions r, t, and f. You can use diff, int, subs, and other Symbolic Math Toolbox functions to manipulate such expressions.

Creating an M-File

M-files permit a more general use of functions. Suppose, for example, you want to create the sinc function sin(x)/x. To do this, create an M-file in the @sym directory.

```
function z = sinc(x)
%SINC The symbolic sinc function
%      sin(x)/x. This function
%      accepts a sym as the input argument.
if isequal(x,sym(0))
   z = 1;
else
   z = sin(x)/x;
end
```

You can extend such examples to functions of several variables. See the MATLAB topic "Programming and Data Types" in the MATLAB documentation for a more detailed discussion on object-oriented programming.

Using the Symbolic Math Toolbox

This chapter explains how to use the Symbolic Math Toolbox to perform many common mathematical operations.

Calculus

The Symbolic Math Toolbox provides functions to do the basic operations of calculus. The following sections describe these functions:

- "Differentiation" on page 9-2
- "Limits" on page 9-8
- "Integration" on page 9-10
- "Symbolic Summation" on page 9-18
- "Taylor Series" on page 9-18
- "Calculus Example" on page 9-20
- "Extended Calculus Example" on page 9-27

Differentiation

To illustrate how to take derivatives using the Symbolic Math Toolbox, first create a symbolic expression.

```
syms x
f = sin(5*x)
```

The command

```
diff(f)
```

differentiates f with respect to x.

```
ans =
5*cos(5*x)
```

As another example, let

```
g = exp(x)*cos(x)
```

where exp(x) denotes e^x, and differentiate g.

```
diff(g)
ans =
exp(x)*cos(x)-exp(x)*sin(x)
```

To take the second derivative of g, enter

```
diff(g,2)
```

```
ans =
-2*exp(x)*sin(x)
```

You can get the same result by taking the derivative twice.

```
diff(diff(g))
ans =
-2*exp(x)*sin(x)
```

In this example, MATLAB automatically simplifies the answer. However, in some cases, MATLAB might not simplify an answer, in which case you can use the simplify command. For an example of this, see "More Examples" on page 9-4.

Note that to take the derivative of a constant, you must first define the constant as a symbolic expression. For example, entering

```
c = sym('5');
diff(c)
```

returns

```
ans =
0
```

If you just enter

```
diff(5)
```

MATLAB returns

```
ans =
     []
```

because 5 is not a symbolic expression.

Derivatives of Expressions with Several Variables

To differentiate an expression that contains more than one symbolic variable, you must specify the variable that you want to differentiate with respect to. The diff command then calculates the partial derivative of the expression with respect to that variable. For example, given the symbolic expression

```
syms s t
f = sin(s*t)
```

the command

```
diff(f,t)
```

calculates the partial derivative $\partial f / \partial t$. The result is

```
ans =
cos(s*t)*s
```

To differentiate f with respect to the variable s, enter

```
diff(f,s)
```

which returns

```
ans =
cos(s*t)*t
```

If you do not specify a variable to differentiate with respect to, MATLAB chooses a default variable by the same rule described in "The subs Command" on page 8-10. For one-letter variables, the default variable is the letter closest to x in the alphabet. In the preceding example, diff(f) takes the derivative of f with respect to t because t is closer to x in the alphabet than s is. To determine the default variable that MATLAB differentiates with respect to, use the findsym command.

```
findsym(f,1)
ans =
t
```

To calculate the second derivative of f with respect to t, enter

```
diff(f,t,2)
```

which returns

```
ans =
-sin(s*t)*s^2
```

Note that diff(f,2) returns the same answer because t is the default variable.

More Examples

To further illustrate the diff command, define a, b, x, n, t, and theta in the MATLAB workspace by entering

```
syms a b x n t theta
```

The table below illustrates the results of entering `diff(f)`.

f	diff(f)
x^n	x^n*n/x
sin(a*t+b)	cos(a*t+b)*a
exp(i*theta)	i*exp(i*theta)

In the first example, MATLAB does not automatically simplify the answer. To simplify the answer, enter

```
simplify(diff(x^n))
ans =
x^(n-1)*n
```

To differentiate the Bessel function of the first kind, `besselj(nu,z)`, with respect to z, type

```
syms nu z
b = besselj(nu,z);
db = diff(b)
```

which returns

```
db =
-besselj(nu+1,z)+nu/z*besselj(nu,z)
```

The `diff` function can also take a symbolic matrix as its input. In this case, the differentiation is done element-by-element. Consider the example

```
syms a x
A = [cos(a*x),sin(a*x);-sin(a*x),cos(a*x)]
```

which returns

```
A =
[  cos(a*x),   sin(a*x)]
[ -sin(a*x),   cos(a*x)]
```

The command

```
diff(A)
```

returns

```
ans =
[ -sin(a*x)*a,  cos(a*x)*a]
[ -cos(a*x)*a, -sin(a*x)*a]
```

You can also perform differentiation of a column vector with respect to a row vector. Consider the transformation from Euclidean (x, y, z) to spherical (r, λ, φ) coordinates as given by $x = r\cos\lambda\cos\varphi$, $y = r\cos\lambda\sin\varphi$, and $z = r\sin\lambda$. Note that λ corresponds to elevation or latitude while φ denotes azimuth or longitude.

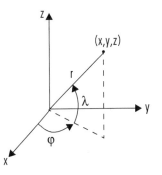

To calculate the Jacobian matrix, J, of this transformation, use the `jacobian` function. The mathematical notation for J is

$$J = \frac{\partial(x, y, x)}{\partial(r, \lambda, \varphi)}$$

For the purposes of toolbox syntax, use l for λ and f for φ. The commands

```
syms r l f
x = r*cos(l)*cos(f); y = r*cos(l)*sin(f); z = r*sin(l);
J = jacobian([x; y; z], [r l f])
```

return the Jacobian

```
J =
[    cos(1)*cos(f),  -r*sin(1)*cos(f),  -r*cos(1)*sin(f)]
[    cos(1)*sin(f),  -r*sin(1)*sin(f),   r*cos(1)*cos(f)]
[           sin(1),         r*cos(1),                  0]
```

and the command

```
detJ = simple(det(J))
```

returns

```
detJ =
-cos(1)*r^2
```

Notice that the first argument of the jacobian function must be a column vector and the second argument a row vector. Moreover, since the determinant of the Jacobian is a rather complicated trigonometric expression, you can use the simple command to make trigonometric substitutions and reductions (simplifications). The section "Simplifications and Substitutions" on page 9-40 discusses simplification in more detail.

A table summarizing diff and jacobian follows.

Mathematical Operator	MATLAB Command
$\dfrac{df}{dx}$	diff(f) or diff(f,x)
$\dfrac{df}{da}$	diff(f,a)
$\dfrac{d^2 f}{db^2}$	diff(f,b,2)
$J = \dfrac{\partial(r, t)}{\partial(u, v)}$	J = jacobian([r;t],[u,v])

Limits

The fundamental idea in calculus is to make calculations on functions as a variable "gets close to" or approaches a certain value. Recall that the definition of the derivative is given by a limit

$$f'(x) = \lim_{h \to 0} \frac{f(x+h) - f(x)}{h}$$

provided this limit exists. The Symbolic Math Toolbox enables you to calculate the limits of functions directly. The commands

```
syms h n x
limit( (cos(x+h) - cos(x))/h,h,0 )
```

which return

```
ans =
-sin(x)
```

and

```
limit( (1 + x/n)^n,n,inf )
```

which returns

```
ans =
exp(x)
```

illustrate two of the most important limits in mathematics: the derivative (in this case of cos x) and the exponential function.

One-Sided Limits

You can also calculate one-sided limits with the Symbolic Math Toolbox. For example, you can calculate the limit of $x/|x|$, whose graph is shown in the following figure, as x approaches 0 from the left or from the right.

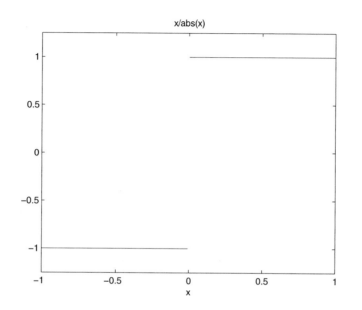

To calculate the limit as x approaches 0 from the left,

$$\lim_{x \to 0^-} \frac{x}{|x|}$$

enter

```
limit(x/abs(x),x,0,'left')
```

This returns

```
ans =
 -1
```

To calculate the limit as x approaches 0 from the right,

$$\lim_{x \to 0^+} \frac{x}{|x|} = 1$$

enter

```
limit(x/abs(x),x,0,'right')
```

This returns

```
ans =
1
```

Since the limit from the left does not equal the limit from the right, the two-sided limit does not exist. In the case of undefined limits, MATLAB returns NaN (not a number). For example,

```
limit(x/abs(x),x,0)
```

returns

```
ans =
NaN
```

Observe that the default case, limit(f) is the same as limit(f,x,0). Explore the options for the limit command in this table, where f is a function of the symbolic object x.

Mathematical Operation	MATLAB Command
$\lim\limits_{x \to 0} f(x)$	limit(f)
$\lim\limits_{x \to a} f(x)$	limit(f,x,a) or limit(f,a)
$\lim\limits_{x \to a-} f(x)$	limit(f,x,a,'left')
$\lim\limits_{x \to a+} f(x)$	limit(f,x,a,'right')

Integration

If f is a symbolic expression, then

```
int(f)
```

attempts to find another symbolic expression, F, so that diff(F) = f. That is, int(f) returns the indefinite integral or antiderivative of f (provided one exists in closed form). Similar to differentiation,

```
int(f,v)
```

uses the symbolic object v as the variable of integration, rather than the variable determined by findsym. See how int works by looking at this table.

Mathematical Operation	MATLAB Command
$\int x^n dx = \dfrac{x^{n+1}}{n+1}$	int(x^n) or int(x^n,x)
$\int\limits_{0}^{\pi/2} \sin(2x)dx = 1$	int(sin(2*x),0,pi/2) or int(sin(2*x),x,0,pi/2)
$g = \cos(at+b)$ $\int g(t)dt = \sin(at+b)/a$	g = cos(a*t + b) int(g) or int(g,t)
$\int J_1(z)dz = -J_0(z)$	int(besselj(1,z)) or int(besselj(1,z),z)

In contrast to differentiation, symbolic integration is a more complicated task. A number of difficulties can arise in computing the integral:

- The antiderivative, F, may not exist in closed form.
- The antiderivative may define an unfamiliar function.
- The antiderivative may exist, but the software can't find it.
- The software could find the antiderivative on a larger computer, but runs out of time or memory on the available machine.

Nevertheless, in many cases, MATLAB can perform symbolic integration successfully. For example, create the symbolic variables:

```
syms a b theta x y n u z
```

The following table illustrates integration of expressions containing those variables.

f	int(f)
x^n	x^(n+1)/(n+1)
y^(-1)	log(y)
n^x	1/log(n)*n^x
sin(a*theta+b)	-1/a*cos(a*theta+b)
1/(1+u^2)	atan(u)
exp(-x^2)	1/2*pi^(1/2)*erf(x)

In the last example, exp(-x^2), there is no formula for the integral involving standard calculus expressions, such as trigonometric and exponential functions. In this case, MATLAB returns an answer in terms of the error function erf.

If MATLAB is unable to find an answer to the integral of a function f, it just returns int(f).

Definite integration is also possible. The commands

```
int(f,a,b)
```

and

```
int(f,v,a,b)
```

are used to find a symbolic expression for

$$\int_a^b f(x)dx \quad \text{and} \quad \int_a^b f(v)dv$$

respectively.

Here are some additional examples.

f	a, b	int(f,a,b)
x^7	0, 1	1/8
1/x	1, 2	log(2)
log(x)*sqrt(x)	0, 1	-4/9
exp(-x^2)	0, inf	1/2*pi^(1/2)
besselj(1,z)^2	0, 1	1/12*hypergeom([3/2, 3/2], [2, 5/2, 3],-1)

For the Bessel function (besselj) example, it is possible to compute a numerical approximation to the value of the integral, using the double function. The commands

```
syms z
a = int(besselj(1,z)^2,0,1)
```

return

```
a =
1/12*hypergeom([3/2, 3/2],[2, 5/2, 3],-1)
```

and the command

```
a = double(a)
```

returns

```
a =
   0.0717
```

Integration with Real Parameters

One of the subtleties involved in symbolic integration is the "value" of various parameters. For example, if a is any positive real number, the expression

$$e^{-ax^2}$$

is the positive, bell shaped curve that tends to 0 as x tends to $\pm\infty$. You can create an example of this curve, for $a = 1/2$, using the following commands.

```
syms x
a = sym(1/2);
f = exp(-a*x^2);
ezplot(f)
```

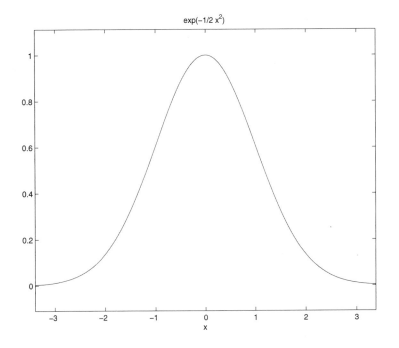

However, if you try to calculate the integral

$$\int\limits_{-\infty}^{\infty} e^{-ax^2} dx$$

without assigning a value to a, MATLAB assumes that a represents a complex number, and therefore returns a complex answer. If you are only interested in the case when a is a positive real number, you can calculate the integral as follows:

```
syms a positive;
```

The argument positive in the syms command restricts a to have positive values. Now you can calculate the preceding integral using the commands

```
syms x;
f = exp(-a*x^2);
int(f,x,-inf,inf)
```

This returns

```
ans =
1/(a)^(1/2)*pi^(1/2)
```

If you want to calculate the integral

$$\int_{-\infty}^{\infty} e^{-ax^2} dx$$

for any real number a, not necessarily positive, you can declare a to be real with the following commands.

```
syms a real
f=exp(-a*x^2);
F = int(f, x, -inf, inf)
```

MATLAB returns

```
F =
PIECEWISE([1/a^(1/2)*pi^(1/2), signum(a) = 1],[Inf, otherwise])
```

You can put this in a more readable form by entering

```
pretty(F)
                              {    1/2
                              { pi
                              {  - - - - -              signum(a~) = 1
                              {    1/2
                              { a~
                              {
                              {  Inf                    otherwise
```

The ~ after a is simply a reminder that a is real, and `signum(a~)` is the sign of a. So the integral is

$$\frac{\sqrt{\pi}}{\sqrt{a}}$$

when a is positive, just as in the preceding example, and ∞ when a is negative.

You can also declare a sequence of symbolic variables w, y, x, z to be real by entering

```
syms w x y z real
```

Integration with Complex Parameters

To calculate the integral

$$\int_{-\infty}^{\infty} e^{-ax^2} dx$$

for complex values of a, enter

```
syms a x unreal %
f = exp(-a*x^2);
F = int(f, x, -inf, inf)
```

Note that `syms` is used with the `unreal` option to clear the `real` property that was assigned to a in the preceding example — see "Clearing Variables in the Maple Workspace" on page 8-14.

The preceding commands produce the complex output

```
F =
PIECEWISE([1/a^(1/2)*pi^(1/2), csgn(a) = 1],[Inf, otherwise])
```

You can make this output more readable by entering

```
pretty(F)
                        {    1/2
                        { pi
                        { -----            csgn(a) = 1
                        {    1/2
                        {  a
                        {
                        {  Inf              otherwise
```

The expression csgn(a) (complex sign of a) is defined by

$$\operatorname{csgn}(a) = \begin{cases} 1 & \text{if } \operatorname{Re}(a) > 0, \text{ or } \operatorname{Re}(a) = 0 \text{ and } \operatorname{Im}(a) > 0 \\ -1 & \text{if } \operatorname{Re}(a) < 0, \text{ or } \operatorname{Re}(a) = 0 \text{ and } \operatorname{Im}(a) < 0 \end{cases}$$

The condition csgn(a) = 1 corresponds to the shaded region of the complex plane shown in the following figure.

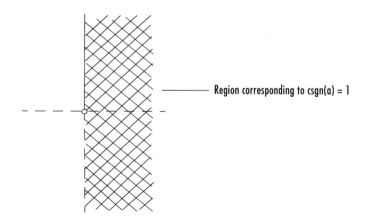

Region corresponding to csgn(a) = 1

The square root of a in the answer is the unique square root lying in the shaded region.

Symbolic Summation

You can compute symbolic summations, when they exist, by using the `symsum` command. For example, the p-series

$$1 + \frac{1}{2^2} + \frac{1}{3^2} + \dots$$

sums to $\pi^2/6$, while the geometric series

$$1 + x + x^2 + \dots$$

sums to $1/(1-x)$, provided $|x| < 1$. Three summations are demonstrated below.

```
syms x k
s1 = symsum(1/k^2,1,inf)
s2 = symsum(x^k,k,0,inf)

s1 =

1/6*pi^2

s2 =

-1/(x-1)
```

Taylor Series

The statements

```
syms x
f = 1/(5+4*cos(x))
T = taylor(f,8)
```

return

```
T =
1/9+2/81*x^2+5/1458*x^4+49/131220*x^6
```

which is all the terms up to, but not including, order eight in the Taylor series for $f(x)$.

$$\sum_{n=0}^{\infty} (x-a)^n \frac{f^{(n)}(a)}{n!}$$

Technically, T is a Maclaurin series, since its basepoint is a = 0.

The command

```
pretty(T)
```

prints T in a format resembling typeset mathematics.

```
              2            4     49    6
1/9 + 2/81 x  + 5/1458 x  + ------ x
                             131220
```

These commands

```
syms x
g = exp(x*sin(x))
t = taylor(g,12,2);
```

generate the first 12 nonzero terms of the Taylor series for g about x = 2.

Next, plot these functions together to see how well this Taylor approximation compares to the actual function g.

```
xd = 1:0.05:3; yd = subs(g,x,xd);
ezplot(t, [1,3]); hold on;
plot(xd, yd, 'r-.')
title('Taylor approximation vs. actual function');
legend('Taylor','Function')
```

9-19

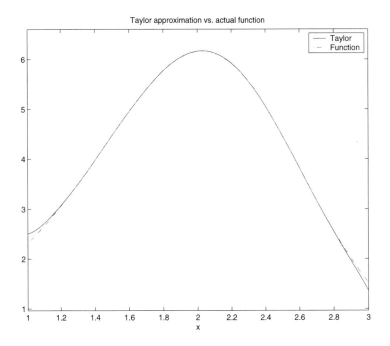

Special thanks to Professor Gunnar Bäckstrøm of UMEA in Sweden for this example.

Calculus Example

This section describes how to analyze a simple function to find its asymptotes, maximum, minimum, and inflection point. The section covers the following topics:

- "Defining the Function" on page 9-20
- "Finding the Asymptotes" on page 9-22
- "Finding the Maximum and Minimum" on page 9-23
- "Finding the Inflection Point" on page 9-25

Defining the Function

The function in this example is

$$f(x) = \frac{3x^2 + 6x - 1}{x^2 + x - 3}$$

To create the function, enter the following commands.

```
syms x
num = 3*x^2 + 6*x -1;
denom = x^2 + x - 3;
f = num/denom
```

This returns

```
f =
(3*x^2+6*x-1)/(x^2+x-3)
```

You can plot the graph of f by entering

```
ezplot(f)
```

This displays the following plot.

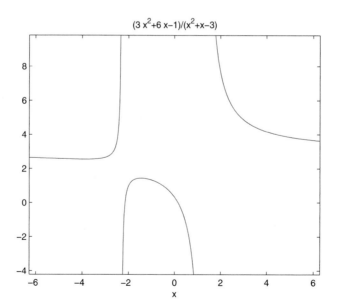

Finding the Asymptotes

To find the horizontal asymptote of the graph of f, take the limit of f as x approaches positive infinity.

```
limit(f, inf)
ans =
3
```

The limit as x approaches negative infinity is also 3. This tells you that the line $y = 3$ is a horizontal asymptote to the graph.

To find the vertical asymptotes of f, set the denominator equal to 0 and solve by entering the following command.

```
roots = solve(denom)
```

This returns two solutions to $x^2 + x - 3 = 0$:

```
roots =
[  -1/2+1/2*13^(1/2)]
[  -1/2-1/2*13^(1/2)]
```

This tells you that vertical asymptotes are the lines

$$x = \frac{-1 + \sqrt{13}}{2}$$

and

$$x = \frac{-1 - \sqrt{13}}{2}$$

You can plot the horizontal and vertical asymptotes with the following commands.

```
ezplot(f)
hold on % Keep the graph of f in the figure
% Plot horizontal asymptote
plot([-2*pi 2*pi], [3 3],'g')
% Plot vertical asymptotes
plot(double(roots(1))*[1 1], [-5 10],'r')
plot(double(roots(2))*[1 1], [-5 10],'r')
title('Horizontal and Vertical Asymptotes')
hold off
```

Note that `roots` must be converted to `double` to use the `plot` command.
The preceding commands display the following figure.

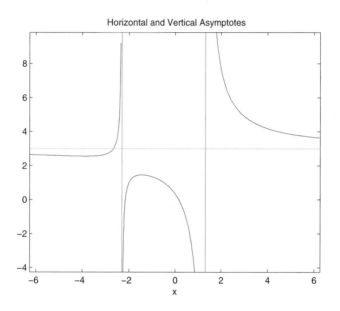

To recover the graph of f without the asymptotes, enter

```
ezplot(f)
```

Finding the Maximum and Minimum

You can see from the graph that f has a local maximum somewhere between
the points $x = 2$ and $x = 3$, and might have a local minimum between $x = -4$ and
$x = -2$. To find the x-coordinates of the maximum and minimum, first take the
derivative of f.

```
f1 = diff(f)
```

This returns

```
f1 = (6*x+6)/(x^2+x-3)-(3*x^2+6*x-1)/(x^2+x-3)^2*(2*x+1)
```

To simplify this expression, enter

```
f1 = simplify(f1)
```

which returns

```
f1 = -(3*x^2+16*x+17)/(x^2+x-3)^2
```

You can display f1 in a more readable form by entering

```
pretty(f1)
```

which returns

```
         2
     3 x   + 16 x + 17
  - ----------------
       2         2
     (x   + x - 3)
```

Next, set the derivative equal to 0 and solve for the critical points:

```
crit_pts = solve(f1)
```

This returns

```
ans =
[ -8/3-1/3*13^(1/2)]
[ -8/3+1/3*13^(1/2)]
```

It is clear from the graph of f that it has a local minimum at

$$x_1 = \frac{-8 - \sqrt{13}}{3}$$

and a local maximum at

$$x_2 = \frac{-8 + \sqrt{13}}{3}$$

Note MATLAB does not always return the roots to an equation in the same order.

You can plot the maximum and minimum of f with the following commands:

```
ezplot(f)
hold on
```

```
plot(double(crit_pts), double(subs(f,crit_pts)),'ro')
title('Maximum and Minimum of f')
text(-5.5,3.2,'Local minimum')
text(-2.5,2,'Local maximum')
hold off
```

This displays the following figure.

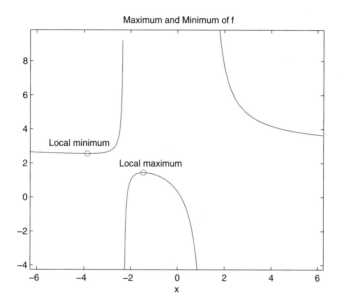

Finding the Inflection Point

To find the inflection point of f, set the second derivative equal to 0 and solve.

```
f2 = diff(f1);
inflec_pt = solve(f2);
double(inflec_pt)
```

This returns

```
ans =
  -5.2635
  -1.3682 - 0.8511i
  -1.3682 + 0.8511i
```

In this example, only the first entry is a real number, so this is the only inflection point. (Note that in other examples, the real solutions might not be the first entries of the answer.) Since you are only interested in the real solutions, you can discard the last two entries, which are complex numbers.

```
inflec_pt = inflec_pt(1)
```

To see the symbolic expression for the inflection point, enter

```
pretty(simplify(inflec_pt))
```

This returns

```
              1/2 2/3                          1/2 1/3
       (676 + 156 13   )    + 52 + 16 (676 + 156 13   )
  - 1/6 -------------------------------------------------
                                    1/2 1/3
                       (676 + 156 13   )
```

To plot the inflection point, enter

```
ezplot(f, [-9 6])
hold on
plot(double(inflec_pt), double(subs(f,inflec_pt)),'ro')
title('Inflection Point of f')
text(-7,2,'Inflection point')
hold off
```

The extra argument, [-9 6], in ezplot extends the range of x values in the plot so that you see the inflection point more clearly, as shown in the following figure.

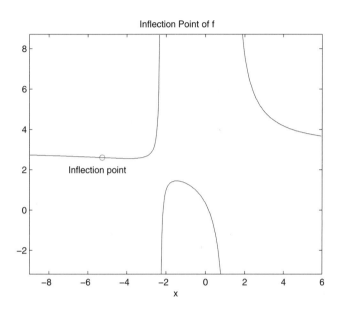

Inflection Point of f

Inflection point

Extended Calculus Example

This section presents an extended example that illustrates how to find the maxima and minima of a function. The section covers the following topics:

- "Defining the Function" on page 9-27
- "Finding the Zeros of f3" on page 9-29
- "Finding the Maxima and Minima of f2" on page 9-32
- "Integrating" on page 9-34

Defining the Function

The starting point for the example is the function

$$f(x) = \frac{1}{5 + 4\cos(x)}$$

You can create the function with the commands

```
syms x
f = 1/(5+4*cos(x))
```

which return

```
f =
1/(5+4*cos(x))
```

The example shows how to find the maximum and minimum of the second derivative of $f(x)$. To compute the second derivative, enter

```
f2 = diff(f,2)
```

which returns

```
f2 =
32/(5+4*cos(x))^3*sin(x)^2+4/(5+4*cos(x))^2*cos(x)
```

Equivalently, you can type f2 = diff(f,x,2). The default scaling in ezplot cuts off part of the graph of f2. You can set the axes limits manually to see the entire function.

```
ezplot(f2)
axis([-2*pi 2*pi -5 2])
title('Graph of f2')
```

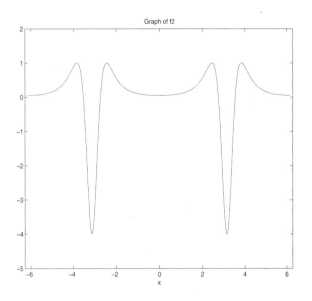

From the graph, it appears that the maximum value of $f''(x)$ is 1 and the minimum value is -4. As you will see, this is not quite true. To find the exact values of the maximum and minimum, you only need to find the maximum and minimum on the interval $(-\pi\ \pi]$. This is true because $f''(x)$ is periodic with period 2π, so that the maxima and minima are simply repeated in each translation of this interval by an integer multiple of 2π. The next two sections explain how to find the maxima and minima.

Finding the Zeros of f3

The maxima and minima of $f''(x)$ occur at the zeros of $f'''(x)$. The statements

```
f3 = diff(f2);
pretty(f3)
```

compute $f'''(x)$ and display it in a more readable form.

```
              3
          sin(x)                sin(x) cos(x)             sin(x)
    384 -------------- + 96 --------------- - 4 ---------------
              4                    3                    2
        (5 + 4 cos(x))        (5 + 4 cos(x))       (5 + 4 cos(x))
```

You can simplify this expression using the statements

```
f3 = simple(f3);
pretty(f3)
```

$$4 \, \frac{\sin(x) \, (96 \sin(x)^2 + 80 \cos(x) + 80 \cos(x)^2 - 25)}{(5 + 4 \cos(x))^4}$$

Now, to find the zeros of $f'''(x)$, enter

```
zeros = solve(f3)
```

This returns a 5-by-1 symbolic matrix

```
zeros =
[                                                         0]
[        atan((-255-60*19^(1/2))^(1/2),10+3*19^(1/2))]
[        atan(-(-255-60*19^(1/2))^(1/2),10+3*19^(1/2))]
[   atan((-255+60*19^(1/2))^(1/2)/(10-3*19^(1/2)))+pi]
[  -atan((-255+60*19^(1/2))^(1/2)/(10-3*19^(1/2)))-pi]
```

each of whose entries is a zero of $f'''(x)$. The commands

```
format; % Default format of 5 digits
zerosd = double(zeros)
```

convert the zeros to double form.

```
zerosd =
         0
         0+ 2.4381i
         0- 2.4381i
    2.4483
   -2.4483
```

So far, you have found three real zeros and two complex zeros. However, as the following graph of f3 shows, these are not all its zeros.

```
ezplot(f3)
hold on;
plot(zerosd,0*zerosd,'ro') % Plot zeros
plot([-2*pi,2*pi], [0,0],'g-.'); % Plot x-axis
title('Graph of f3')
```

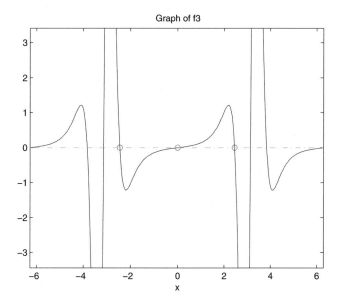

The red circles in the graph correspond to zerosd(1), zerosd(4), and zerosd(5). As you can see in the graph, there are also zeros at $\pm\pi$. The additional zeros occur because $f'''(x)$ contains a factor of $\sin(x)$, which is zero at integer multiples of π. The function solve(sin(x)), however, only finds the zero at $x = 0$.

A complete list of the zeros of $f'''(x)$ in the interval $(-\pi\ \pi]$ is

```
zerosd = [zerosd(1) zerosd(4) zerosd(5) pi];
```

You can display these zeros on the graph of $f'''(x)$ with the following commands.

```
ezplot(f3)
hold on;
plot(zerosd,0*zerosd,'ro')
plot([-2*pi,2*pi], [0,0],'g-.'); % Plot x-axis
title('Zeros of f3')
hold off;
```

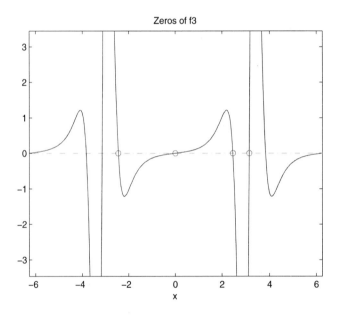

Finding the Maxima and Minima of f2

To find the maxima and minima of $f''(x)$, calculate the value of $f''(x)$ at each of the zeros of $f'''(x)$. To do so, substitute zeros into f2 and display the result below zeros.

```
[zerosd; subs(f2,zerosd)]
ans =
         0    2.4483   -2.4483    3.1416
    0.0494    1.0051    1.0051   -4.0000
```

This shows the following:

- $f''(x)$ has an absolute maximum at $x = \pm 2.4483$, whose value is 1.0051.
- $f''(x)$ has an absolute minimum at $x = \pi$, whose value is -4.
- $f''(x)$ has a local minimum at $x = \pi$, whose value is 0.0494.

You can display the maxima and minima with the following commands.

```
clf
ezplot(f2)
axis([-2*pi 2*pi -4.5 1.5])
ylabel('f2');
title('Maxima and Minima of f2')
hold on
plot(zeros, subs(f2,zeros), 'ro')
text(-4, 1.25, 'Absolute maximum')
text(-1,-0.25,'Local minimum')
text(.9, 1.25, 'Absolute maximum')
text(1.6, -4.25, 'Absolute minimum')
hold off;
```

This displays the following figure.

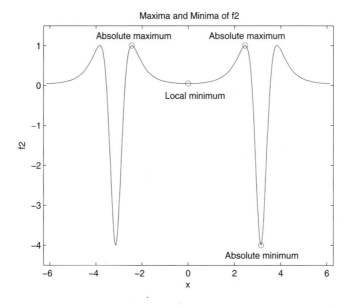

The preceding analysis shows that the actual range of $f''(x)$ is [-4, 1.0051].

Integrating

To see whether integrating $f''(x)$ twice with respect to x recovers the original function $f(x) = 1/(5 + 4\cos x)$, enter the command

```
g = int(int(f2))
```

which returns

```
g =
-8/(tan(1/2*x)^2+9)
```

This is certainly not the original expression for $f(x)$. Now look at the difference $f(x) - g(x)$.

```
d = f - g
pretty(d)
```

$$\frac{1}{5 + 4\cos(x)} + \frac{8}{\tan(1/2\ x)^2 + 9}$$

You can simplify this using `simple(d)` or `simplify(d)`. Either command produces

```
ans =
1
```

This illustrates the concept that differentiating $f(x)$ twice, then integrating the result twice, produces a function that may differ from $f(x)$ by a linear function of x.

Finally, integrate $f(x)$ once more.

```
F = int(f)
```

The result

```
F =
2/3*atan(1/3*tan(1/2*x))
```

involves the arctangent function.

Note that $F(x)$ is not an antiderivative of $f(x)$ for all real numbers, since it is discontinuous at odd multiples of π, where $\tan x$ is singular. You can see the gaps in $F(x)$ in the following figure.

```
ezplot(F)
```

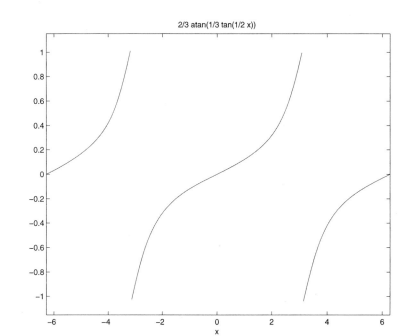

To change $F(x)$ into a true antiderivative of $f(x)$ that is differentiable everywhere, you can add a step function to $F(x)$. The height of the steps is the height of the gaps in the graph of $F(x)$. You can determine the height of the gaps by taking the limits of $F(x)$ as x approaches π from the left and from the right. The limit from the left is

```
limit(F, x, pi, 'left')
ans =
1/3*pi
```

The limit from the right is

```
limit(F, x, pi, 'right')
ans =-1/3*pi
```

The height of the gap is the distance between the left and right limits, which is $2\pi/3$, as shown in the following figure.

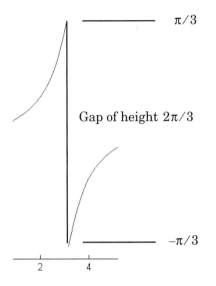

You can create the step function using the round function, which rounds numbers to the nearest integer, as follows:

```
J = sym(2*pi/3)*sym('round(x/(2*pi))');
```

Each step has width 2π and the jump from one step to the next is $2\pi/3$, as shown in the following figure.

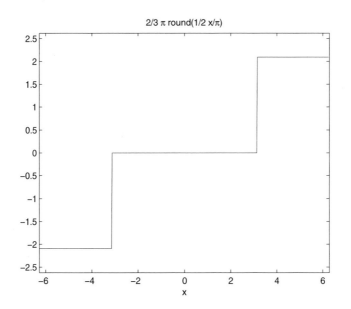

Next, add the step function $J(x)$ to $F(x)$ with the following code.

```
F1 = F+J
F1 =
2/3*atan(1/3*tan(1/2*x))+2/3*pi*round(1/2*x/pi)
```

Adding the step function raises the section of the graph of $F(x)$ on the interval $[\pi \quad 3\pi)$ up by $2\pi/3$, lowers the section on the interval $(-3\pi \quad -\pi]$ down by $2\pi/3$, and so on, as shown in the following figure.

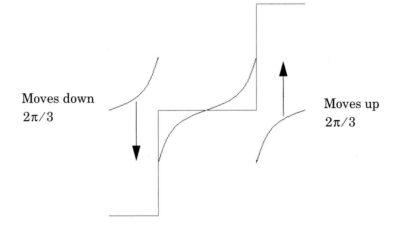

Moves down
$2\pi/3$

Moves up
$2\pi/3$

When you plot the result by entering

```
ezplot(F1)
```

you see that this representation does have a continuous graph.

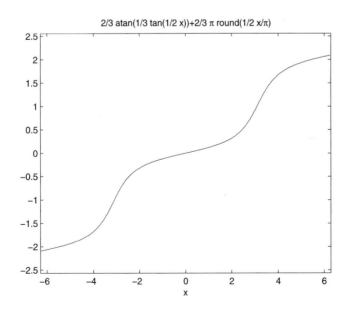

$2/3 \ \text{atan}(1/3 \ \text{tan}(1/2 \ x)) + 2/3 \ \pi \ \text{round}(1/2 \ x/\pi)$

Simplifications and Substitutions

There are several functions that simplify symbolic expressions and are used to perform symbolic substitutions.

Simplifications

Here are three different symbolic expressions.

```
syms x
f = x^3-6*x^2+11*x-6
g = (x-1)*(x-2)*(x-3)
h = -6+(11+(-6+x)*x)*x
```

Here are their pretty-printed forms, generated by

```
pretty(f), pretty(g), pretty(h)
```

```
 3     2
x - 6 x  + 11 x - 6


(x - 1) (x - 2) (x - 3)


-6 + (11 + (-6 + x) x) x
```

These expressions are three different representations of the same mathematical function, a cubic polynomial in x.

Each of the three forms is preferable to the others in different situations. The first form, f, is the most commonly used representation of a polynomial. It is simply a linear combination of the powers of x. The second form, g, is the factored form. It displays the roots of the polynomial and is the most accurate for numerical evaluation near the roots. But, if a polynomial does not have such simple roots, its factored form may not be so convenient. The third form, h, is the Horner, or nested, representation. For numerical evaluation, it involves the fewest arithmetic operations and is the most accurate for some other ranges of x.

The symbolic simplification problem involves the verification that these three expressions represent the same function. It also involves a less clearly defined objective — which of these representations is "the simplest"?

This toolbox provides several functions that apply various algebraic and trigonometric identities to transform one representation of a function into another, possibly simpler, representation. These functions are collect, expand, horner, factor, simplify, and simple.

collect

The statement

```
collect(f)
```

views f as a polynomial in its symbolic variable, say x, and collects all the coefficients with the same power of x. A second argument can specify the variable in which to collect terms if there is more than one candidate. Here are a few examples.

f	collect(f)
(x-1)*(x-2)*(x-3)	x^3-6*x^2+11*x-6
x*(x*(x-6)+11)-6	x^3-6*x^2+11*x-6
(1+x)*t + x*t	2*x*t+t

expand

The statement

```
expand(f)
```

distributes products over sums and applies other identities involving functions of sums as shown in the examples below.

f	expand(f)
a*(x + y)	a*x + a*y
(x-1)*(x-2)*(x-3)	x^3-6*x^2+11*x-6
x*(x*(x-6)+11)-6	x^3-6*x^2+11*x-6
exp(a+b)	exp(a)*exp(b)
cos(x+y)	cos(x)*cos(y)-sin(x)*sin(y)
cos(3*acos(x))	4*x^3-3*x

horner

The statement

```
horner(f)
```

transforms a symbolic polynomial f into its Horner, or nested, representation as shown in the following examples.

f	horner(f)
x^3-6*x^2+11*x-6	-6+(11+(-6+x)*x)*x
1.1+2.2*x+3.3*x^2	11/10+(11/5+33/10*x)*x

factor

If f is a polynomial with rational coefficients, the statement

```
factor(f)
```

expresses f as a product of polynomials of lower degree with rational coefficients. If f cannot be factored over the rational numbers, the result is f itself. Here are several examples.

f	factor(f)
x^3-6*x^2+11*x-6	(x-1)*(x-2)*(x-3)
x^3-6*x^2+11*x-5	x^3-6*x^2+11*x-5
x^6+1	(x^2+1)*(x^4-x^2+1)

Here is another example involving factor. It factors polynomials of the form x^n + 1. This code

```
syms x;
n = (1:9)';
p = x.^n + 1;
f = factor(p);
[p, f]
```

returns a matrix with the polynomials in its first column and their factored forms in its second.

```
[                    x+1,                                 x+1 ]
[                  x^2+1,                               x^2+1 ]
[                  x^3+1,                    (x+1)*(x^2-x+1) ]
[                  x^4+1,                               x^4+1 ]
[                  x^5+1,         (x+1)*(x^4-x^3+x^2-x+1) ]
[                  x^6+1,              (x^2+1)*(x^4-x^2+1) ]
[                  x^7+1, (x+1)*(1-x+x^2-x^3+x^4-x^5+x^6) ]
[                  x^8+1,                               x^8+1 ]
[                  x^9+1,       (x+1)*(x^2-x+1)*(x^6-x^3+1) ]
```

As an aside at this point, `factor` can also factor symbolic objects containing integers. This is an alternative to using the `factor` function in the MATLAB specfun directory. For example, the following code segment

```
N = sym(1);
for k = 2:11
    N(k) = 10*N(k-1)+1;
end
[N' factor(N')]
```

displays the factors of symbolic integers consisting of 1s.

```
[                           1,                              1]
[                          11,                           (11)]
[                         111,                       (3)*(37)]
[                        1111,                     (11)*(101)]
[                       11111,                     (41)*(271)]
[                      111111, (3)*(7)*(11)*(13)*(37)]
[                     1111111,                   (239)*(4649)]
[                    11111111,    (11)*(73)*(101)*(137)]
[                   111111111,       (3)^2*(37)*(333667)]
[                  1111111111, (11)*(41)*(271)*(9091)]
[                 11111111111,           (513239)*(21649)]
```

simplify

The `simplify` function is a powerful, general purpose tool that applies a number of algebraic identities involving sums, integral powers, square roots and other fractional powers, as well as a number of functional identities involving trig functions, exponential and log functions, Bessel functions, hypergeometric functions, and the gamma function. Here are some examples.

f	simplify(f)
`x*(x*(x-6)+11)-6`	`x^3-6*x^2+11*x-6`
`(1-x^2)/(1-x)`	`x+1`
`(1/a^3+6/a^2+12/a+8)^(1/3)`	`((2*a+1)^3/a^3)^(1/3)`
`syms x y positive` `log(x*y)`	`log(x)+log(y)`
`exp(x) * exp(y)`	`exp(x+y)`
`besselj(2,x) + besselj(0,x)`	`2/x*besselj(1,x)`
`gamma(x+1)-x*gamma(x)`	`0`
`cos(x)^2 + sin(x)^2`	`1`

simple

The `simple` function has the unorthodox mathematical goal of finding a simplification of an expression that has the fewest number of characters. Of course, there is little mathematical justification for claiming that one expression is "simpler" than another just because its ASCII representation is shorter, but this often proves satisfactory in practice.

The `simple` function achieves its goal by independently applying `simplify`, `collect`, `factor`, and other simplification functions to an expression and keeping track of the lengths of the results. The `simple` function then returns the shortest result.

The `simple` function has several forms, each returning different output. The form

```
simple(f)
```

displays each trial simplification and the simplification function that produced it in the MATLAB command window. The `simple` function then returns the shortest result. For example, the command

```
simple(cos(x)^2 + sin(x)^2)
```

displays the following alternative simplifications in the MATLAB Command Window

```
simplify:
1

radsimp:
cos(x)^2+sin(x)^2

combine(trig):
1

factor:
 cos(x)^2+sin(x)^2

expand:
cos(x)^2+sin(x)^2

combine:
1

convert(exp):
 (1/2*exp(i*x)+1/2/exp(i*x))^2-1/4*(exp(i*x)-1/exp(i*x))^2

convert(sincos):
cos(x)^2+sin(x)^2

convert(tan):
(1-tan(1/2*x)^2)^2/(1+tan(1/2*x)^2)^2+
4*tan(1/2*x)^2/(1+tan(1/2*x)^2)^2

collect(x):
cos(x)^2+sin(x)^2
```

and returns

```
ans =
1
```

This form is useful when you want to check, for example, whether the shortest form is indeed the simplest. If you are not interested in how `simple` achieves its result, use the form

```
f = simple(f)
```

This form simply returns the shortest expression found. For example, the statement

```
f = simple(cos(x)^2+sin(x)^2)
```

returns

```
f =
1
```

If you want to know which simplification returned the shortest result, use the multiple output form.

```
[F, how] = simple(f)
```

This form returns the shortest result in the first variable and the simplification method used to achieve the result in the second variable. For example, the statement

```
[f, how] = simple(cos(x)^2+sin(x)^2)
```

returns

```
f =
1

how =
combine
```

The `simple` function sometimes improves on the result returned by `simplify`, one of the simplifications that it tries. For example, when applied to the examples given for `simplify`, `simple` returns a simpler (or at least shorter) result in two cases.

f	simplify(f)	simple(f)
`(1/a^3+6/a^2+12/a+8)^(1/3)`	`((2*a+1)^3/a^3)^(1/3)`	`(2*a+1)/a`
`syms x y positive` `log(x*y)`	`log(x)+log(y)`	`log(x*y)`

In some cases, it is advantageous to apply `simple` twice to obtain the effect of two different simplification functions. For example, the statements

```
f = (1/a^3+6/a^2+12/a+8)^(1/3);
simple(simple(f))
```

return

```
2+1/a
```

The first application, `simple(f)`, uses `radsimp` to produce `(2*a+1)/a`; the second application uses `combine(trig)` to transform this to `1/a+2`.

The `simple` function is particularly effective on expressions involving trigonometric functions. Here are some examples.

f	simple(f)
`cos(x)^2+sin(x)^2`	`1`
`2*cos(x)^2-sin(x)^2`	`3*cos(x)^2-1`
`cos(x)^2-sin(x)^2`	`cos(2*x)`
`cos(x)+(-sin(x)^2)^(1/2)`	`cos(x)+i*sin(x)`
`cos(x)+i*sin(x)`	`exp(i*x)`
`cos(3*acos(x))`	`4*x^3-3*x`

Substitutions

There are two functions for symbolic substitution: subexpr and subs.

subexpr

These commands

```
syms a x
s = solve(x^3+a*x+1)
```

solve the equation x^3+a*x+1 = 0 for x.

```
s =
[                            1/6*(-108+12*(12*a^3+81)^(1/2))^(1/3)-2*a/
                               (-108+12*(12*a^3+81)^(1/2))^(1/3)]
[ -1/12*(-108+12*(12*a^3+81)^(1/2))^(1/3)+a/
     (-108+12*(12*a^3+81)^(1/2))^(1/3)+1/2*i*3^(1/2)*(1/
     6*(-108+12*(12*a^3+81)^(1/2))^(1/3)+2*a/
     (-108+12*(12*a^3+81)^(1/2))^(1/3))]
[ -1/12*(-108+12*(12*a^3+81)^(1/2))^(1/3)+a/
     (-108+12*(12*a^3+81)^(1/2))^(1/3)-1/2*i*3^(1/2)*(1/
     6*(-108+12*(12*a^3+81)^(1/2))^(1/3)+2*a/
     (-108+12*(12*a^3+81)^(1/2))^(1/3))]
```

Use the `pretty` function to display s in a more readable form.

```
pretty(s)

s =
                                            .
                    [                    1/3        a              ]
                    [            1/6 %1      - 2 -----             ]
                    [                              1/3             ]
                    [                              %1              ]
                    [                                             ]
                    [       1/3     a            1/2 /      1/3      a  \]
                    [- 1/12 %1    + ----- + 1/2 i 3  |1/6 %1    + 2 -----|]
                    [              1/3              |                1/3|]
                    [              %1               \               %1   /]
                    [                                             ]
                    [       1/3     a            1/2 /      1/3      a  \]
                    [- 1/12 %1    + ----- - 1/2 i 3  |1/6 %1    + 2 -----|]
                    [              1/3              |                1/3|]
                    [              %1               \               %1   /]

                                              3      1/2
                %1 := -108 + 12 (12 a  + 81)
```

The `pretty` command inherits the `%n` (n, an integer) notation from Maple to denote subexpressions that occur multiple times in the symbolic object. The `subexpr` function allows you to save these common subexpressions as well as the symbolic object rewritten in terms of the subexpressions. The subexpressions are saved in a column vector called `sigma`.

Continuing with the example

```
    r = subexpr(s)
```

returns

```
sigma =
-108+12*(12*a^3+81)^(1/2)
r =
[                                    1/6*sigma^(1/3)-2*a/sigma^(1/3)]
[ -1/12*sigma^(1/3)+a/sigma^(1/3)+1/2*i*3^(1/2)*(1/6*sigma^
    (1/3)+2*a/sigma^(1/3))]
```

```
[ -1/12*sigma^(1/3)+a/sigma^(1/3)-1/2*i*3^(1/2)*(1/6*sigma^
    (1/3)+2*a/sigma^(1/3))]
```

Notice that subexpr creates the variable sigma in the MATLAB workspace. You can verify this by typing whos, or the command

```
    sigma
```

which returns

```
sigma =
-108+12*(12*a^3+81)^(1/2)
```

subs

The following code finds the eigenvalues and eigenvectors of a circulant matrix A.

```
syms a b c
A = [a b c; b c a; c a b];
[v,E] = eig(A)

v =

[ -(a+(b^2-b*a-c*b-c*a+a^2+c^2)^(1/2)-b)/(a-c),
        -(a-(b^2-b*a-c*b-c*a+a^2+c^2)^(1/2)-b)/(a-c),   1]
[ -(b-c-(b^2-b*a-c*b-c*a+a^2+c^2)^(1/2))/(a-c),
        -(b-c+(b^2-b*a-c*b-c*a+a^2+c^2)^(1/2))/(a-c),   1]
[ 1,
        1,                                              1]


E =

[ (b^2-b*a-c*b-
    c*a+a^2+c^2)^(1/2),                    0,           0]
[                   0,    -(b^2-b*a-c*b-
                            c*a+a^2+c^2)^(1/2),          0]
[                   0,                    0,       b+c+a]
```

Note MATLAB might return the eigenvalues that appear on the diagonal of E in a different order. In this case, the corresponding eigenvectors, which are the columns of v, will also appear in a different order.

Suppose you want to replace the rather lengthy expression

```
(b^2-b*a-c*b-c*a+a^2+c^2)^(1/2)
```

throughout v and E. First, use `subexpr`

```
v = subexpr(v,'S')
```

which returns

```
S =
(b^2-b*a-c*b-c*a+a^2+c^2)^(1/2)

v =
[ -(a+S-b)/(a-c), -(a-S-b)/(a-c),          1]
[ -(b-c-S)/(a-c), -(b-c+S)/(a-c),          1]
[             1,              1,          1]
```

Next, substitute the symbol S into E with

```
E = subs(E,S,'S')

E =
[    S,    0,    0]
[    0,   -S,    0]
[    0,    0, b+c+a]
```

Now suppose you want to evaluate v at a = 10. You can do this using the subs command.

```
subs(v,a,10)
```

This replaces all occurrences of a in v with 10.

```
[ -(10+S-b)/(10-c), -(10-S-b)/(10-c),          1]
[  -(b-c-S)/(10-c),  -(b-c+S)/(10-c),          1]
[               1,               1,          1]
```

Notice, however, that the symbolic expression that S represents is unaffected by this substitution. That is, the symbol a in S is not replaced by 10. The subs command is also a useful function for substituting in a variety of values for several variables in a particular expression. For example, suppose that in addition to substituting a = 10 in S, you also want to substitute the values for 2 and 10 for b and c, respectively. The way to do this is to set values for a, b, and c in the workspace. Then subs evaluates its input using the existing symbolic and double variables in the current workspace. In the example, you first set

```
a = 10; b = 2; c = 10;
subs(S)

ans =
8
```

To look at the contents of the workspace, type whos, which gives

Name	Size	Bytes	Class
A	3x3	878	sym object
E	3x3	888	sym object
S	1x1	186	sym object
a	1x1	8	double array
ans	1x1	140	sym object
b	1x1	8	double array
c	1x1	8	double array
v	3x3	982	sym object

a, b, and c are now variables of class double while A, E, S, and v remain symbolic expressions (class sym).

If you want to preserve a, b, and c as symbolic variables, but still alter their value within S, use this procedure.

```
syms a b c
subs(S,{a,b,c},{10,2,10})

ans =
8
```

Typing whos reveals that a, b, and c remain 1-by-1 sym objects.

The subs command can be combined with double to evaluate a symbolic expression numerically. Suppose you have the following expressions

```
syms t
M = (1-t^2)*exp(-1/2*t^2);
P = (1-t^2)*sech(t);
```

and want to see how M and P differ graphically.

One approach is to type

```
ezplot(M); hold on; ezplot(P); hold off;
```

but this plot does not readily help us identify the curves.

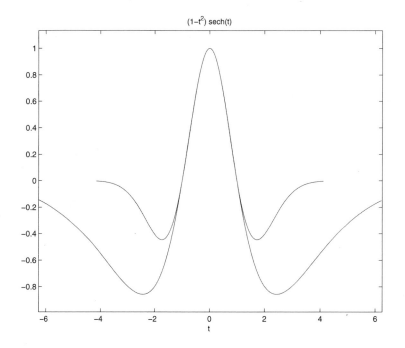

Instead, combine subs, double, and plot

```
T = -6:0.05:6;
MT = double(subs(M,t,T));
PT = double(subs(P,t,T));
plot(T,MT,'b',T,PT,'r-.')
title(' ')
legend('M','P')
xlabel('t'); grid
```

to produce a multicolored graph that indicates the difference between M and P.

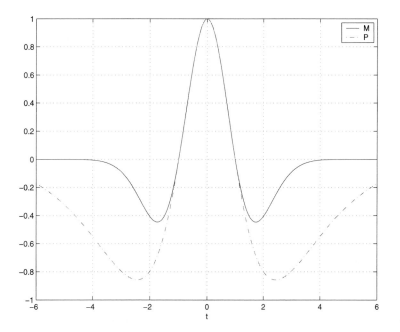

Finally the use of subs with strings greatly facilitates the solution of problems involving the Fourier, Laplace, or z-transforms.

Variable-Precision Arithmetic

Overview

There are three different kinds of arithmetic operations in this toolbox:

Numeric   MATLAB floating-point arithmetic

Rational   Maple's exact symbolic arithmetic

VPA   Maple's variable-precision arithmetic

For example, the MATLAB statements

```
format long
1/2+1/3
```

use numeric computation to produce

```
0.83333333333333
```

With the Symbolic Math Toolbox, the statement

```
sym(1/2)+1/3
```

uses symbolic computation to yield

```
5/6
```

And, also with the toolbox, the statements

```
digits(25)
vpa('1/2+1/3')
```

use variable-precision arithmetic to return

```
.8333333333333333333333333
```

The floating-point operations used by numeric arithmetic are the fastest of the three, and require the least computer memory, but the results are not exact. The number of digits in the printed output of MATLAB double quantities is controlled by the format statement, but the internal representation is always the eight-byte floating-point representation provided by the particular computer hardware.

In the computation of the numeric result above, there are actually three roundoff errors, one in the division of 1 by 3, one in the addition of 1/2 to the result of the division, and one in the binary to decimal conversion for the printed output. On computers that use IEEE floating-point standard arithmetic, the resulting internal value is the binary expansion of 5/6, truncated to 53 bits. This is approximately 16 decimal digits. But, in this particular case, the printed output shows only 15 digits.

The symbolic operations used by rational arithmetic are potentially the most expensive of the three, in terms of both computer time and memory. The results are exact, as long as enough time and memory are available to complete the computations.

Variable-precision arithmetic falls in between the other two in terms of both cost and accuracy. A global parameter, set by the function digits, controls the number of significant decimal digits. Increasing the number of digits increases the accuracy, but also increases both the time and memory requirements. The default value of digits is 32, corresponding roughly to floating-point accuracy.

The Maple documentation uses the term "hardware floating-point" for what you are calling "numeric" or "floating-point" and uses the term "floating-point arithmetic" for what you are calling "variable-precision arithmetic."

Example: Using the Different Kinds of Arithmetic

Rational Arithmetic

By default, the Symbolic Math Toolbox uses rational arithmetic operations, i.e., the exact symbolic arithmetic of Maple. Rational arithmetic is invoked when you create symbolic variables using the sym function.

The sym function converts a double matrix to its symbolic form. For example, if the double matrix is

```
A =
    1.1000    1.2000    1.3000
    2.1000    2.2000    2.3000
    3.1000    3.2000    3.3000
```

its symbolic form, S = sym(A), is

```
S =
[11/10,  6/5, 13/10]
[21/10, 11/5, 23/10]
[31/10, 16/5, 33/10]
```

For this matrix A, it is possible to discover that the elements are the ratios of small integers, so the symbolic representation is formed from those integers. On the other hand, the statement

```
E = [exp(1) (1+sqrt(5))/2; log(3) rand]
```

returns a matrix

```
E =
    2.71828182845905    1.61803398874989
    1.09861228866811    0.76209683302739
```

whose elements are not the ratios of small integers, so sym(E) reproduces the floating-point representation in a symbolic form.

```
ans =
[ 6121026514868074*2^(-51),  7286977268806824*2^(-52)]
[ 4947709893870346*2^(-52),  6864358026484820*2^(-53)]
```

Variable-Precision Numbers

Variable-precision numbers are distinguished from the exact rational representation by the presence of a decimal point. A power of 10 scale factor, denoted by 'e', is allowed. To use variable-precision instead of rational arithmetic, create your variables using the vpa function.

For matrices with purely double entries, the vpa function generates the representation that is used with variable-precision arithmetic. For example, if you apply vpa to the matrix S defined in the preceding section, with digits(4), by entering

```
vpa(S)
```

MATLAB returns the output

```
S =
[1.100, 1.200, 1.300]
[2.100, 2.200, 2.300]
[3.100, 3.200, 3.300]
```

Applying vpa to the matrix E defined in the preceding section with digits(25), by entering

```
digits(25)
F = vpa(E)
```

returns

```
F =
[2.718281828459045534884808, 1.414213562373094923430017]
[1.098612288668110004152823, .2189591863280899719512718]
```

Converting to Floating-Point

To convert a rational or variable-precision number to its MATLAB floating-point representation, use the double function.

In the example, both double(sym(E)) and double(vpa(E)) return E.

Another Example

The next example is perhaps more interesting. Start with the symbolic expression

```
f = sym('exp(pi*sqrt(163))')
```

The statement

```
double(f)
```

produces the printed floating-point value

```
ans =
    2.625374126407687e+017
```

Using the second argument of vpa to specify the number of digits,

```
vpa(f,18)
```

returns

    262537412640768744.

whereas

    vpa(f,25)

returns

    262537412640768744.0000000

You suspect that f might actually have an integer value. This suspicion is reinforced by the 30 digit value, vpa(f,30)

    262537412640768743.999999999999

Finally, the 40 digit value, vpa(f,40)

    262537412640768743.9999999999992500725944

shows that f is very close to, but not exactly equal to, an integer.

Linear Algebra

Basic Algebraic Operations

Basic algebraic operations on symbolic objects are the same as operations on MATLAB objects of class double. This is illustrated in the following example.

The Givens transformation produces a plane rotation through the angle t. The statements

```
syms t;
G = [cos(t) sin(t); -sin(t) cos(t)]
```

create this transformation matrix.

```
G =
[  cos(t),  sin(t) ]
[ -sin(t),  cos(t) ]
```

Applying the Givens transformation twice should simply be a rotation through twice the angle. The corresponding matrix can be computed by multiplying G by itself or by raising G to the second power. Both

```
A = G*G
```

and

```
A = G^2
```

produce

```
A =
[cos(t)^2-sin(t)^2,   2*cos(t)*sin(t)]
[ -2*cos(t)*sin(t), cos(t)^2-sin(t)^2]
```

The simple function

```
A = simple(A)
```

uses a trigonometric identity to return the expected form by trying several different identities and picking the one that produces the shortest representation.

```
A =
[ cos(2*t), sin(2*t)]
[-sin(2*t), cos(2*t)]
```

The Givens rotation is an orthogonal matrix, so its transpose is its inverse. Confirming this by

```
I = G.' *G
```

which produces

```
I =
[cos(t)^2+sin(t)^2,                 0]
[                0, cos(t)^2+sin(t)^2]
```

and then

```
I = simple(I)
I =
[1, 0]
[0, 1]
```

Linear Algebraic Operations

The following examples show several basic linear algebraic operations using the Symbolic Math Toolbox.

The command

```
H = hilb(3)
```

generates the 3-by-3 Hilbert matrix. With format short, MATLAB prints

```
H =
1.0000    0.5000    0.3333
0.5000    0.3333    0.2500
0.3333    0.2500    0.2000
```

The computed elements of H are floating-point numbers that are the ratios of small integers. Indeed, H is a MATLAB array of class double. Converting H to a symbolic matrix

```
H = sym(H)
```

gives

```
[  1, 1/2, 1/3]
[1/2, 1/3, 1/4]
[1/3, 1/4, 1/5]
```

This allows subsequent symbolic operations on H to produce results that correspond to the infinitely precise Hilbert matrix, sym(hilb(3)), not its floating-point approximation, hilb(3). Therefore,

```
inv(H)
```

produces

```
[  9,  -36,   30]
[-36,  192, -180]
[ 30, -180,  180]
```

and

```
det(H)
```

yields

```
1/2160
```

You can use the backslash operator to solve a system of simultaneous linear equations, for example, the commands

```
b = [1 1 1]'
x = H\b     % Solve Hx = b
```

produce the solution

```
[   3]
[-24]
[ 30]
```

All three of these results, the inverse, the determinant, and the solution to the linear system, are the exact results corresponding to the infinitely precise, rational, Hilbert matrix. Using digits(16), the command

```
V = vpa(hilb(3))
```

returns

```
[                1., .5000000000000000, .3333333333333333]
[.5000000000000000, .3333333333333333, .2500000000000000]
[.3333333333333333, .2500000000000000, .2000000000000000]
```

The decimal points in the representation of the individual elements are the signal to use variable-precision arithmetic. The result of each arithmetic operation is rounded to 16 significant decimal digits. When inverting the matrix, these errors are magnified by the matrix condition number, which for hilb(3) is about 500. Consequently,

```
inv(V)
```

which returns

```
ans =
[   9.000000000000179,  -36.00000000000080,   30.00000000000067]
[  -36.00000000000080,  192.0000000000042,  -180.0000000000040]
[   30.00000000000067, -180.0000000000040,  180.0000000000038]
```

shows the loss of two digits. So does

```
det(V)
```

which gives

```
.462962962962953e-3
```

and

```
V\b
```

which is

```
[ 3.000000000000041]
[-24.00000000000021]
[ 30.00000000000019]
```

Since H is nonsingular, calculating the null space of H with the command

```
null(H)
```

returns an empty matrix, and calculating the column space of H with

```
colspace(H)
```

returns a permutation of the identity matrix. A more interesting example, which the following code shows, is to find a value s for H(1,1) that makes H singular. The commands

```
syms s
H(1,1) = s
Z = det(H)
sol = solve(Z)
```

produce

```
H =
[   s, 1/2, 1/3]
[1/2, 1/3, 1/4]
[1/3, 1/4, 1/5]

Z =
1/240*s-1/270

sol =
8/9
```

Then

```
H = subs(H,s,sol)
```

substitutes the computed value of sol for s in H to give

```
H =
[8/9, 1/2, 1/3]
[1/2, 1/3, 1/4]
[1/3, 1/4, 1/5]
```

Now, the command

```
det(H)
```

returns

```
ans =
0
```

and

```
inv(H)
```

produces an error message

```
??? error using ==> inv
Error, (in inverse) singular matrix
```

because H is singular. For this matrix, Z = null(H) and C = colspace(H) are nontrivial.

```
Z =
[    1]
[   -4]
[10/3]

C =
[    1,    0]
[    0,    1]
[ -3/10,  6/5]
```

It should be pointed out that even though H is singular, vpa(H) is not. For any integer value d, setting

```
digits(d)
```

and then computing

```
det(vpa(H))
inv(vpa(H))
```

results in a determinant of size 10^(-d) and an inverse with elements on the order of 10^d.

Eigenvalues

The symbolic eigenvalues of a square matrix A or the symbolic eigenvalues and eigenvectors of A are computed, respectively, using the commands

```
E = eig(A)
[V,E] = eig(A)
```

The variable-precision counterparts are

```
E = eig(vpa(A))
[V,E] = eig(vpa(A))
```

The eigenvalues of A are the zeros of the characteristic polynomial of A, det(A-x*I), which is computed by

```
poly(A)
```

The matrix H from the last section provides the first example.

```
H =
[8/9, 1/2, 1/3]
[1/2, 1/3, 1/4]
[1/3, 1/4, 1/5]
```

The matrix is singular, so one of its eigenvalues must be zero. The statement

```
[T,E] = eig(H)
```

produces the matrices T and E. The columns of T are the eigenvectors of H.

```
T =

[    1, 28/153+2/153*12589^(1/2),  28/153-2/153*12589^(12)]
[   -4,                        1,                        1]
[ 10/3, 92/255-1/255*12589^(1/2), 292/255+1/255*12589^(12)]
```

Similarly, the diagonal elements of E are the eigenvalues of H:

```
E =

[0,                        0,                        0]
[0, 32/45+1/180*12589^(1/2),                        0]
[0,                        0, 32/45-1/180*12589^(1/2)]
```

It may be easier to understand the structure of the matrices of eigenvectors, T, and eigenvalues, E, if you convert T and E to decimal notation. To do so, proceed as follows. The commands

```
Td = double(T)
Ed = double(E)
```

return

```
Td =
      1.0000    1.6497   -1.2837
     -4.0000    1.0000    1.0000
      3.3333    0.7051    1.5851
```

```
Ed =
     0         0          0
     0      1.3344        0
     0         0       0.0878
```

The first eigenvalue is zero. The corresponding eigenvector (the first column of Td) is the same as the basis for the null space found in the last section. The other two eigenvalues are the result of applying the quadratic formula to

```
x^2-64/45*x+253/2160
```

which is the quadratic factor in `factor(poly(H))`.

```
syms x
g = simple(factor(poly(H))/x);
solve(g)

ans =
[ 32/45+1/180*12589^(1/2)]
[ 32/45-1/180*12589^(1/2)]
```

Closed form symbolic expressions for the eigenvalues are possible only when the characteristic polynomial can be expressed as a product of rational polynomials of degree four or less. The Rosser matrix is a classic numerical analysis test matrix that illustrates this requirement. The statement

```
R = sym(gallery('rosser'))
```

generates

```
R =
[ 611    196   -192    407     -8    -52    -49     29]
[ 196    899    113   -192    -71    -43     -8    -44]
[-192    113    899    196     61     49      8     52]
[ 407   -192    196    611      8     44     59    -23]
[  -8    -71     61      8    411   -599    208    208]
[ -52    -43     49     44   -599    411    208    208]
[ -49     -8      8     59    208    208     99   -911]
[  29    -44     52    -23    208    208   -911     99]
```

The commands

```
p = poly(R);
pretty(factor(p))
```

produce

$$x \, (x - 1020) \, (x^2 - 1020 \, x + 100) (x^2 - 1040500) \, (x - 1000)^2$$

The characteristic polynomial (of degree 8) factors nicely into the product of two linear terms and three quadratic terms. You can see immediately that four of the eigenvalues are 0, 1020, and a double root at 1000. The other four roots are obtained from the remaining quadratics. Use

```
eig(R)
```

to find all these values

```
ans =
[                0]
[             1020]
[   10*10405^(1/2)]
[  -10*10405^(1/2)]
[ 510+100*26^(1/2)]
[ 510-100*26^(1/2)]
[             1000]
[             1000]
```

The Rosser matrix is not a typical example; it is rare for a full 8-by-8 matrix to have a characteristic polynomial that factors into such simple form. If you change the two "corner" elements of R from 29 to 30 with the commands

```
S = R;   S(1,8) = 30;   S(8,1) = 30;
```

and then try

```
p = poly(S)
```

you find

```
p =
  x^8-4040*x^7+5079941*x^6+82706090*x^5-5327831918568*x^4+
4287832912719760*x^3-1082699388411166000*x^2+51264008540948000*x
+40250968213600000
```

You also find that factor(p) is p itself. That is, the characteristic polynomial cannot be factored over the rationals.

For this modified Rosser matrix

```
F = eig(S)
```

returns

```
F =
[    .21803980548301606860857564424981]
[   999.94691786044276755320289228602]
[  1000.12069829338413357128170754454]
[  1019.52435526320163583249332782910]
[  1019.99355012916292573480918081730]
[  1020.42018820150472781854574988400]
[ -1020.05321425589151659318942526000]
[    -.17053529728768998575200874607757]
```

Notice that these values are close to the eigenvalues of the original Rosser matrix. Further, the numerical values of F are a result of Maple's floating-point arithmetic. Consequently, different settings of digits do not alter the number of digits to the right of the decimal place.

It is also possible to try to compute eigenvalues of symbolic matrices, but closed form solutions are rare. The Givens transformation is generated as the matrix exponential of the elementary matrix

$$A = \begin{bmatrix} 0 & 1 \\ -1 & 0 \end{bmatrix}$$

The Symbolic Math Toolbox commands

```
syms t
A = sym([0 1; -1 0]);
G = expm(t*A)
```

return

```
[  cos(t),  sin(t)]
[ -sin(t),  cos(t)]
```

Next, the command

```
g = eig(G)
```

produces

```
g =
[ cos(t)+(cos(t)^2-1)^(1/2)]
[ cos(t)-(cos(t)^2-1)^(1/2)]
```

You can use `simple` to simplify this form of g. Indeed, a repeated application of `simple`

```
for  j = 1:4
    [g,how] = simple(g)
end
```

produces the best result.

```
g =
[ cos(t)+(-sin(t)^2)^(1/2)]
[ cos(t)-(-sin(t)^2)^(1/2)]

how =
mwcos2sin

g =
[ cos(t)+i*sin(t)]
[ cos(t)-i*sin(t)]

how =
radsimp

g =
[   exp(i*t)]
[ 1/exp(i*t)]

how =
convert(exp)

g =
[  exp(i*t)]
[ exp(-i*t)]

how =
simplify
```

Notice the first application of `simple` uses `mwcos2sin` to produce a sum of sines and cosines. Next, `simple` invokes `radsimp` to produce `cos(t) + i*sin(t)` for the first eigenvector. The third application of `simple` uses `convert(exp)` to change the sines and cosines to complex exponentials. The last application of `simple` uses `simplify` to obtain the final form.

Jordan Canonical Form

The Jordan canonical form results from attempts to diagonalize a matrix by a similarity transformation. For a given matrix A, find a nonsingular matrix V, so that `inv(V)*A*V`, or, more succinctly, `J = V\A*V`, is "as close to diagonal as possible." For almost all matrices, the Jordan canonical form is the diagonal matrix of eigenvalues and the columns of the transformation matrix are the eigenvectors. This always happens if the matrix is symmetric or if it has distinct eigenvalues. Some nonsymmetric matrices with multiple eigenvalues cannot be diagonalized. The Jordan form has the eigenvalues on its diagonal, but some of the superdiagonal elements are one, instead of zero. The statement

```
J = jordan(A)
```

computes the Jordan canonical form of A. The statement

```
[V,J] = jordan(A)
```

also computes the similarity transformation. The columns of V are the generalized eigenvectors of A.

The Jordan form is extremely sensitive to perturbations. Almost any change in A causes its Jordan form to be diagonal. This makes it very difficult to compute the Jordan form reliably with floating-point arithmetic. It also implies that A must be known exactly (i.e., without round-off error, etc.). Its elements must be integers, or ratios of small integers. In particular, the variable-precision calculation, `jordan(vpa(A))`, is not allowed.

For example, let

```
A = sym([12,32,66,116;-25,-76,-164,-294;
        21,66,143,256;-6,-19,-41,-73])
A =
[   12,    32,    66,    116]
[  -25,   -76,  -164,   -294]
[   21,    66,   143,    256]
[   -6,   -19,   -41,    -73]
```

Then

```
[V,J] = jordan(A)
```

produces

```
V =
[    4,   -2,    4,    3]
[   -6,    8,  -11,   -8]
[    4,   -7,   10,    7]
[   -1,    2,   -3,   -2]

J =
[ 1,  1,  0,  0]
[ 0,  1,  0,  0]
[ 0,  0,  2,  1]
[ 0,  0,  0,  2]
```

Therefore A has a double eigenvalue at 1, with a single Jordan block, and a double eigenvalue at 2, also with a single Jordan block. The matrix has only two eigenvectors, V(:,1) and V(:,3). They satisfy

```
A*V(:,1) = 1*V(:,1)
A*V(:,3) = 2*V(:,3)
```

The other two columns of V are generalized eigenvectors of grade 2. They satisfy

```
A*V(:,2) = 1*V(:,2) + V(:,1)
A*V(:,4) = 2*V(:,4) + V(:,3)
```

In mathematical notation, with $\mathbf{v}_j$ = v(:,j), the columns of V and eigenvalues satisfy the relationships

$$(A - \lambda_1 I)\mathbf{v}_2 = \mathbf{v}_1$$

$$(A - \lambda_2 I)\mathbf{v}_4 = \mathbf{v}_3$$

Singular Value Decomposition

Only the variable-precision numeric computation of the complete singular vector decomposition is available in the toolbox. One reason for this is that the formulas that result from symbolic computation are usually too long and complicated to be of much use. If A is a symbolic matrix of floating-point or variable-precision numbers, then

```
S = svd(A)
```

computes the singular values of A to an accuracy determined by the current setting of digits. And

```
[U,S,V] = svd(A);
```

produces two orthogonal matrices, U and V, and a diagonal matrix, S, so that

```
A = U*S*V';
```

Consider the n-by-n matrix A with elements defined by

```
A(i,j) = 1/(i-j+1/2)
```

For n = 5, the matrix is

```
[  2    -2   -2/3   -2/5   -2/7]
[2/3     2    -2   -2/3   -2/5]
[2/5   2/3     2    -2   -2/3]
[2/7   2/5   2/3     2    -2]
[2/9   2/7   2/5   2/3     2]
```

It turns out many of the singular values of these matrices are close to π.

The most obvious way of generating this matrix is

```
for i=1:n
    for j=1:n
        A(i,j) = sym(1/(i-j+1/2));
    end
end
```

The most efficient way to generate the matrix is

```
[J,I] = meshgrid(1:n);
A = sym(1./(I - J+1/2));
```

Since the elements of A are the ratios of small integers, vpa(A) produces a variable-precision representation, which is accurate to digits precision. Hence

```
S = svd(vpa(A))
```

computes the desired singular values to full accuracy. With n = 16 and digits(30), the result is

```
S =
[ 1.20968137605668985332455685357 ]
[ 2.69162158686066606774782763594 ]
[ 3.07790297231119748658424727354 ]
[ 3.13504054399744654843898901261 ]
[ 3.14106044663470063805218371924 ]
[ 3.14155754359918083691050658260 ]
[ 3.14159075458605848728982577119 ]
[ 3.14159256925492306470284863102 ]
[ 3.14159265052654880815569479613 ]
[ 3.14159265349961053143856838564 ]
[ 3.14159265358767361712392612384 ]
[ 3.14159265358975439206849907220 ]
[ 3.14159265358979270342635559051 ]
[ 3.14159265358979323325290142781 ]
[ 3.14159265358979323843066846712 ]
[ 3.14159265358979323846255035974 ]
```

There are two ways to compare S with pi, the floating-point representation of π. In the vector below, the first element is computed by subtraction with variable-precision arithmetic and then converted to a double. The second element is computed with floating-point arithmetic.

```
format short e
[double(pi*ones(16,1)-S)  pi-double(S)]
```

The results are

1.9319e+00	1.9319e+00
4.4997e-01	4.4997e-01
6.3690e-02	6.3690e-02
6.5521e-03	6.5521e-03
5.3221e-04	5.3221e-04
3.5110e-05	3.5110e-05
1.8990e-06	1.8990e-06
8.4335e-08	8.4335e-08
3.0632e-09	3.0632e-09
9.0183e-11	9.0183e-11
2.1196e-12	2.1196e-12
3.8846e-14	3.8636e-14
5.3504e-16	4.4409e-16
5.2097e-18	0
3.1975e-20	0
9.3024e-23	0

Since the relative accuracy of `pi` is `pi*eps`, which is `6.9757e-16`, either column confirms the suspicion that four of the singular values of the 16-by-16 example equal π to floating-point accuracy.

Eigenvalue Trajectories

This example applies several numeric, symbolic, and graphic techniques to study the behavior of matrix eigenvalues as a parameter in the matrix is varied. This particular setting involves numerical analysis and perturbation theory, but the techniques illustrated are more widely applicable.

In this example, you consider a 3-by-3 matrix A whose eigenvalues are 1, 2, 3. First, you perturb A by another matrix E and parameter t: $A \rightarrow A + tE$. As t increases from 0 to 10^{-6}, the eigenvalues $\lambda_1 = 1$, $\lambda_2 = 2$, $\lambda_3 = 3$ change to $\lambda_1' \approx 1.5596 + 0.2726i$, $\lambda_2' \approx 1.5596 - 0.2726i$, $\lambda_3' \approx 2.8808$.

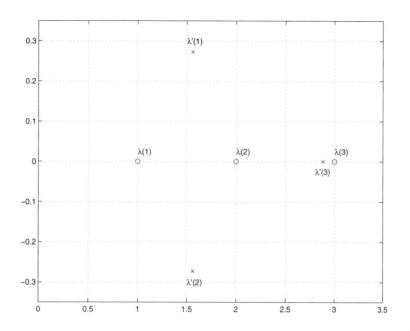

This, in turn, means that for some value of $t = \tau$, $0 < \tau < 10^{-6}$, the perturbed matrix $A(t) = A + tE$ has a double eigenvalue $\lambda_1 = \lambda_2$. The example shows how to find the value of t, called τ, where this happens.

The starting point is a MATLAB test example, known as gallery(3).

```
A = gallery(3)
A =
   -149      -50     -154
    537      180      546
    -27       -9      -25
```

This is an example of a matrix whose eigenvalues are sensitive to the effects of roundoff errors introduced during their computation. The actual computed eigenvalues may vary from one machine to another, but on a typical workstation, the statements

```
format long
e = eig(A)
```

produce

```
e =
    1.00000000001122
    1.99999999999162
    2.99999999999700
```

Of course, the example was created so that its eigenvalues are actually 1, 2, and 3. Note that three or four digits have been lost to roundoff. This can be easily verified with the toolbox. The statements

```
B = sym(A);
e = eig(B)'
p = poly(B)
f = factor(p)
```

produce

```
e =
[1,   2,   3]

p =
x^3-6*x^2+11*x-6

f =
(x-1)*(x-2)*(x-3)
```

Are the eigenvalues sensitive to the perturbations caused by roundoff error because they are "close together"? Ordinarily, the values 1, 2, and 3 would be regarded as "well separated." But, in this case, the separation should be viewed on the scale of the original matrix. If A were replaced by A/1000, the eigenvalues, which would be .001, .002, .003, would "seem" to be closer together.

But eigenvalue sensitivity is more subtle than just "closeness." With a carefully chosen perturbation of the matrix, it is possible to make two of its eigenvalues coalesce into an actual double root that is extremely sensitive to roundoff and other errors.

One good perturbation direction can be obtained from the outer product of the left and right eigenvectors associated with the most sensitive eigenvalue. The following statement creates

```
E = [130,-390,0;43,-129,0;133,-399,0]
```

the perturbation matrix

```
E =
130   -390      0
 43   -129      0
133   -399      0
```

The perturbation can now be expressed in terms of a single, scalar parameter t. The statements

```
syms x t
A = A+t*E
```

replace A with the symbolic representation of its perturbation.

```
A =
[-149+130*t,  -50-390*t,  -154]
[  537+43*t,  180-129*t,   546]
[ -27+133*t,   -9-399*t,   -25]
```

Computing the characteristic polynomial of this new A

```
p = poly(A)
```

gives

```
p =
x^3-6*x^2+11*x-t*x^2+492512*t*x-6-1221271*t
```

Prettyprinting

```
pretty(collect(p,x))
```

shows more clearly that p is a cubic in x whose coefficients vary linearly with t.

$$x^3 + (-t - 6) x^2 + (492512\ t + 11)\ x - 6 - 1221271\ t$$

It turns out that when t is varied over a very small interval, from 0 to 1.0e-6, the desired double root appears. This can best be seen graphically. The first figure shows plots of p, considered as a function of x, for three different values of t: t = 0, t = 0.5e-6, and t = 1.0e-6. For each value, the eigenvalues are computed numerically and also plotted.

```
x = .8:.01:3.2;
for k = 0:2
  c = sym2poly(subs(p,t,k*0.5e-6));
  y = polyval(c,x);
  lambda = eig(double(subs(A,t,k*0.5e-6)));
  subplot(3,1,3-k)
  plot(x,y,'-',x,0*x,':',lambda,0*lambda,'o')
  axis([.8 3.2 -.5 .5])
  text(2.25,.35,['t = ' num2str( k*0.5e-6 )]);
end
```

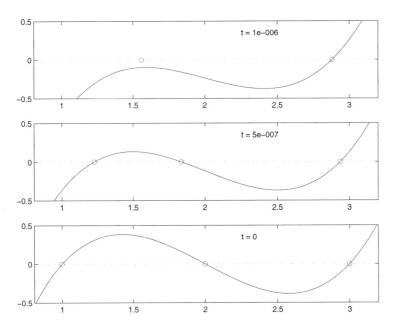

The bottom subplot shows the unperturbed polynomial, with its three roots at 1, 2, and 3. The middle subplot shows the first two roots approaching each other. In the top subplot, these two roots have become complex and only one real root remains.

The next statements compute and display the actual eigenvalues

```
e = eig(A);
pretty(e)
```

showing that e(2) and e(3) form a complex conjugate pair.

```
[                                               2              ]
[         1/3         492508/3 t - 1/3 - 1/9 t                 ]
[1/3 %1       - 3 --------------------------- + 1/3 t + 2]
[                               1/3                           ]
[                              %1                              ]


[                                               2
[         1/3         492508/3 t - 1/3 - 1/9 t
[- 1/6 %1      + 3/2 --------------------------- + 1/3 t + 2
[                                 1/3
[                                %1

                      /                                    2\]
              1/2 |         1/3         492508/3 t - 1/3 - 1/9 t |]
      + 1/2 I 3    |1/3 %1       + 3 ---------------------------|]
                      |                                 1/3          |]
                      \                                %1           /]


[                                               2
[         1/3         492508/3 t - 1/3 - 1/9 t
[- 1/6 %1      + 3/2 --------------------------- + 1/3 t + 2
[                                 1/3
[                                %1

                      /                                    2\]
              1/2 |         1/3         492508/3 t - 1/3 - 1/9 t |]
      - 1/2 I 3    |1/3 %1       + 3 ---------------------------|]
                      |                                 1/3          |]
                      \                                %1           /]
```

$$
\begin{aligned}
\%1 := -2216286 \; t^2 + 3189393 \; t^3 + t^3 + 3 \, (358392752910068940 \; t^3 \\
- 1052829647418 \; t^2 - 181922388795 \; t^4 + 4432572 \; t - 3)^{1/2}
\end{aligned}
$$

Next, the symbolic representations of the three eigenvalues are evaluated at many values of t

```
tvals = (2:-.02:0)' * 1.e-6;
r = size(tvals,1);
c = size(e,1);
lambda = zeros(r,c);
for k = 1:c
   lambda(:,k) = double(subs(e(k),t,tvals));
end
plot(lambda,tvals)
xlabel('\lambda'); ylabel('t');
title('Eigenvalue Transition')
```

to produce a plot of their trajectories.

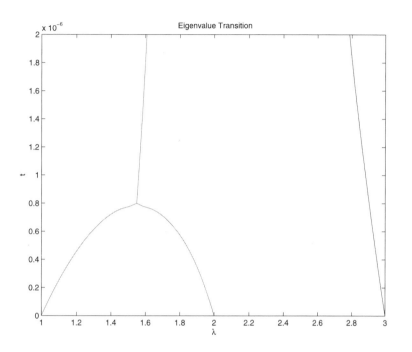

Above $t = 0.8e^{-6}$, the graphs of two of the eigenvalues intersect, while below $t = 0.8e^{-6}$, two real roots become a complex conjugate pair. What is the precise value of t that marks this transition? Let τ denote this value of t.

One way to find τ is based on the fact that, at a double root, both the function and its derivative must vanish. This results in two polynomial equations to be solved for two unknowns. The statement

```
sol = solve(p,diff(p,'x'))
```

solves the pair of algebraic equations $p = 0$ and $dp/dx = 0$ and produces

```
sol =
    t: [4x1 sym]
    x: [4x1 sym]
```

Find τ now by

```
tau = double(sol.t(2))
```

which reveals that the second element of sol.t is the desired value of τ:

```
format short
tau =
   7.8379e-07
```

Therefore, the second element of sol.x

```
sigma = double(sol.x(2))
```

is the double eigenvalue

```
sigma =
    1.5476
```

Let's verify that this value of τ does indeed produce a double eigenvalue at $\sigma = 1.5476$. To achieve this, substitute τ for t in the perturbed matrix $A(t) = A + tE$ and find the eigenvalues of $A(t)$. That is,

```
e = eig(double(subs(A,t,tau)))

e =
    1.5476 + 0.0000i
    1.5476 - 0.0000i
    2.9048
```

confirms that $\sigma = 1.5476$ is a double eigenvalue of $A(t)$ for $t = 7.8379$e-07.

Solving Equations

Algebraic Equations

If S is a symbolic expression,

```
solve(S)
```

attempts to find values of the symbolic variable in S (as determined by findsym) for which S is zero. For example,

```
syms a b c x
S = a*x^2 + b*x + c;
solve(S)
```

uses the familiar quadratic formula to produce

```
ans =
[1/2/a*(-b+(b^2-4*a*c)^(1/2))]
[1/2/a*(-b-(b^2-4*a*c)^(1/2))]
```

This is a symbolic vector whose elements are the two solutions.

If you want to solve for a specific variable, you must specify that variable as an additional argument. For example, if you want to solve S for b, use the command

```
b = solve(S,b)
```

which returns

```
b =
-(a*x^2+c)/x
```

Note that these examples assume equations of the form $f(x) = 0$. If you need to solve equations of the form $f(x) = q(x)$, you must use quoted strings. In particular, the command

```
s = solve('cos(2*x)+sin(x)=1')
```

returns a vector with four solutions.

```
s =
[      0]
[     pi]
[ 1/6*pi]
[ 5/6*pi]
```

Several Algebraic Equations

You can solve systems of equations using the Symbolic Math Toolbox. Suppose you have the system

$$x^2 y^2 = 0$$

$$x - \frac{y}{2} = \alpha$$

and you want to solve for x and y. First create the necessary symbolic objects.

```
syms x y alpha
```

There are several ways to address the output of solve. One is to use a two-output call

```
[x,y] = solve(x^2*y^2, x-y/2-alpha)
```

which returns

```
x =
[     0]
[     0]
[ alpha]
[ alpha]

y =
[ -2*alpha]
[ -2*alpha]
[        0]
[        0]
```

Consequently, the solution vector

```
v = [x, y]
```

appears to have redundant components. This is due to the first equation $x^2 y^2 = 0$, which has two solutions in x and y: $x = \pm 0$, $y = \pm 0$. Changing the equations to

```
eqs1 = 'x^2*y^2=1, x-y/2-alpha'
[x,y] = solve(eqs1)
```

produces four distinct solutions

```
x =
[ 1/2*alpha+1/2*(alpha^2+2)^(1/2)]
[ 1/2*alpha-1/2*(alpha^2+2)^(1/2)]
[ 1/2*alpha+1/2*(alpha^2-2)^(1/2)]
[ 1/2*alpha-1/2*(alpha^2-2)^(1/2)]


y =
[ -alpha+(alpha^2+2)^(1/2)]
[ -alpha-(alpha^2+2)^(1/2)]
[ -alpha+(alpha^2-2)^(1/2)]
[ -alpha-(alpha^2-2)^(1/2)]
```

Since you did not specify the dependent variables, solve uses findsym to determine the variables.

This way of assigning output from solve is quite successful for "small" systems. Plainly, if you had, say, a 10-by-10 system of equations, typing

```
[x1,x2,x3,x4,x5,x6,x7,x8,x9,x10] = solve(...)
```

is both awkward and time consuming. To circumvent this difficulty, solve can return a structure whose fields are the solutions. In particular, consider the system u^2-v^2 = a^2, u + v = 1, a^2-2*a = 3. The command

```
S = solve('u^2-v^2 = a^2','u + v = 1','a^2-2*a = 3')
```

returns

```
S =
    a: [2x1 sym]
    u: [2x1 sym]
    v: [2x1 sym]
```

The solutions for a reside in the "a-field" of S. That is,

```
S.a
```

produces

```
ans =
[   3]
[  -1]
```

Similar comments apply to the solutions for u and v. The structure S can now be manipulated by field and index to access a particular portion of the solution. For example, if you want to examine the second solution, you can use the following statement

```
s2 = [S.a(2), S.u(2), S.v(2)]
```

to extract the second component of each field.

```
s2 =
[  -1,   1,   0]
```

The following statement

```
M = [S.a, S.u, S.v]
```

creates the solution matrix M

```
M =
[   3,   5,  -4]
[  -1,   1,   0]
```

whose rows comprise the distinct solutions of the system.

Linear systems of simultaneous equations can also be solved using matrix division. For example,

```
clear u v x y
syms u v x y
S = solve(x+2*y-u, 4*x+5*y-v);
sol = [S.x;S.y]
```

and

```
A = [1 2; 4 5];
b = [u; v];
z = A\b
```

result in

```
sol =

[ -5/3*u+2/3*v]
[  4/3*u-1/3*v]

z =
[ -5/3*u+2/3*v]
[  4/3*u-1/3*v]
```

Thus s and z produce the same solution, although the results are assigned to different variables.

Single Differential Equation

The function dsolve computes symbolic solutions to ordinary differential equations. The equations are specified by symbolic expressions containing the letter D to denote differentiation. The symbols D2, D3, ... DN, correspond to the second, third, ..., Nth derivative, respectively. Thus, D2y is the Symbolic Math Toolbox equivalent of d^2y/dt^2. The dependent variables are those preceded by D and the default independent variable is t. Note that names of symbolic variables should not contain D. The independent variable can be changed from t to some other symbolic variable by including that variable as the last input argument.

Initial conditions can be specified by additional equations. If initial conditions are not specified, the solutions contain constants of integration, C1, C2, etc.

The output from dsolve parallels the output from solve. That is, you can call dsolve with the number of output variables equal to the number of dependent variables or place the output in a structure whose fields contain the solutions of the differential equations.

Example 1

The following call to dsolve

```
dsolve('Dy=1+y^2')
```

uses y as the dependent variable and t as the default independent variable. The output of this command is

```
ans =
tan(t+C1)
```

To specify an initial condition, use

```
y = dsolve('Dy=1+y^2','y(0)=1')
```

This produces

```
y =
tan(t+1/4*pi)
```

Notice that y is in the MATLAB workspace, but the independent variable t is not. Thus, the command diff(y,t) returns an error. To place t in the workspace, type syms t.

Example 2

Nonlinear equations may have multiple solutions, even when initial conditions are given.

```
x = dsolve('(Dx)^2+x^2=1','x(0)=0')
```

results in

```
x =
[ sin(t)]
[ -sin(t)]
```

Example 3

Here is a second order differential equation with two initial conditions. The commands

```
y = dsolve('D2y=cos(2*x)-y','y(0)=1','Dy(0)=0', 'x')
simplify(y)
```

produce

```
ans =
4/3*cos(x)-2/3*cos(x)^2+1/3
```

The key issues in this example are the order of the equation and the initial conditions. To solve the ordinary differential equation

$$\frac{d^3 u}{dx^3} = u$$

$$u(0) = 1, u'(0) = -1, u''(0) = \pi$$

simply type

```
u = dsolve('D3u=u','u(0)=1','Du(0)=-1','D2u(0) = pi','x')
```

Use D3u to represent $d^3 u/dx^3$ and D2u(0) for $u''(0)$.

Several Differential Equations

The function dsolve can also handle several ordinary differential equations in several variables, with or without initial conditions. For example, here is a pair of linear, first-order equations.

```
S = dsolve('Df = 3*f+4*g', 'Dg = -4*f+3*g')
```

The computed solutions are returned in the structure S. You can determine the values of f and g by typing

```
f = S.f
f =
exp(3*t)*(C1*sin(4*t)+C2*cos(4*t))

g = S.g
g =
exp(3*t)*(C1*cos(4*t)-C2*sin(4*t))
```

If you prefer to recover f and g directly as well as include initial conditions, type

```
[f,g] = dsolve('Df=3*f+4*g, Dg =-4*f+3*g', 'f(0) = 0, g(0) = 1')
```

```
f =
exp(3*t)*sin(4*t)

g =
exp(3*t)*cos(4*t)
```

This table details some examples and Symbolic Math Toolbox syntax. Note that the final entry in the table is the Airy differential equation whose solution is referred to as the Airy function.

Differential Equation	MATLAB Command
$\dfrac{dy}{dt} + 4y(t) = e^{-t}$ $y(0) = 1$	`y = dsolve('Dy+4*y = exp(-t)',` `'y(0) = 1')`
$\dfrac{d^2y}{dx^2} + 4y(x) = e^{-2x}$ $y(0) = 0, y(\pi) = 0$	`y = dsolve('D2y+4*y = exp(-2*x)',` `'y(0)=0', 'y(pi) = 0', 'x')`

$\dfrac{d^2y}{dx^2} = xy(x)$
 	
 $y(0) = 0, y(3) = \dfrac{1}{\pi}K_{\frac{1}{3}}(2\sqrt{3})$
 	
 (The Airy equation)
	`y = dsolve('D2y = x*y','y(0) = 0',`
	 `'y(3) = besselk(1/3, 2*sqrt(3))/pi',`
	 `'x')`

The Airy function plays an important role in the mathematical modeling of the dispersion of water waves.

MATLAB Quick Reference

This appendix lists the MATLAB functions as they are grouped in Help by category. For complete information about any of these functions, refer to Help and either

- Select the function from Functions — By Category or Functions — Alphabetical List, or
- From the **Search** tab in the Help Navigator, select **Function Name** as **Search type**, type the function name in the **Search for** field, and click **Go**.

If you are viewing this book from Help, you can click on any function name and jump directly to the corresponding MATLAB function page.

Select a category from the following table to see a list of related functions.

Development Environment (p. A-2)	Startup, Command Window, help, editing and debugging, other general functions
Mathematics (p. A-6)	Arrays and matrices, linear algebra, data analysis, other areas of mathematics
Programming and Data Types (p. A-19)	Function/expression evaluation, program control, function handles, object oriented programming, error handling, operators, data types, dates and times, timers
File I/O (p. A-30)	General and low-level file I/O, plus specific file formats, like audio, spreadsheet, HDF, images
Graphics (p. A-34)	Line plots, annotating graphs, specialized plots, images, printing, Handle Graphics
3-D Visualization (p. A-39)	Surface and mesh plots, view control, lighting and transparency, volume visualization
Creating Graphical User Interfaces (p. A-43)	GUIDE, programming graphical user interfaces

Development Environment

General functions for working in MATLAB, including functions for startup, Command Window, help, and editing and debugging.

Starting and Quitting

exit	Terminate MATLAB (same as quit)
finish	MATLAB termination M-file
matlab	Start MATLAB (UNIX systems only)
matlabrc	MATLAB startup M-file for single user systems or administrators
quit	Terminate MATLAB
startup	MATLAB startup M-file for user-defined options

Command Window

clc	Clear Command Window
diary	Save session to file
dos	Execute DOS command and return result
format	Control display format for output
home	Move cursor to upper left corner of Command Window
more	Control paged output for Command Window
notebook	Open M-book in Microsoft Word (Windows only)
perl	Call Perl script using appropriate operating system executable
system	Execute operating system command and return result
unix	Execute UNIX command and return result

Getting Help

doc	Display online documentation in MATLAB Help browser
demo	Access product demos via Help browser
docopt	Location of help file directory for UNIX platforms
docroot	Get or set root directory for MATLAB help files
help	Display help for MATLAB functions in Command Window
helpbrowser	Display Help browser for access to extensive online help
helpwin	Display M-file help, with access to M-file help for all functions
info	Display information about The MathWorks or products
lookfor	Search for specified keyword in all help entries
support	Open MathWorks Technical Support Web page
web	Point Help browser or Web browser to file or Web site
whatsnew	Display information about MATLAB and toolbox releases

Workspace, File, and Search Path

Workspace

assignin	Assign value to workspace variable
clear	Remove items from workspace, freeing up system memory
evalin	Execute string containing MATLAB expression in a workspace
exist	Check if variable or file exists
openvar	Open workspace variable in Array Editor for graphical editing
pack	Consolidate workspace memory
which	Locate functions and files
who, whos	List variables in the workspace
workspace	Display Workspace browser, a tool for managing the workspace

File

cd	Change working directory
copyfile	Copy file or directory
delete	Delete files or graphics objects
dir	Display directory listing
exist	Check if a variable or file exists
fileattrib	Set or get attributes of file or directory
filebrowser	Display Current Directory browser, a tool for viewing files
lookfor	Search for specified keyword in all help entries
ls	List directory on UNIX
matlabroot	Return root directory of MATLAB installation
mkdir	Make new directory
movefile	Move file or directory
pwd	Display current directory
rehash	Refresh function and file system caches
rmdir	Remove directory
type	List file
what	List MATLAB specific files in current directory
which	Locate functions and files

See also "File I/O" functions.

Search Path

addpath	Add directories to MATLAB search path
genpath	Generate path string
partialpath	Partial pathname
path	View or change the MATLAB directory search path
path2rc	Save current MATLAB search path to pathdef.m file

pathtool	Open **Set Path** dialog box to view and change MATLAB path
rmpath	Remove directories from MATLAB search path

Programming Tools

Editing and Debugging

dbclear	Clear breakpoints
dbcont	Resume execution
dbdown	Change local workspace context
dbquit	Quit debug mode
dbstack	Display function call stack
dbstatus	List all breakpoints
dbstep	Execute one or more lines from current breakpoint
dbstop	Set breakpoints in M-file function
dbtype	List M-file with line numbers
dbup	Change local workspace context
edit	Edit or create M-file
keyboard	Invoke the keyboard in an M-file

Source Control

checkin	Check file into source control system
checkout	Check file out of source control system
cmopts	Get name of source control system
customverctrl	Allow custom source control system
undocheckout	Undo previous checkout from source control system
verctrl	Version control operations on PC platforms

Notebook

notebook	Open M-book in Microsoft Word (Windows only)

System

computer	Identify information about computer on which MATLAB is running
javachk	Generate error message based on Java feature support
license	Show license number for MATLAB
prefdir	Return directory containing preferences, history, and .ini files
usejava	Determine if a Java feature is supported in MATLAB
ver	Display version information for MathWorks products
version	Get MATLAB version number

Performance Improvement Tools and Techniques

memory	Help for memory limitations
pack	Consolidate workspace memory
profile	Optimize performance of M-file code
profreport	Generate profile report
rehash	Refresh function and file system caches
sparse	Create sparse matrix
zeros	Create array of all zeros

Mathematics

Functions for working with arrays and matrices, linear algebra, data analysis, and other areas of mathematics.

Arrays and Matrices

Basic Information

disp	Display array
display	Display array
isempty	True for empty matrix
isequal	True if arrays are identical
islogical	True for logical array
isnumeric	True for numeric arrays
issparse	True for sparse matrix
length	Length of vector
ndims	Number of dimensions
numel	Number of elements
size	Size of matrix

Operators

+	Addition
+	Unary plus
-	Subtraction
-	Unary minus
*	Matrix multiplication
^	Matrix power
\	Backslash or left matrix divide
/	Slash or right matrix divide
'	Transpose
.'	Nonconjugated transpose
.*	Array multiplication (elementwise)
.^	Array power (elementwise)
.\	Left array divide (elementwise)
./	Right array divide (elementwise)

Operations and Manipulation

: (colon)	Index into array, rearrange array
blkdiag	Block diagonal concatenation
cat	Concatenate arrays

cross	Vector cross product
cumprod	Cumulative product
cumsum	Cumulative sum
diag	Diagonal matrices and diagonals of matrix
dot	Vector dot product
end	Last index
find	Find indices of nonzero elements
fliplr	Flip matrices left-right
flipud	Flip matrices up-down
flipdim	Flip matrix along specified dimension
horzcat	Horizontal concatenation
ind2sub	Multiple subscripts from linear index
ipermute	Inverse permute dimensions of multidimensional array
kron	Kronecker tensor product
max	Maximum elements of array
min	Minimum elements of array
permute	Rearrange dimensions of multidimensional array
prod	Product of array elements
repmat	Replicate and tile array
reshape	Reshape array
rot90	Rotate matrix 90 degrees
sort	Sort elements in ascending order
sortrows	Sort rows in ascending order
sum	Sum of array elements
sqrtm	Matrix square root
sub2ind	Linear index from multiple subscripts
tril	Lower triangular part of matrix
triu	Upper triangular part of matrix
vertcat	Vertical concatenation

See also "Linear Algebra" for other matrix operations.
See also "Elementary Math" for other array operations.

Elementary Matrices and Arrays

: (colon)	Regularly spaced vector
blkdiag	Construct block diagonal matrix from input arguments
diag	Diagonal matrices and diagonals of matrix
eye	Identity matrix
freqspace	Frequency spacing for frequency response
linspace	Generate linearly spaced vectors
logspace	Generate logarithmically spaced vectors
meshgrid	Generate X and Y matrices for three-dimensional plots

ndgrid	Arrays for multidimensional functions and interpolation
ones	Create array of all ones
rand	Uniformly distributed random numbers and arrays
randn	Normally distributed random numbers and arrays
repmat	Replicate and tile array
zeros	Create array of all zeros

Specialized Matrices

compan	Companion matrix
gallery	Test matrices
hadamard	Hadamard matrix
hankel	Hankel matrix
hilb	Hilbert matrix
invhilb	Inverse of Hilbert matrix
magic	Magic square
pascal	Pascal matrix
rosser	Classic symmetric eigenvalue test problem
toeplitz	Toeplitz matrix
vander	Vandermonde matrix
wilkinson	Wilkinson's eigenvalue test matrix

Linear Algebra

Matrix Analysis

cond	Condition number with respect to inversion
condeig	Condition number with respect to eigenvalues
det	Determinant
norm	Matrix or vector norm
normest	Estimate matrix 2-norm
null	Null space
orth	Orthogonalization
rank	Matrix rank
rcond	Matrix reciprocal condition number estimate
rref	Reduced row echelon form
subspace	Angle between two subspaces
trace	Sum of diagonal elements

Linear Equations

\ and /	Linear equation solution
chol	Cholesky factorization
cholinc	Incomplete Cholesky factorization

cond	Condition number with respect to inversion
condest	1-norm condition number estimate
funm	Evaluate general matrix function
inv	Matrix inverse
lscov	Least squares solution in presence of known covariance
lsqnonneg	Nonnegative least squares
lu	LU matrix factorization
luinc	Incomplete LU factorization
pinv	Moore-Penrose pseudoinverse of matrix
qr	Orthogonal-triangular decomposition
rcond	Matrix reciprocal condition number estimate

Eigenvalues and Singular Values

balance	Improve accuracy of computed eigenvalues
cdf2rdf	Convert complex diagonal form to real block diagonal form
condeig	Condition number with respect to eigenvalues
eig	Eigenvalues and eigenvectors
eigs	Eigenvalues and eigenvectors of sparse matrix
gsvd	Generalized singular value decomposition
hess	Hessenberg form of matrix
poly	Polynomial with specified roots
polyeig	Polynomial eigenvalue problem
qz	QZ factorization for generalized eigenvalues
rsf2csf	Convert real Schur form to complex Schur form
schur	Schur decomposition
svd	Singular value decomposition
svds	Singular values and vectors of sparse matrix

Matrix Logarithms and Exponentials

expm	Matrix exponential
logm	Matrix logarithm
sqrtm	Matrix square root

Factorization

balance	Diagonal scaling to improve eigenvalue accuracy
cdf2rdf	Complex diagonal form to real block diagonal form
chol	Cholesky factorization
cholinc	Incomplete Cholesky factorization
cholupdate	Rank 1 update to Cholesky factorization
lu	LU matrix factorization
luinc	Incomplete LU factorization
planerot	Givens plane rotation

qr	Orthogonal-triangular decomposition
qrdelete	Delete column or row from QR factorization
qrinsert	Insert column or row into QR factorization
qrupdate	Rank 1 update to QR factorization
qz	QZ factorization for generalized eigenvalues
rsf2csf	Real block diagonal form to complex diagonal form

Elementary Math

Trigonometric

acos	Inverse cosine
acosh	Inverse hyperbolic cosine
acot	Inverse cotangent
acoth	Inverse hyperbolic cotangent
acsc	Inverse cosecant
acsch	Inverse hyperbolic cosecant
asec	Inverse secant
asech	Inverse hyperbolic secant
asin	Inverse sine
asinh	Inverse hyperbolic sine
atan	Inverse tangent
atanh	Inverse hyperbolic tangent
atan2	Four-quadrant inverse tangent
cos	Cosine
cosh	Hyperbolic cosine
cot	Cotangent
coth	Hyperbolic cotangent
csc	Cosecant
csch	Hyperbolic cosecant
sec	Secant
sech	Hyperbolic secant
sin	Sine
sinh	Hyperbolic sine
tan	Tangent
tanh	Hyperbolic tangent

Exponential

exp	Exponential
log	Natural logarithm
log2	Base 2 logarithm and dissect floating-point numbers into exponent and mantissa
log10	Common (base 10) logarithm
nextpow2	Next higher power of 2
pow2	Base 2 power and scale floating-point number

`reallog`	Natural logarithm for nonnegative real arrays
`realpow`	Array power for real-only output
`realsqrt`	Square root for nonnegative real arrays
`sqrt`	Square root

Complex

`abs`	Absolute value
`angle`	Phase angle
`complex`	Construct complex data from real and imaginary parts
`conj`	Complex conjugate
`cplxpair`	Sort numbers into complex conjugate pairs
`i`	Imaginary unit
`imag`	Complex imaginary part
`isreal`	True for real array
`j`	Imaginary unit
`real`	Complex real part
`unwrap`	Unwrap phase angle

Rounding and Remainder

`fix`	Round towards zero
`floor`	Round towards minus infinity
`ceil`	Round towards plus infinity
`round`	Round towards nearest integer
`mod`	Modulus after division
`rem`	Remainder after division
`sign`	Signum

Discrete Math (e.g., Prime Factors)

`factor`	Prime factors
`factorial`	Factorial function
`gcd`	Greatest common divisor
`isprime`	True for prime numbers
`lcm`	Least common multiple
`nchoosek`	All combinations of N elements taken K at a time
`perms`	All possible permutations
`primes`	Generate list of prime numbers
`rat, rats`	Rational fraction approximation

Data Analysis and Fourier Transforms

Basic Operations

cumprod	Cumulative product
cumsum	Cumulative sum
cumtrapz	Cumulative trapezoidal numerical integration
max	Maximum elements of array
mean	Average or mean value of arrays
median	Median value of arrays
min	Minimum elements of array
prod	Product of array elements
sort	Sort elements in ascending order
sortrows	Sort rows in ascending order
std	Standard deviation
sum	Sum of array elements
trapz	Trapezoidal numerical integration
var	Variance

Finite Differences

del2	Discrete Laplacian
diff	Differences and approximate derivatives
gradient	Numerical gradient

Correlation

corrcoef	Correlation coefficients
cov	Covariance matrix
subspace	Angle between two subspaces

Filtering and Convolution

conv	Convolution and polynomial multiplication
conv2	Two-dimensional convolution
convn	N-dimensional convolution
deconv	Deconvolution and polynomial division
detrend	Linear trend removal
filter	Filter data with infinite impulse response (IIR) or finite impulse response (FIR) filter
filter2	Two-dimensional digital filtering

Fourier Transforms

abs	Absolute value and complex magnitude

angle	Phase angle
fft	One-dimensional discrete Fourier transform
fft2	Two-dimensional discrete Fourier transform
fftn	N-dimensional discrete Fourier Transform
fftshift	Shift DC component of discrete Fourier transform to center of spectrum
ifft	Inverse one-dimensional discrete Fourier transform
ifft2	Inverse two-dimensional discrete Fourier transform
ifftn	Inverse multidimensional discrete Fourier transform
ifftshift	Inverse fast Fourier transform shift
nextpow2	Next power of two
unwrap	Correct phase angles

Polynomials

conv	Convolution and polynomial multiplication
deconv	Deconvolution and polynomial division
poly	Polynomial with specified roots
polyder	Polynomial derivative
polyeig	Polynomial eigenvalue problem
polyfit	Polynomial curve fitting
polyint	Analytic polynomial integration
polyval	Polynomial evaluation
polyvalm	Matrix polynomial evaluation
residue	Convert between partial fraction expansion and polynomial coefficients
roots	Polynomial roots

Interpolation and Computational Geometry

Interpolation

dsearch	Search for nearest point
dsearchn	Multidimensional closest point search
griddata	Data gridding
griddata3	Data gridding and hypersurface fitting for three-dimensional data
griddatan	Data gridding and hypersurface fitting (dimension >= 2)
interp1	One-dimensional data interpolation (table lookup)
interp2	Two-dimensional data interpolation (table lookup)
interp3	Three-dimensional data interpolation (table lookup)
interpft	One-dimensional interpolation using fast Fourier transform method

interpn	Multidimensional data interpolation (table lookup)
meshgrid	Generate X and Y matrices for three-dimensional plots
mkpp	Make piecewise polynomial
ndgrid	Generate arrays for multidimensional functions and interpolation
pchip	Piecewise Cubic Hermite Interpolating Polynomial (PCHIP)
ppval	Piecewise polynomial evaluation
spline	Cubic spline data interpolation
tsearchn	Multidimensional closest simplex search
unmkpp	Piecewise polynomial details

Delaunay Triangulation and Tessellation

delaunay	Delaunay triangulation
delaunay3	Three-dimensional Delaunay tessellation
delaunayn	Multidimensional Delaunay tessellation
dsearch	Search for nearest point
dsearchn	Multidimensional closest point search
tetramesh	Tetrahedron mesh plot
trimesh	Triangular mesh plot
triplot	Two-dimensional triangular plot
trisurf	Triangular surface plot
tsearch	Search for enclosing Delaunay triangle
tsearchn	Multidimensional closest simplex search

Convex Hull

convhull	Convex hull
convhulln	Multidimensional convex hull
patch	Create patch graphics object
plot	Linear two-dimensional plot
trisurf	Triangular surface plot

Voronoi Diagrams

dsearch	Search for nearest point
patch	Create patch graphics object
plot	Linear two-dimensional plot
voronoi	Voronoi diagram
voronoin	Multidimensional Voronoi diagrams

Domain Generation

meshgrid	Generate X and Y matrices for three-dimensional plots
ndgrid	Generate arrays for multidimensional functions and interpolation

Coordinate System Conversion

Cartesian

cart2sph	Transform Cartesian to spherical coordinates
cart2pol	Transform Cartesian to polar coordinates
pol2cart	Transform polar to Cartesian coordinates
sph2cart	Transform spherical to Cartesian coordinates

Nonlinear Numerical Methods

Ordinary Differential Equations (IVP)

deval	Evaluate solution of differential equation problem
ode113	Solve non-stiff differential equations, variable order method
ode15s	Solve stiff ODEs and DAEs Index 1, variable order method
ode23	Solve non-stiff differential equations, low order method
ode23s	Solve stiff differential equations, low order method
ode23t	Solve moderately stiff ODEs and DAEs Index 1, trapezoidal rule
ode23tb	Solve stiff differential equations, low order method
ode45	Solve non-stiff differential equations, medium order method
odeget	Get ODE options parameters
odeset	Create/alter ODE options structure

Delay Differential Equations

dde23	Solve delay differential equations with constant delays
ddeget	Get DDE options parameters
ddeset	Create/alter DDE options structure

Boundary Value Problems

bvp4c	Solve two-point boundary value problems for ODEs by collocation
bvpget	Get BVP options parameters
bvpset	Create/alter BVP options structure
deval	Evaluate solution of differential equation problem

Partial Differential Equations

`pdepe`	Solve initial-boundary value problems for parabolic-elliptic PDEs
`pdeval`	Evaluates by interpolation solution computed by `pdepe`

Optimization

`fminbnd`	Scalar bounded nonlinear function minimization
`fminsearch`	Multidimensional unconstrained nonlinear minimization, by Nelder-Mead direct search method
`fzero`	Scalar nonlinear zero finding
`lsqnonneg`	Linear least squares with nonnegativity constraints
`optimset`	Create or alter optimization `options` structure
`optimget`	Get optimization parameters from `options` structure

Numerical Integration (Quadrature)

`quad`	Numerically evaluate integral, adaptive Simpson quadrature (low order)
`quadl`	Numerically evaluate integral, adaptive Lobatto quadrature (high order)
`dblquad`	Numerically evaluate double integral
`triplequad`	Numerically evaluate triple integral

Specialized Math

`airy`	Airy functions
`besselh`	Bessel functions of third kind (Hankel functions)
`besseli`	Modified Bessel function of first kind
`besselj`	Bessel function of first kind
`besselk`	Modified Bessel function of second kind
`bessely`	Bessel function of second kind
`beta`	Beta function
`betainc`	Incomplete beta function
`betaln`	Logarithm of beta function
`ellipj`	Jacobi elliptic functions
`ellipke`	Complete elliptic integrals of first and second kind
`erf`	Error function
`erfc`	Complementary error function
`erfcinv`	Inverse complementary error function
`erfcx`	Scaled complementary error function
`erfinv`	Inverse error function
`expint`	Exponential integral
`gamma`	Gamma function

gammainc	Incomplete gamma function
gammaln	Logarithm of gamma function
legendre	Associated Legendre functions
psi	Psi (polygamma) function

Sparse Matrices

Elementary Sparse Matrices

spdiags	Sparse matrix formed from diagonals
speye	Sparse identity matrix
sprand	Sparse uniformly distributed random matrix
sprandn	Sparse normally distributed random matrix
sprandsym	Sparse random symmetric matrix

Full to Sparse Conversion

find	Find indices of nonzero elements
full	Convert sparse matrix to full matrix
sparse	Create sparse matrix
spconvert	Import from sparse matrix external format

Working with Sparse Matrices

issparse	True for sparse matrix
nnz	Number of nonzero matrix elements
nonzeros	Nonzero matrix elements
nzmax	Amount of storage allocated for nonzero matrix elements
spalloc	Allocate space for sparse matrix
spfun	Apply function to nonzero matrix elements
spones	Replace nonzero sparse matrix elements with ones
spparms	Set parameters for sparse matrix routines
spy	Visualize sparsity pattern

Reordering Algorithms

colamd	Column approximate minimum degree permutation
colmmd	Column minimum degree permutation
colperm	Column permutation
dmperm	Dulmage-Mendelsohn permutation
randperm	Random permutation
symamd	Symmetric approximate minimum degree permutation
symmmd	Symmetric minimum degree permutation
symrcm	Symmetric reverse Cuthill-McKee permutation

Linear Algebra

cholinc	Incomplete Cholesky factorization
condest	1-norm condition number estimate
eigs	Eigenvalues and eigenvectors of sparse matrix
luinc	Incomplete LU factorization
normest	Estimate matrix 2-norm
sprank	Structural rank
svds	Singular values and vectors of sparse matrix

Linear Equations (Iterative Methods)

bicg	BiConjugate Gradients method
bicgstab	BiConjugate Gradients Stabilized method
cgs	Conjugate Gradients Squared method
gmres	Generalized Minimum Residual method
lsqr	LSQR implementation of Conjugate Gradients on Normal Equations
minres	Minimum Residual method
pcg	Preconditioned Conjugate Gradients method
qmr	Quasi-Minimal Residual method
spaugment	Form least squares augmented system
symmlq	Symmetric LQ method

Tree Operations

etree	Elimination tree
etreeplot	Plot elimination tree
gplot	Plot graph, as in "graph theory"
symbfact	Symbolic factorization analysis
treelayout	Lay out tree or forest
treeplot	Plot picture of tree

Math Constants

eps	Floating-point relative accuracy
i	Imaginary unit
Inf	Infinity, ∞
j	Imaginary unit
NaN	Not-a-Number
pi	Ratio of a circle's circumference to its diameter, π
realmax	Largest positive floating-point number
realmin	Smallest positive floating-point number

Programming and Data Types

Functions to store and operate on data at either the MATLAB command line or in programs and scripts. Functions to write, manage, and execute MATLAB programs.

Data Types

Numeric

[ ]	Array constructor
cat	Concatenate arrays
class	Return object's class name (e.g., numeric)
find	Find indices and values of nonzero array elements
ipermute	Inverse permute dimensions of multidimensional array
isa	Detect object of given class (e.g., numeric)
isequal	Determine if arrays are numerically equal
isequalwithequalnans	Test for equality, treating NaNs as equal
isnumeric	Determine if item is numeric array
isreal	Determine if all array elements are real numbers
permute	Rearrange dimensions of multidimensional array
reshape	Reshape array
squeeze	Remove singleton dimensions from array
zeros	Create array of all zeros

Characters and Strings

Description of Strings in MATLAB

strings	Describes MATLAB string handling

Creating and Manipulating Strings

blanks	Create string of blanks
char	Create character array (string)
cellstr	Create cell array of strings from character array
datestr	Convert to date string format
deblank	Strip trailing blanks from the end of string
lower	Convert string to lower case
sprintf	Write formatted data to string
sscanf	Read string under format control
strcat	String concatenation
strjust	Justify character array

`strread`	Read formatted data from string
`strrep`	String search and replace
`strvcat`	Vertical concatenation of strings
`upper`	Convert string to upper case

Comparing and Searching Strings

`class`	Return object's class name (e.g., char)
`findstr`	Find string within another, longer string
`isa`	Detect object of given class (e.g., char)
`iscellstr`	Determine if item is cell array of strings
`ischar`	Determine if item is character array
`isletter`	Detect array elements that are letters of the alphabet
`isspace`	Detect elements that are ASCII white spaces
`regexp`	Match regular expression
`regexpi`	Match regular expression, ignoring case
`regexprep`	Replace string using regular expression
`strcmp`	Compare strings
`strcmpi`	Compare strings, ignoring case
`strfind`	Find one string within another
`strmatch`	Find possible matches for string
`strncmp`	Compare first n characters of strings
`strncmpi`	Compare first n characters of strings, ignoring case
`strtok`	First token in string

Evaluating String Expressions

`eval`	Execute string containing MATLAB expression
`evalc`	Evaluate MATLAB expression with capture
`evalin`	Execute string containing MATLAB expression in workspace

Structures

`cell2struct`	Cell array to structure array conversion
`class`	Return object's class name (e.g., struct)
`deal`	Deal inputs to outputs
`fieldnames`	Field names of structure
`isa`	Detect object of given class (e.g., struct)
`isequal`	Determine if arrays are numerically equal
`isfield`	Determine if item is structure array field
`isstruct`	Determine if item is structure array
`orderfields`	Order fields of a structure array
`rmfield`	Remove structure fields
`struct`	Create structure array
`struct2cell`	Structure to cell array conversion

Cell Arrays

{ }	Construct cell array
cell	Construct cell array
cellfun	Apply function to each element in cell array
cellstr	Create cell array of strings from character array
cell2mat	Convert cell array of matrices into single matrix
cell2struct	Cell array to structure array conversion
celldisp	Display cell array contents
cellplot	Graphically display structure of cell arrays
class	Return object's class name (e.g., cell)
deal	Deal inputs to outputs
isa	Detect object of given class (e.g., cell)
iscell	Determine if item is cell array
iscellstr	Determine if item is cell array of strings
isequal	Determine if arrays are numerically equal
mat2cell	Divide matrix up into cell array of matrices
num2cell	Convert numeric array into cell array
struct2cell	Structure to cell array conversion

Data Type Conversion

Numeric

double	Convert to double-precision
int8	Convert to signed 8-bit integer
int16	Convert to signed 16-bit integer
int32	Convert to signed 32-bit integer
int64	Convert to signed 64-bit integer
single	Convert to single-precision
uint8	Convert to unsigned 8-bit integer
uint16	Convert to unsigned 16-bit integer
uint32	Convert to unsigned 32-bit integer
uint64	Convert to unsigned 64-bit integer

String to Numeric

base2dec	Convert base N number string to decimal number
bin2dec	Convert binary number string to decimal number
hex2dec	Convert hexadecimal number string to decimal number
hex2num	Convert hexadecimal number string to double number
str2double	Convert string to double-precision number
str2num	Convert string to number

Numeric to String

char	Convert to character array (string)
dec2base	Convert decimal to base N number in string
dec2bin	Convert decimal to binary number in string
dec2hex	Convert decimal to hexadecimal number in string
int2str	Convert integer to string
mat2str	Convert a matrix to string
num2str	Convert number to string

Other Conversions

cell2mat	Convert cell array of matrices into single matrix
cell2struct	Convert cell array to structure array
datestr	Convert serial date number to string
func2str	Convert function handle to function name string
logical	Convert numeric to logical array
mat2cell	Divide matrix up into cell array of matrices
num2cell	Convert a numeric array to cell array
str2func	Convert function name string to function handle
struct2cell	Convert structure to cell array

Determine Data Type

is*	Detect state
isa	Detect object of given MATLAB class or Java class
iscell	Determine if item is cell array
iscellstr	Determine if item is cell array of strings
ischar	Determine if item is character array
isfield	Determine if item is character array
isjava	Determine if item is Java object
islogical	Determine if item is logical array
isnumeric	Determine if item is numeric array
isobject	Determine if item is MATLAB OOPs object
isstruct	Determine if item is MATLAB structure array

Arrays

Array Operations

[ ]	Array constructor
,	Array row element separator
;	Array column element separator
:	Specify range of array elements

`end`	Indicate last index of array
`+`	Addition or unary plus
`-`	Subtraction or unary minus
`.*`	Array multiplication
`./`	Array right division
`.\`	Array left division
`.^`	Array power
`.'`	Array (nonconjugated) transpose

Basic Array Information

`disp`	Display text or array
`display`	Overloaded method to display text or array
`isempty`	Determine if array is empty
`isequal`	Determine if arrays are numerically equal
`isequalwithequalnans`	Test for equality, treating NaNs as equal
`isnumeric`	Determine if item is numeric array
`islogical`	Determine if item is logical array
`length`	Length of vector
`ndims`	Number of array dimensions
`numel`	Number of elements in matrix or cell array
`size`	Array dimensions

Array Manipulation

`:`	Specify range of array elements
`blkdiag`	Construct block diagonal matrix from input arguments
`cat`	Concatenate arrays
`circshift`	Shift array circularly
`find`	Find indices and values of nonzero elements
`fliplr`	Flip matrices left-right
`flipud`	Flip matrices up-down
`flipdim`	Flip array along specified dimension
`horzcat`	Horizontal concatenation
`ind2sub`	Subscripts from linear index
`ipermute`	Inverse permute dimensions of multidimensional array
`permute`	Rearrange dimensions of multidimensional array
`repmat`	Replicate and tile array
`reshape`	Reshape array
`rot90`	Rotate matrix 90 degrees
`shiftdim`	Shift dimensions
`sort`	Sort elements in ascending order
`sortrows`	Sort rows in ascending order
`squeeze`	Remove singleton dimensions

A-23

sub2ind	Single index from subscripts
vertcat	Horizontal concatenation

Elementary Arrays

:	Regularly spaced vector
blkdiag	Construct block diagonal matrix from input arguments
eye	Identity matrix
linspace	Generate linearly spaced vectors
logspace	Generate logarithmically spaced vectors
meshgrid	Generate X and Y matrices for three-dimensional plots
ndgrid	Generate arrays for multidimensional functions and interpolation
ones	Create array of all ones
rand	Uniformly distributed random numbers and arrays
randn	Normally distributed random numbers and arrays
zeros	Create array of all zeros

Operators and Operations

Special Characters

:	Specify range of array elements
( )	Pass function arguments, or prioritize operations
[ ]	Construct array
{ }	Construct cell array
.	Decimal point, or structure field separator
...	Continue statement to next line
,	Array row element separator
;	Array column element separator
%	Insert comment line into code
!	Command to operating system
=	Assignment

Arithmetic Operations

+	Plus
-	Minus
.	Decimal point
=	Assignment
*	Matrix multiplication
/	Matrix right division
\	Matrix left division
^	Matrix power

'	Matrix transpose
.*	Array multiplication (elementwise)
./	Array right division (elementwise)
.\	Array left division (elementwise)
.^	Array power (elementwise)
.'	Array transpose

Bitwise Operations

bitand	Bitwise AND
bitcmp	Bitwise complement
bitor	Bitwise OR
bitmax	Maximum floating-point integer
bitset	Set bit at specified position
bitshift	Bitwise shift
bitget	Get bit at specified position
bitxor	Bitwise XOR

Relational Operations

<	Less than
<=	Less than or equal to
>	Greater than
>=	Greater than or equal to
==	Equal to
~=	Not equal to

Logical Operations

&&	Logical AND
||	Logical OR
&	Logical AND for arrays
|	Logical OR for arrays
~	Logical NOT
all	Test to determine if all elements are nonzero
any	Test for any nonzero elements
false	False array
find	Find indices and values of nonzero elements
is*	Detect state
isa	Detect object of given class
iskeyword	Determine if string is MATLAB keyword
isvarname	Determine if string is valid variable name
logical	Convert numeric values to logical
true	True array
xor	Logical EXCLUSIVE OR

Set Operations

`intersect`	Set intersection of two vectors
`ismember`	Detect members of set
`setdiff`	Return set difference of two vectors
`issorted`	Determine if set elements are in sorted order
`setxor`	Set exclusive or of two vectors
`union`	Set union of two vectors
`unique`	Unique elements of vector

Date and Time Operations

`calendar`	Calendar for specified month
`clock`	Current time as date vector
`cputime`	Elapsed CPU time
`date`	Current date string
`datenum`	Serial date number
`datestr`	Convert serial date number to string
`datevec`	Date components
`eomday`	End of month
`etime`	Elapsed time
`now`	Current date and time
`tic, toc`	Stopwatch timer
`weekday`	Day of the week

Programming in MATLAB

M-File Functions and Scripts

`( )`	Pass function arguments
`%`	Insert comment line into code
`...`	Continue statement to next line
`depfun`	List dependent functions of M-file or P-file
`depdir`	List dependent directories of M-file or P-file
`function`	Function M-files
`input`	Request user input
`inputname`	Input argument name
`mfilename`	Name of currently running M-file
`namelengthmax`	Return maximum identifier length
`nargin`	Number of function input arguments
`nargout`	Number of function output arguments
`nargchk`	Check number of input arguments
`nargoutchk`	Validate number of output arguments
`pcode`	Create preparsed pseudocode file (P-file)

script	Describes script M-file
varargin	Accept variable number of arguments
varargout	Return variable number of arguments

Evaluation of Expressions and Functions

builtin	Execute builtin function from overloaded method
cellfun	Apply function to each element in cell array
eval	Interpret strings containing MATLAB expressions
evalc	Evaluate MATLAB expression with capture
evalin	Evaluate expression in workspace
feval	Evaluate function
iskeyword	Determine if item is MATLAB keyword
isvarname	Determine if item is valid variable name
pause	Halt execution temporarily
run	Run script that is not on current path
script	Describes script M-file
symvar	Determine symbolic variables in expression
tic, toc	Stopwatch timer

Timer Functions

delete	Delete timer object from memory
disp	Display information about timer object
get	Retrieve information about timer object properties
isvalid	Determine if timer object is valid
set	Display or set timer object properties
start	Start a timer
startat	Start a timer at a specific timer
stop	Stop a timer
timer	Create a timer object
timerfind	Return an array of all timer object in memory
wait	Block command line until timer completes

Variables and Functions in Memory

assignin	Assign value to workspace variable
global	Define global variables
inmem	Return names of functions in memory
isglobal	Determine if item is global variable
mislocked	True if M-file cannot be cleared
mlock	Prevent clearing M-file from memory
munlock	Allow clearing M-file from memory
namelengthmax	Return maximum identifier length
pack	Consolidate workspace memory

| persistent | Define persistent variable |
| rehash | Refresh function and file system caches |

Control Flow

break	Terminate execution of `for` loop or `while` loop
case	Case switch
catch	Begin catch block
continue	Pass control to next iteration of `for` or `while` loop
else	Conditionally execute statements
elseif	Conditionally execute statements
end	Terminate conditional statements, or indicate last index
error	Display error messages
for	Repeat statements specific number of times
if	Conditionally execute statements
otherwise	Default part of `switch` statement
return	Return to invoking function
switch	Switch among several cases based on expression
try	Begin `try` block
while	Repeat statements indefinite number of times

Function Handles

class	Return object's class name (e.g. function_handle)
feval	Evaluate function
function_handle	Describes function handle data type
functions	Return information about function handle
func2str	Constructs function name string from function handle
isa	Detect object of given class (e.g. function_handle)
isequal	Determine if function handles are equal
str2func	Constructs function handle from function name string

Object-Oriented Programming

MATLAB Classes and Objects

class	Create object or return class of object
fieldnames	List public fields belonging to object,
inferiorto	Establish inferior class relationship
isa	Detect object of given class
isobject	Determine if item is MATLAB OOPs object
loadobj	User-defined extension of `load` function for user objects
methods	Display method names
methodsview	Displays information on all methods implemented by class

saveobj	User-defined extension of save function for user objects
subsasgn	Overloaded method for A(I)=B, A{I}=B, and A.field=B
subsindex	Overloaded method for X(A)
subsref	Overloaded method for A(I), A{I} and A.field
substruct	Create structure argument for subsasgn or subsref
superiorto	Establish superior class relationship

Java Classes and Objects

cell	Convert Java array object to cell array
class	Return class name of Java object
clear	Clear Java packages import list
depfun	List Java classes used by M-file
exist	Detect if item is Java class
fieldnames	List public fields belonging to object
im2java	Convert image to instance of Java image object
import	Add package or class to current Java import list
inmem	List names of Java classes loaded into memory
isa	Detect object of given class
isjava	Determine whether object is Java object
javaArray	Constructs Java array
javaMethod	Invokes Java method
javaObject	Constructs Java object
methods	Display methods belonging to class
methodsview	Display information on all methods implemented by class
which	Display package and class name for method

Error Handling

catch	Begin catch block of try/catch statement
error	Display error message
ferror	Query MATLAB about errors in file input or output
lasterr	Return last error message generated by MATLAB
lasterror	Last error message and related information
lastwarn	Return last warning message issued by MATLAB
rethrow	Reissue error
try	Begin try block of try/catch statement
warning	Display warning message

MEX Programming

dbmex	Enable MEX-file debugging
inmem	Return names of currently loaded MEX-files
mex	Compile MEX-function from C or Fortran source code
mexext	Return MEX-filename extension

File I/O

Functions to read and write data to files of different format types.

To see a listing of file formats that are readable from MATLAB, go to file formats.

Filename Construction

fileparts	Return parts of filename
filesep	Return directory separator for this platform
fullfile	Build full filename from parts
tempdir	Return name of system's temporary directory
tempname	Return unique string for use as temporary filename

Opening, Loading, Saving Files

importdata	Load data from various types of files
load	Load all or specific data from MAT or ASCII file
open	Open files of various types using appropriate editor or program
save	Save all or specific data to MAT or ASCII file
winopen	Open file in appropriate application (Windows only)

Low-Level File I/O

fclose	Close one or more open files
feof	Test for end-of-file
ferror	Query MATLAB about errors in file input or output
fgetl	Return next line of file as string without line terminator(s)
fgets	Return next line of file as string with line terminator(s)
fopen	Open file or obtain information about open files
fprintf	Write formatted data to file
fread	Read binary data from file
frewind	Rewind open file
fscanf	Read formatted data from file
fseek	Set file position indicator
ftell	Get file position indicator
fwrite	Write binary data to file

Text Files

csvread	Read numeric data from text file, using comma delimiter
csvwrite	Write numeric data to text file, using comma delimiter

dlmread	Read numeric data from text file, specifying your own delimiter
dlmwrite	Write numeric data to text file, specifying your own delimiter
textread	Read data from text file, specifying format for each value

XML Documents

xmlread	Parse XML document
xmlwrite	Serialize XML Document Object Model node
xslt	Transform XML document using XSLT engine

Spreadsheets

Microsoft Excel Functions

xlsfinfo	Determine if file contains Microsoft Excel (.xls) spreadsheet
xlsread	Read Microsoft Excel spreadsheet file (.xls)

Lotus123 Functions

wk1read	Read Lotus123 WK1 spreadsheet file into matrix
wk1write	Write matrix to Lotus123 WK1 spreadsheet file

Scientific Data

Common Data Format (CDF)

cdfepoch	Convert MATLAB date number or date string into CDF epoch
cdfinfo	Return information about CDF file
cdfread	Read CDF file
cdfwrite	Write CDF file

Flexible Image Transport System

fitsinfo	Return information about FITS file
fitsread	Read FITS file

Hierarchical Data Format (HDF)

hdf	Interface to HDF files
hdfinfo	Return information about HDF or HDF-EOS file
hdfread	Read HDF file
hdftool	Start HDF Import Tool

Band-Interleaved Data

multibandread	Read band-interleaved data from file
multibandwrite	Write band-interleaved data to file

Audio and Audio/Video

General

audioplayer	Create audio player object
audiorecorder	Perform real-time audio capture
beep	Produce beep sound
lin2mu	Convert linear audio signal to mu-law
mu2lin	Convert mu-law audio signal to linear
sound	Convert vector into sound
soundsc	Scale data and play as sound

SPARCstation-Specific Sound Functions

auread	Read NeXT/SUN (.au) sound file
auwrite	Write NeXT/SUN (.au) sound file

Microsoft WAVE Sound Functions

wavplay	Play sound on PC-based audio output device
wavread	Read Microsoft WAVE (.wav) sound file
wavrecord	Record sound using PC-based audio input device
wavwrite	Write Microsoft WAVE (.wav) sound file

Audio Video Interleaved (AVI) Functions

addframe	Add frame to AVI file
avifile	Create new AVI file
aviinfo	Return information about AVI file
aviread	Read AVI file
close	Close AVI file
movie2avi	Create AVI movie from MATLAB movie

Images

im2java	Convert image to instance of Java image object
imfinfo	Return information about graphics file
imread	Read image from graphics file
imwrite	Write image to graphics file

Internet Exchange

sendmail	Send e-mail message (attachments optional) to list of addresses
unzip	Extract contents of zip file
urlread	Read contents at URL
urlwrite	Save contents of URL to file
zip	Create compressed version of files in zip format

Graphics

2-D graphs, specialized plots (e.g., pie charts, histograms, and contour plots), function plotters, and Handle Graphics functions.

Basic Plots and Graphs

box	Axis box for 2-D and 3-D plots
errorbar	Plot graph with error bars
hold	Hold current graph
LineSpec	Line specification syntax
loglog	Plot using log-log scales
polar	Polar coordinate plot
plot	Plot vectors or matrices.
plot3	Plot lines and points in 3-D space
plotyy	Plot graphs with Y tick labels on the left and right
semilogx	Semi-log scale plot
semilogy	Semi-log scale plot
subplot	Create axes in tiled positions

Annotating Plots

clabel	Add contour labels to contour plot
datetick	Date formatted tick labels
gtext	Place text on 2-D graph using mouse
legend	Graph legend for lines and patches
texlabel	Produce the TeX format from character string
title	Titles for 2-D and 3-D plots
xlabel	X-axis labels for 2-D and 3-D plots
ylabel	Y-axis labels for 2-D and 3-D plots
zlabel	Z-axis labels for 3-D plots

Specialized Plotting

Area, Bar, and Pie Plots

area	Area plot
bar	Vertical bar chart
barh	Horizontal bar chart
bar3	Vertical 3-D bar chart
bar3h	Horizontal 3-D bar chart
pareto	Pareto char
pie	Pie plot

`pie3`	3-D pie plot

Contour Plots

`contour`	Contour (level curves) plot
`contour3`	3-D contour plot
`contourc`	Contour computation
`contourf`	Filled contour plot
`ezcontour`	Easy to use contour plotter
`ezcontourf`	Easy to use filled contour plotter

Direction and Velocity Plots

`comet`	Comet plot
`comet3`	3-D comet plot
`compass`	Compass plot
`feather`	Feather plot
`quiver`	Quiver (or velocity) plot
`quiver3`	3-D quiver (or velocity) plot

Discrete Data Plots

`stem`	Plot discrete sequence data
`stem3`	Plot discrete surface data
`stairs`	Stairstep graph

Function Plots

`ezcontour`	Easy to use contour plotter
`ezcontourf`	Easy to use filled contour plotter
`ezmesh`	Easy to use 3-D mesh plotter
`ezmeshc`	Easy to use combination mesh/contour plotter
`ezplot`	Easy to use function plotter
`ezplot3`	Easy to use 3-D parametric curve plotter
`ezpolar`	Easy to use polar coordinate plotter
`ezsurf`	Easy to use 3-D colored surface plotter
`ezsurfc`	Easy to use combination surface/contour plotter
`fplot`	Plot a function

Histograms

`hist`	Plot histograms
`histc`	Histogram count
`rose`	Plot rose or angle histogram

A-35

Polygons and Surfaces

convhull	Convex hull
cylinder	Generate cylinder
delaunay	Delaunay triangulation
dsearch	Search Delaunay triangulation for nearest point
ellipsoid	Generate ellipsoid
fill	Draw filled 2-D polygons
fill3	Draw filled 3-D polygons in 3-space
inpolygon	True for points inside a polygonal region
pcolor	Pseudocolor (checkerboard) plot
polyarea	Area of polygon
ribbon	Ribbon plot
slice	Volumetric slice plot
sphere	Generate sphere
tsearch	Search for enclosing Delaunay triangle
voronoi	Voronoi diagram
waterfall	Waterfall plot

Scatter Plots

plotmatrix	Scatter plot matrix
scatter	Scatter plot
scatter3	3-D scatter plot

Animation

frame2im	Convert movie frame to indexed image
getframe	Capture movie frame
im2frame	Convert image to movie frame
movie	Play recorded movie frames
noanimate	Change EraseMode of all objects to normal

Bit-Mapped Images

frame2im	Convert movie frame to indexed image
image	Display image object
imagesc	Scale data and display image object
imfinfo	Information about graphics file
imformats	Manage file format registry
im2frame	Convert image to movie frame
im2java	Convert image to instance of Java image object
imread	Read image from graphics file
imwrite	Write image to graphics file
ind2rgb	Convert indexed image to RGB image

Printing

frameedit	Edit print frame for Simulink and Stateflow diagram
orient	Hardcopy paper orientation
pagesetupdlg	Page position dialog box
print	Print graph or save graph to file
printdlg	Print dialog box
printopt	Configure local printer defaults
printpreview	Preview figure to be printed
saveas	Save figure to graphic file

Handle Graphics

Finding and Identifying Graphics Objects

allchild	Find all children of specified objects
copyobj	Make copy of graphics object and its children
delete	Delete files or graphics objects
findall	Find all graphics objects (including hidden handles)
figflag	Test if figure is on screen
findfigs	Display off-screen visible figure windows
findobj	Find objects with specified property values
gca	Get current Axes handle
gcbo	Return object whose callback is currently executing
gcbf	Return handle of figure containing callback object
gco	Return handle of current object
get	Get object properties
ishandle	True if value is valid object handle
set	Set object properties

Object Creation Functions

axes	Create axes object
figure	Create figure (graph) windows
image	Create image (2-D matrix)
light	Create light object (illuminates Patch and Surface)
line	Create line object (3-D polylines)
patch	Create patch object (polygons)
rectangle	Create rectangle object (2-D rectangle)
rootobject	List of root properties
surface	Create surface (quadrilaterals)
text	Create text object (character strings)
uicontextmenu	Create context menu (popup associated with object)

Figure Windows

capture	Screen capture of the current figure
clc	Clear figure window
clf	Clear figure
close	Close specified window
closereq	Default close request function
drawnow	Complete any pending drawing
figflag	Test if figure is on screen
gcf	Get current figure handle
hgload	Load graphics object hierarchy from a FIG-file
hgsave	Save graphics object hierarchy to a FIG-file
newplot	Graphics M-file preamble for NextPlot property
opengl	Change automatic selection mode of OpenGL rendering
refresh	Refresh figure
saveas	Save figure or model to desired output format

Axes Operations

axis	Plot axis scaling and appearance
box	Display axes border
cla	Clear Axes
gca	Get current Axes handle
grid	Grid lines for 2-D and 3-D plots
ishold	Get the current hold state

3-D Visualization

Create and manipulate graphics that display 2-D matrix and 3-D volume data, controlling the view, lighting and transparency.

Surface and Mesh Plots

Creating Surfaces and Meshes

hidden	Mesh hidden line removal mode
meshc	Combination mesh/contourplot
mesh	3-D mesh with reference plane
peaks	A sample function of two variables
surf	3-D shaded surface graph
surface	Create surface low-level objects
surfc	Combination surf/contourplot
surfl	3-D shaded surface with lighting
tetramesh	Tetrahedron mesh plot
trimesh	Triangular mesh plot
triplot	2-D triangular plot
trisurf	Triangular surface plot

Domain Generation

griddata	Data gridding and surface fitting
meshgrid	Generation of X and Y arrays for 3-D plots

Color Operations

brighten	Brighten or darken colormap
caxis	Pseudocolor axis scaling
colormapeditor	Start colormap editor
colorbar	Display color bar (color scale)
colordef	Set up color defaults
colormap	Set the color look-up table (list of colormaps)
ColorSpec	Ways to specify color
graymon	Graphics figure defaults set for grayscale monitor
hsv2rgb	Hue-saturation-value to red-green-blue conversion
rgb2hsv	RGB to HSVconversion
rgbplot	Plot colormap
shading	Color shading mode
spinmap	Spin the colormap
surfnorm	3-D surface normals

whitebg	Change axes background color for plots

Colormaps

autumn	Shades of red and yellow colormap
bone	Gray-scale with a tinge of blue colormap
contrast	Gray colormap to enhance image contrast
cool	Shades of cyan and magenta colormap
copper	Linear copper-tone colormap
flag	Alternating red, white, blue, and black colormap
gray	Linear gray-scale colormap
hot	Black-red-yellow-white colormap
hsv	Hue-saturation-value (HSV) colormap
jet	Variant of HSV
lines	Line color colormap
prism	Colormap of prism colors
spring	Shades of magenta and yellow colormap
summer	Shades of green and yellow colormap
winter	Shades of blue and green colormap

View Control

Controlling the Camera Viewpoint

camdolly	Move camera position and target
camlookat	View specific objects
camorbit	Orbit about camera target
campan	Rotate camera target about camera position
campos	Set or get camera position
camproj	Set or get projection type
camroll	Rotate camera about viewing axis
camtarget	Set or get camera target
camup	Set or get camera up-vector
camva	Set or get camera view angle
camzoom	Zoom camera in or out
view	3-D graph viewpoint specification.
viewmtx	Generate view transformation matrices

Setting the Aspect Ratio and Axis Limits

daspect	Set or get data aspect ratio
pbaspect	Set or get plot box aspect ratio
xlim	Set or get the current x-axis limits
ylim	Set or get the current y-axis limits

zlim   Set or get the current *z*-axis limits

Object Manipulation

reset   Reset axis or figure
rotate   Rotate objects about specified origin and direction
rotate3d   Interactively rotate the view of a 3-D plot
selectmoveresize   Interactively select, move, or resize objects
zoom   Zoom in and out on a 2-D plot

Selecting Region of Interest

dragrect   Drag XOR rectangles with mouse
rbbox   Rubberband box

Lighting

camlight   Create or position light
light   Light object creation function
lightangle   Position light in spherical coordinates
lighting   Lighting mode
material   Material reflectance mode

Transparency

alpha   Set or query transparency properties for objects in current axes
alphamap   Specify the figure alphamap
alim   Set or query the axes alpha limits

Volume Visualization

coneplot   Plot velocity vectors as cones in 3-D vector field
contourslice   Draw contours in volume slice plane
curl   Compute curl and angular velocity of vector field
divergence   Compute divergence of vector field
flow   Generate scalar volume data
interpstreamspeed   Interpolate streamline vertices from vector-field magnitudes
isocaps   Compute isosurface end-cap geometry
isocolors   Compute colors of isosurface vertices
isonormals   Compute normals of isosurface vertices
isosurface   Extract isosurface data from volume data
reducepatch   Reduce number of patch faces
reducevolume   Reduce number of elements in volume data set

`shrinkfaces`	Reduce size of patch faces
`slice`	Draw slice planes in volume
`smooth3`	Smooth 3-D data
`stream2`	Compute 2-D stream line data
`stream3`	Compute 3-D stream line data
`streamline`	Draw stream lines from 2- or 3-D vector data
`streamparticles`	Draws stream particles from vector volume data
`streamribbon`	Draws stream ribbons from vector volume data
`streamslice`	Draws well-spaced stream lines from vector volume data
`streamtube`	Draws stream tubes from vector volume data
`surf2patch`	Convert surface data to patch data
`subvolume`	Extract subset of volume data set
`volumebounds`	Return coordinate and color limits for volume (scalar and vector)

Creating Graphical User Interfaces

Predefined dialog boxes and functions to control GUI programs.

Predefined Dialog Boxes

dialog	Create dialog box
errordlg	Create error dialog box
helpdlg	Display help dialog box
inputdlg	Create input dialog box
listdlg	Create list selection dialog box
msgbox	Create message dialog box
pagedlg	Display page layout dialog box
printdlg	Display print dialog box
questdlg	Create question dialog box
uigetdir	Display dialog box to retrieve name of directory
uigetfile	Display dialog box to retrieve name of file for reading
uiputfile	Display dialog box to retrieve name of file for writing
uisetcolor	Set ColorSpec using dialog box
uisetfont	Set font using dialog box
waitbar	Display wait bar
warndlg	Create warning dialog box

Deploying User Interfaces

guidata	Store or retrieve application data
guihandles	Create a structure of handles
movegui	Move GUI figure onscreen
openfig	Open or raise GUI figure

Developing User Interfaces

guide	Open GUI Layout Editor
inspect	Display Property Inspector

Working with Application Data

getappdata	Get value of application data
isappdata	True if application data exists
rmappdata	Remove application data
setappdata	Specify application data

A-43

Interactive User Input

ginput	Graphical input from a mouse or cursor
waitfor	Wait for conditions before resuming execution
waitforbuttonpress	Wait for key/buttonpress over figure

User Interface Objects

menu	Generate menu of choices for user input
uicontextmenu	Create context menu
uicontrol	Create user interface control
uimenu	Create user interface menu

Finding Objects from Callbacks

findall	Find all graphics objects
findfigs	Display off-screen visible figure windows
findobj	Find specific graphics object
gcbf	Return handle of figure containing callback object
gcbo	Return handle of object whose callback is executing

GUI Utility Functions

selectmoveresize	Select, move, resize, or copy axes and uicontrol graphics objects
textwrap	Return wrapped string matrix for given uicontrol

Controlling Program Execution

uiresume	Resumes program execution halted with uiwait
uiwait	Halts program execution, restart with uiresume

Symbolic Math Toolbox Quick Reference

This appendix lists the Symbolic Math Toolbox functions that are available in the MATLAB Student Version. For complete information about any of these functions, use Help and select **Function Reference** from the **Symbolic Math Toolbox**.

All of the functions listed in Symbolic Math Toolbox "Reference" are available in the MATLAB Student Version except maple, mapleinit, mfun, mfunlist, and mhelp.

Basic Operations

ccode	C code representation of a symbolic expression
conj	Complex conjugate
findsym	Determine symbolic variables
fortran	Fortran representation of a symbolic expression
imag	Imaginary part of a complex number
latex	LaTeX representation of a symbolic expression
pretty	Pretty print a symbolic expression
real	Real part of an imaginary number
sym	Create symbolic object
syms	Shortcut for creating multiple symbolic objects

Calculus

diff	Differentiate
int	Integrate
jacobian	Jacobian matrix
limit	Limit of an expression
symsum	Summation of series
taylor	Taylor series expansion

Conversions

char	Convert sym object to string
double	Convert symbolic matrix to double
poly2sym	Function calculator
sym2poly	Symbolic polynomial to coefficient vector

Integral Transforms

fourier	Fourier transform
ifourier	Inverse Fourier transform
ilaplace	Inverse Laplace transform
iztrans	Inverse Z-transform
laplace	Laplace transform
ztrans	Z-transform

Linear Algebra

colspace	Basis for column space
det	Determinant
diag	Create or extract diagonals
eig	Eigenvalues and eigenvectors
expm	Matrix exponential
inv	Matrix inverse
jordan	Jordan canonical form
null	Basis for null space
poly	Characteristic polynomial
rank	Matrix rank
rref	Reduced row echelon form
svd	Singular value decomposition
tril	Lower triangle
triu	Upper triangle

Pedagogical and Graphical Applications

ezcontour	Contour plotter
ezcontourf	Filled contour plotter
ezmesh	Mesh plotter
ezmeshc	Combined mesh and contour plotter
ezplot	Function plotter
ezplot	Easy-to-use function plotter
ezplot3	Three-dimensional curve plotter
ezpolar	Polar coordinate plotter
ezsurf	Surface plotter
ezsurfc	Combined surface and contour plotter
funtool	Function calculator
rsums	Riemann sums
taylortool	Taylor series calculator

Simplification

collect	Collect common terms
expand	Expand polynomials and elementary functions
factor	Factorization
horner	Nested polynomial representation
numden	Numerator and denominator
simple	Search for shortest form

simplify	Simplification
subexpr	Rewrite in terms of subexpressions

Solution of Equations

compose	Functional composition
dsolve	Solution of differential equations
finverse	Functional inverse
solve	Solution of algebraic equations

Special Functions

cosint	Cosine integral, $Ci(x)$
hypergeom	Generalized hypergeometric function
lambertw	Solution of $\lambda(x)e^{\lambda(x)} = x$
sinint	Sine integral, $Si(x)$
zeta	Riemann zeta function

Variable-Precision Arithmetic

digits	Set variable-precision accuracy
vpa	Variable-precision arithmetic

Index

Symbols

A

B

C